COACH

COACH

DARREN LEHMANN

WITH BRIAN MURGATROYD

EBURY
PRESS

An Ebury Press book
Published by Penguin Random House Australia Pty Ltd
Level 3, 100 Pacific Highway, North Sydney NSW 2060
www.penguin.com.au

Penguin
Random House
Australia

First published by Ebury Press in 2016

Addresses for the Penguin Random House group of companies can be found at global.penguinrandomhouse.com/offices.

National Library of Australia
Cataloguing-in-Publication entry

Lehmann, Darren, 1970– author
Coach/Darren Lehmann

ISBN 978 1 92532 477 8 (hardback)

Lehmann, Darren, 1970–
Cricket coaches – Australia – Biography
Cricket players – Australia
Cricket – Australia
Sports teams – Australia

796.358092

Cover design by Luke Causby/Blue Cork
Front cover photo: Richard Whitfield
Back cover photo © Robert Cianflone/Getty Images
Typesetting and internal design by Midland Typesetters, Australia
Printed in Australia by Griffin Press, an accredited ISO AS/NZS 14001:2004
Environmental Management System printer

Penguin Random House Australia uses papers that are natural, renewable and recyclable products and made from wood grown in sustainable forests. The logging and manufacturing processes are expected to conform to the environmental regulations of the country of origin.

CONTENTS

ACKNOWLEDGEMENTS

This book would not have been possible without the amount of love and support I have received from my beautiful family. To my wife, Andrea, who has always encouraged me to follow my dreams, thank you for being with me on the journey and, despite me being away for 300 days a year, thank you for bringing up our children in a great way. Thank you, love, for everything.

To not only Andrea, but also my children, Ethan, Amy, Jake and Tori, thank you for allowing me to do the job of Australia's head coach, a role I regard as the best job in the world. Your support in the background has been behind any success I may have had. I know I have not been there enough for all of you and for that I am sorry. When I finally get off the merry-go-round then I will be able to do the things that dads do, but in the meantime you are making me proud by turning into great young men and women. To the rest of my family, thanks for helping Andrea and me run things whilst I have been on the road for so long. The times you are there for both of us are another reason I can do the job.

To all our friends, thank you for your support and I am looking forward to sharing more good times with everyone. You know who you are. The times you have helped Andrea and the children out, whether it is with a school run or going to the cricket, makes it easier for us to do what we do and I cannot thank you enough.

To Adam Gilchrist – 'Gilly' – thanks for taking me on this journey, mate, by giving me my first break in coaching and for always encouraging me and challenging me throughout. And thanks, too, for writing the foreword to this book. I can think of no-one better or more appropriate to have done it. And to my manager Andrew McRitchie, thanks for being you and always being there for me through my journey, not only as a player but now as a coach as well.

To the players that have been with me on this journey, thank you for making it fun and entertaining along the way and also for challenging me – and yourselves – and usually in a good way. I love you all as you know and hope your families enjoy the way we go about our business. I have always loved having the children, wives and partners of the players and staff around when we are in action. It helps make for a good, fun environment, wherever the team may be.

Thanks to the Deccan Chargers, the Kings XI Punjab, the Australian Cricketers' Association, Queensland Cricket and Cricket Australia for providing me with the opportunity to coach and to put my ideas into practice and for the support you have given me along the way to make my job as easy as possible. And to all the sponsors of our great game, thank you for helping to keep our sport healthy so that it can be enjoyed by everyone.

To Brian 'Steady' Murgatroyd, I cannot thank you enough for your endeavour in capturing all our chats over the years and helping me put together this really good read that captures the essence of what it is like to live the life of Australia's head coach. I hope this book will provide food for thought for other coaches out there, although I do not claim that all my ideas are right! Thanks, too, to Brian's wife, Aarti, daughter, Aariana, and father, Walter, for putting up with his long hours in my company. Hopefully the end product is worthwhile.

To the publishers of this book, Penguin Random House Australia, and in particular Alison Urquhart, editor Patrick Mangan, Gabrielle Coyne, Nikki Christer, Julie Burland and Emily Craker, as well as Michael Epis, thank you for backing this project and having the patience to see it to its climax. It was a terrific idea and hopefully you are just as pleased with the end result as I am.

To John, Jennifer, Jack, Jemima and Pippi Gayleard, Olympia Walker Galt, Jessica, Charlie and Matilda Crane, Garry Rainford, Jaswant and Reena Singh Dabas, Padam, Pooja, Praniti and Prapti Singh Janghu, Doctors John Orchard, Phil Lucas, Mohammed Sobeh and Bhavna Khan, Trader Grenfell and the staff of PRP Diagnostic Imaging at Moore Park in Sydney, the Belmont and Royal Newcastle Hospitals, Jonathan Rose of Cricket Australia, and the

Catho Bowlo Club at Catherine Hill Bay, you all played a pivotal role in this book coming to life.

The media deserve a word of thanks, too, for helping to make this coaching caper an interesting one. You are always questioning but, to me, that is a good thing, as that impartial view from outside the bubble of the team environment helps us to strive to be better every day.

And to all the people who will read this book, hopefully it gives you as much pleasure as I get from doing a job I love, watching players and staff grow alongside me and become better people.

It has been a bloody good journey as a coach so far. A lot has happened in a relatively short space of time and hopefully there will be a few more chapters to add to the story in the years to come.

Coach
Darren Lehmann

FOREWORD
ADAM GILCHRIST

The first time 'Boof' and I met on a cricket field was hardly an auspicious occasion for either of us.

It was the Mercantile Mutual Cup final at the Sydney Cricket Ground in the summer of 1992–93, the showpiece limited-overs event of the domestic season. I was playing just my second game for New South Wales and Darren was representing Victoria at the time.

We both made ducks – he was leg before wicket first ball to Brad McNamara, who went on to work as executive producer on Channel Nine's cricket coverage, while I was bowled by Damien Fleming in the closing stages of a match we won by four wickets in the final over.

I reckon you would have got long odds at that stage that the pair of us would play alongside each other in two ICC Cricket World Cup-winning sides and that Darren would become a successful coach at domestic, franchise and international level, helping Australia to the game's biggest prize on home soil in 2015 and in doing so becoming just the second person after Geoff Marsh to win the World Cup as a player and a coach.

But, on the face of it, his success should not come as a surprise to anyone, and for two reasons: he is a terrific cricket person and an equally great people person too.

You would not label him a 'cricket tragic' in the way that former Prime Minister John Howard describes himself, but Darren is someone who lives and breathes the game. Growing up in a dressing room under David Hookes was the start of his life soaking up cricketing knowledge, and his continuing desire to do that marks him out as an ideal person to learn from and a great role model for young players. He has got the life and the cricketing experiences to be able to guide his players on the right path.

At the same time, Darren is not what you would call a know-it-all and he makes no secret of the fact he does not have all the answers, something that is refreshing in a leader. As you will see in the pages that follow, he has a clear idea about how he sees his role in helping the captain to run a side and he is very much from a collaborative school of coaching. He challenges you as players to help come up with the answers, as that is the best way for players to learn. Whether you are a debutant or a 200-game veteran, your views are equally valid as far as he is concerned.

Darren is a social animal too, there is no doubt about that, and we have had many great nights out as well as sharing plenty of laughs along the way in dressing rooms from Perth to Johannesburg, Mohali to Mumbai and plenty of other places besides. He has the enviable ability to make people relax in his company and put them at their ease. He makes you smile and, as a coach, he makes you want to play for him and run through a brick wall if you have to.

When you put all those characteristics together and throw in the fact he was an outstanding player, then it is absolutely no surprise to me that Boof has proved to be such a good and such a successful coach.

And although he credits me in this book with helping to kick-start his coaching career by encouraging him to apply for the role at the Deccan Chargers, I think of that as unnecessary praise, because with his knowledge of the game and his ability to make people want to listen to and follow him, his rise up the coaching ranks would have been inevitable whether or not he got that opportunity. The fact that he helped transform us from easy-beats to champions in one season sums up the effect he can have.

The idea of a book like this, one that lifts the lid on what coaching at the top end of the game actually involves, is long overdue and I cannot think of anyone who is better qualified than Boof to write it.

Enjoy the wisdom, the anecdotes and the insights – they are well worth it – just as I have enjoyed his company for the past two decades.

PREFACE

Before we get started, it might be a good idea to offer a word of warning, about what this book is not.

It is *not* the book of someone who claims to be the perfect international cricket coach. The qualification to write a book along those lines would be for me never to have made a mistake, got a decision wrong, lost a match – let alone a series – or said a word out of place. That certainly does not reflect either my journey to the job with the Australian cricket team or my experiences in that role.

To set myself up as some sort of master coach would be arrogant, conceited and downright wrong because I have made mistakes and plenty of them, and will continue to do so. The best I can hope for is to learn from those mistakes and make my team and myself better human beings as a result of that learning process. Hopefully, as you turn the pages that follow, you will learn from my mistakes too.

This book is also *not* a handbook on how to become an international coach. That is for the simple reason that there is no set formula to achieving that end. The one thing most people at my elite end of the coaching spectrum have in common is that we have sat for our qualifications and obtained them, but aside from that, if you speak with all the coaches at the highest level they will each have their own story of how they have ended up where they are – some have played at the highest level and some have not, some have coached in the Indian Premier League and some have not, some have coached in countries across the world, while others have simply run sides within their countries of origin. This book is simply my story along that road.

What this book *is* intended to be is an explanation of what I do and why I do it. It is an attempt to demystify my role, pull back the curtain and offer an insight into all the work and all the thought that goes on behind the scenes to try to ensure the Australian cricket team is the best in the world.

In the absence of being able to play any more, the position of Australia's head coach is my perfect job and has reminded me why I love this great game. It is a role that is time-consuming, challenging and tiring, but also immensely rewarding and enjoyable. And by the time you turn the final page I hope you will understand why it is all those things and much more besides.

1

'CAN YOU MAKE A DIFFERENCE?'

'Can you make a difference?'

It took my wife, Andrea, to cut right to the heart of the matter, as she so often does, in working out whether or not I should take what I regard as the best job in cricket outside of actually playing the game – the role of Australia's head coach.

I wanted the job, I knew that much, but in my own mind it was more a case of whether I was up to coping with the challenge and whether it was going to be fair on my family. After all, as myself, Andrea and our two children, Amy and Ethan, discussed the offer made by Cricket Australia's Executive General Manager of Team Performance Pat Howard, there was a realisation I would be on the road and out of home for up to 300 days every year.

The point at which we were discussing that offer was almost the perfect illustration of the pressure that top-level cricket puts on the family unit. We were in Bristol, it was 23 June 2013 and just a short while earlier I had been strolling around the boundary of the county ground on the final day of Australia A's match against English side Gloucestershire, the last game of a brief tour of the United Kingdom. I was involved as one of the staff under the trip's head coach, Troy Cooley, in what was a chance for me to extend my horizons and have a look at the national set-up after a couple of successful seasons with Queensland.

Although the match turned into a really tight contest I was still feeling pretty relaxed. The tour had gone well on two levels, as it had served as a good tune-up in unfamiliar conditions for several players who were set to take part in the Ashes series beginning the following month and, at the same time, it had allowed for a closer look at a few promising individuals who were on the fringes of international honours.

From a personal point of view I was looking forward to some much-needed rest, having been on the road for the best part of four months. I had just finished the first season of a two-year contract coaching Kings XI Punjab in the Indian Premier League (IPL), and that had come off the back of a domestic season in Australia looking after Queensland and the Brisbane Heat, a season in which we finished as runner-up in the Sheffield Shield, won the second edition of the Twenty20 Big Bash League, and the Ryobi Cup, the domestic 50-over per side competition.

I was ready for a break and Andrea, Amy and Ethan had arrived in England to meet up with me at the end of the tour match in Bristol, head to London and then on to Paris for what we had planned as a family holiday away from the game. Now, though, there was the prospect of a rapid change of plans.

Pat's offer came out of the blue. It was true that the national team was experiencing a serious crisis of confidence, that results had been poor and the perception, at least in the media I had seen, appeared to be of a side struggling on every level.

Just a matter of months earlier Australia had been white-washed in a four-Test series in India that included the suspension of four players – Shane Watson, James Pattinson, Mitchell Johnson and Usman Khawaja – for not completing an assignment on how the team could improve following the losses in the first two matches. And then, in early June, the limited-overs side had failed to progress from the group stage of the International Cricket Council (ICC) Champions Trophy in the United Kingdom.

Added to that were the facts that captain Michael Clarke was struggling with a long-standing back injury that sidelined him during the Champions Trophy and David Warner had been suspended after throwing a punch at England batsman Joe Root following an altercation in a bar in Birmingham after a defeat against Alastair Cook's side. It all added up to an impression that the ship was rudderless heading into the Ashes series starting in July.

Whatever the truth behind that view, I still did not expect Cricket Australia to change the head coach so close to the series. I knew Mickey Arthur and knew him to be a hard-working and diligent operator – you do not get to coach three national sides without being good at your job. But as coaches, in cricket as in other sports, tend to live and die by results, I suspected he would be on very thin ice if the Ashes were not regained or if the side was not competitive, especially after the events both on and off the field in India and at the Champions Trophy.

All the same, when I got a call from Pat that he wanted to catch up with me for lunch on that final day of the match in Bristol, I had no inkling about what he was about to offer me. I thought it would simply be a case of some sort of debrief from the A tour, getting my impressions of the players and the usefulness of the trip and picking my brains about any thoughts I may have on the future direction of the game in Australia.

I was actually quite pleased to have the chance to chat with him, as during the previous home summer there had been some to-ing and fro-ing between us in the media. I was frustrated that, despite the success we had been having in Queensland, very few of my players were getting a chance with the national side. And although Pat wasn't a selector, he was the man in charge of them, so I thought the catch-up would be a chance to get the inside track on what was happening.

All that soon went out the window, though, as Pat cut to the chase pretty quickly: 'How would you like to coach the Australian team?' he said. My answer as I recall it now was pretty vague: 'Obviously I'd love to have a crack at it down the track as that's what you're in the game for, to take on big jobs like that and test yourself at the top level.'

'Well, how would you like to take on the job right now?'

My response to that was a pretty good illustration of the shock I felt. 'F*** off!' Thankfully, having played and worked in top-level sport for most of his life, Pat was used to earthy language and allowed it to go through to the keeper.

'Well, if you do want to do the job then you've got the rest of the day to think about it and give me an answer.'

Andrea, Ethan and Amy had just arrived in Bristol, about a 90-minute drive west of London, and I quickly contacted them and arranged a catch-up of our own as I drove back to the hotel in the city centre. I rang Andrea from the car and as she knew the match was still going on, she realised something out of the ordinary had happened. 'What have you done now?' were her first words to me!

I told her about Pat's offer and by the time I arrived back at the hotel, the twins, both 11 years old at this point in time, were waiting for me in the foyer and bolted out to meet me. 'You've got to take it!' they said, not necessarily realising the amount of time I would be away from home.

We took a stroll along the canal that runs through the centre of the city to a restaurant for a late lunch and kicked the situation around for a couple of hours. I don't remember much about the meal but I do remember it was a lovely sunny day as we weighed up our options as a family. I explained the situation in detail and waited for their feedback. I knew I wanted the job but needed to hear two things from them:

their blessing to go for it and also their reassurance they felt I was up to the challenge.

A reluctance to think I was capable of rising to that challenge was behind my failure to apply for the role the previous time it had come up, in 2011. Pat had asked me to throw my hat in the ring back then, but I decided against it, reckoning I was too inexperienced as a coach and that I needed to get some more miles in my legs before I considered taking on the biggest and most prestigious position in Australian cricket, aside from the captaincy.

Now, fast forward less than two years, and here I was in the same position, albeit with a little extra schooling, and we had a big decision to make as a family.

Even after hearing all that the job entailed, Ethan and Amy were all for me taking it on – the thought of their dad overseeing the Australian cricket team was exciting. Although the role involved lots of travel for me, they were happy at the prospect of visiting me overseas when studies and time allowed, having been globetrotters from an early age alongside their mother, given my earlier nomadic lifestyle as a player. Andrea, though, was more measured, asking that key question.

So, could I make a difference? I thought for a moment, thought about the results the team was having, thought about the perception of the team in the media and the public, thought about my own experiences as a player, and my conclusion was a simple one: 'What's the worst that could happen?'

Yes, I was still relatively inexperienced – I had had a handful of seasons in the Indian Premier League with the

Deccan Chargers and Kings XI Punjab, plus a couple of years with Queensland, so I could hardly be said to be the equivalent of a Leigh Matthews or a Kevin Sheedy, two seemingly immortal figures in Australian Rules football coaching of the recent past, but as the four of us chatted I quickly came to the realisation this was one of those sliding door moments. If I didn't take on the role now, while I was still relatively young and healthy, would I regret it later in life? Would I get the chance again?

The side was losing anyway so almost anything would be an improvement on that and, by joining less than three weeks before the Ashes series started, it actually afforded me an unprecedented honeymoon period. Everyone knew I had not had a hand in the squad selected, so even if losses happened I knew I would be cut some slack. And if it did go wrong, as long as I could look myself in the mirror and say I had given it my best shot then that would be enough for me.

Andrea knew the sacrifices that were involved, as many of them seemed to fall to her. She had spent much of her life bringing up Amy and Ethan on her own thanks to my time away from home and, having created a degree of normality in our lives through the move to Queensland, there was the prospect of her having to cope with the same scenario all over again.

But she's a strong woman and wants what's best for me. As soon as I was clear in my own mind that I *could* make a difference – and a positive one, too – our minds were made up.

I called Pat Howard, accepted his offer subject to agreeing terms, and then the whirlwind of changing plans started: for me it was all about calling those close to me beyond Andrea and the twins – including key people I'd worked with at Queensland Cricket like captain James Hopes – to let them know the situation. I think my biggest regret about the whole scenario was that I didn't get a chance to say a proper goodbye – and thank you – to those people, the players and administrators in Brisbane, who had backed me and given me the chance to succeed which had, in turn, earned me the opportunity to take on the role with the Australia team. It had been a superb couple of years for me, moulding a hungry group of predominantly young players into a significant force in domestic cricket, and it was thanks to their buy-in to what I wanted to do that I'd secured my new gig.

Now, though, things were moving in a different direction. For me it was a case of heading to Taunton to meet up with the Australia Test squad, then preparing for a tour game against Somerset ahead of the Ashes series. For Andrea, Ethan and Amy, there was the prospect of the trip to London and then on to Paris without me.

2

RISE OF THE COACH

If you had suggested to me when I began my playing career that I would become a coach, let alone the coach of the Australian cricket team, I suspect you would have received in response a few expletives mixed in with some laughter and incredulity.

Back then, in the late 1980s, cricket was for playing. The idea of a full-time coach was a relatively recent phenomenon. And as for the concept of the myriad support staff that sit under the coach these days, well, that was light years away.

There was – and still is – an old-school perception about coaching: that players, especially at the higher levels of the game, should not need it. They have, so the argument goes, reached the top by working out their own game and finding out what works best for them. They have had success with that approach and, having reached that level, if something goes wrong they should be good enough to figure things out for themselves. That was certainly the feeling when I came in to the game.

When I made my first-class debut for South Australia in December 1987, in a Sheffield Shield game against Victoria at the Melbourne Cricket Ground, there was no coach. It was senior players such as David Hookes, Andrew Hilditch and Wayne Phillips who were the go-to men within the dressing room. It was only the following season that former South Africa opening batsman Barry Richards was appointed to coach the squad. Hookes, in particular, dictated the mood and the approach of the side, and he was the oracle when it came to tactics and technique. There can be no better illustration of his approach than that match at the MCG, when he declared on the final day to try to fashion a result out of what looked set to be a certain draw. We lost the game by six wickets as Victoria chased down the 282 we set them, with a young Jamie Siddons making an unbeaten 124, but it was an early illustration to me of how Hookes wanted us to play the game, always looking for a way to win any match we took part in. Off the field he was an open book, and in those days players learnt not through formal team meetings and video analysis – there was none of the latter – but through discussions over a beer or two in the dressing room following a day's play.

After I made 228 against a full-strength New South Wales side at the Adelaide Oval in my third season as a first-class cricketer in November 1989, an innings that helped catapult me into Test contention for the first time in my career, Hookesy asked me what I thought were, at first, a very strange series of questions: 'What did you have to eat in the run-up to the innings? What time did you go to bed beforehand? What practice did you do before the match?'

I could not figure out why he was asking me all those questions when all I really wanted was a pat on the back from him, but it soon became clear. 'If you figure out how you prepared for what was your best innings, you can try and replicate it next time,' he said. 'The secret is to get a routine that works for you and then stick to it.' It was, as was usually the case with Hookesy, sound advice.

Of course, in the days since senior players like Hookesy were the go-to men in dressing rooms across the country, the game, especially at international level, has changed markedly and the need for a coaching framework has never been more pressing. As an example of that change you only have to look at the profile of the players who are now coming into the Australian team. At the start of the 21st century players such as myself, Mike Hussey and Matthew Hayden became established in the side off the back of literally thousands of first-class runs. Each of us went to play county cricket in England, where we had the opportunity to bat three or four times each week on different surfaces against different bowlers and in a variety of match conditions and situations. It meant that when we finally graduated to becoming regular members of the side at national level we knew our games inside-out.

Fast-forward to the current era and that situation no longer exists because of the higher volume of international cricket and the nature of overseas tours. The international calendar is incessant, but while tours take place in far greater numbers, the opportunity for cricket outside of the international matches has been reduced. Gone are the days when a player like Hayden could go on an Ashes tour as he did in 1993 and rack up 1150 runs in 13 first-class matches outside the Test series. Nowadays if teams play two or three first-class matches outside their international commitments, that is considered a significant amount of action. And gone, too, is the chance for a young player in and around the Australia set-up to spend a season playing in England safe in the knowledge it will not conflict with any other commitments, as there are now numerous lucrative Twenty20 leagues across the world as well as an enlarged A team schedule.

There is no longer the chance for teams to take promising youngsters or 'project players' on tour. Those players that are part of a touring party need to be ready to play, and in order to make that as seamless as possible then individuals with potential are often fast-tracked into the system through age-group and A team selection. That has its advantages, as it means that if or when individuals do make the leap to the senior side they are more familiar with the set-up, and walking into the Australian dressing room is less of a culture shock.

The downside, however, is that the young players who make that leap have far less match experience than someone of my era. Steve Smith's Test debut against Pakistan in 2010 was just his 14th first-class match; Mike Hussey, by contrast, played more than 170 games before he pulled on the baggy green cap for the first time, while, for me, the third Test against India in Bangalore in 1998 was my 123rd match at first-class level. Players play much more international cricket now, but they play a lot less at the level below that, and so have not been exposed to the myriad different scenarios that may confront them at the game's top table. And that is where the coach and his staff, as well as senior players within the set-up, play a key role in helping a player make that transition a smooth one. My coaching staff and I are not there to show a player how to play a forward defensive stroke or how to bowl a leg-break. Our role is to spot if little tweaks are needed to players' techniques, respond to questions, offer advice and be sounding boards for the players, given we have been there, done that and got the T-shirt.

One of the best feelings I have as a coach is when a young player steps up not only on the field but also in a team meeting, volunteering his opinion. That is an affirmation that we have created a culture in which even the most junior player can feel comfortable and not overawed by his surroundings, and also a culture in which players are developing their thoughts about the game.

As for the modern concept of the coach at international level, I think it is fair to say that Australia was the country behind it thanks to Bobby Simpson's appointment as the first full-time person in that role in 1986. The appointment of 'Simmo' was a reaction to the loss of a host of experienced players to retirement and the rebel tours of South Africa, and he was exactly what a callow bunch of cricketers not used to the rough and tumble of international cricket needed. Alongside captain Allan Border, he brought in a strong emphasis on fitness, discipline, fielding, planning and preparation, and on doing the basics well. And that was important because you have to remember that at that time cricket was still very much a part-time occupation in Australia. Many players still worked jobs outside of the game. The days of individuals being completely dedicated to the sport were still a few years ahead. At the start of my first-class career I combined cricket with working on the assembly line of the Holden car plant in Elizabeth, before switching to the Rowe and Jarman sporting goods store in Adelaide.

My day at the car plant ran from 7 am to 3 pm five days a week, building struts for the wheels of the cars coming off the line, as well as helping to put together the automatic and manual transmission gearboxes. It was hard, monotonous and tiring, and in the summer, inside the factory, it was roasting hot, but it was great discipline that has served me well for the rest of my working life. It certainly made me appreciate the opportunity to play cricket for a living when that chance came along, as there were plenty of people within that factory who certainly didn't have the chance to look elsewhere as I did.

Working on an assembly line like that gave me my first real insight into what being part of a team was all about. Each vehicle was put together in a specific order with my job forming part of that order. If my work wasn't done in a timely and accurate way, it held everyone else up, so we all had to look out for each other to keep things moving smoothly.

Although what I did was tiring it actually made me enjoy practice and playing cricket even more, as that was an escape from the reality of life as a worker. Holden, for their part, were supportive of me taking time off to play the game, but by the same token when I did miss work to play, that was leave without pay – not that I minded at that time of my life. I was just revelling in playing cricket, it was as simple as that. And my colleagues on the line were terrific as well. They enjoyed having a sportsman in their midst and treated me the same whether I got a hundred or a duck. It was a great environment for a young bloke to do some growing up.

As for Simpson, the reward for his no-nonsense approach was a victory in the World Cup less than two years after he became coach. His tenure ultimately lasted 10 years, and although it ended with the disappointment of defeat in another World Cup final, against Sri Lanka in 1996, he still had the satisfaction of leaving the side at the top of the pile in Test cricket, having backed up an Ashes win by ending the West Indies' 22-year run without a series defeat by downing them on their home turf in 1995.

It is fair to say that Simpson started the cult of the coach in international cricket, although it is equally fair to say it was not all his creation. The media was happy to paint him as Australian cricket's supremo and off the back of the team's success other sides, most notably England with Micky Stewart, quickly followed suit by making full-time appointments of their own.

Coaches were given responsibility for not only running training sessions but were also involved in selection, consulted on playing schedules, given a say in assessing players' fitness levels and had a handle on everything around the team. They became the side's top dog, and I suspect that is where someone like Ian Chappell, a long-time critic of the role at international level, has an issue.

Chappell's often-quoted view that 'an international coach is something the Australian team travels in around England' is based on that idea that the captain has become inferior to the coach in terms of power and responsibility within the team environment. His view – and I can understand it – is that if a captain at international level needs anything above and beyond someone to organise a practice session or the occasional suggestion on tactics, then the team needs to be looking for a new captain because the leader is not up to the job.

There is some truth in that and I am sure it is based on Chappell's own experiences as Australia captain in the 1970s, when he was given a team for each match and then it was his responsibility to get the best out of his players.

However, it ignores the fact that times have changed and, for better or worse, the game has moved on. The levels of scrutiny are far greater and the pressures and penalties of winning and losing are far greater too. The sport is now fully professionalised and players earn millions of dollars for doing what they do but, at the same time, failure brings with it the prospect of losing those rewards.

In those circumstances, the coach becomes an important facilitator, running the behind-the-scenes events so that the captain can focus as much of his energy as possible on getting things right on the field. And if there is anything wrong with that then I am yet to discover what that is. I am certainly no puppet-master pulling the team's strings in secret. For sure, I make suggestions and the coach's box is a good spot to get a perspective away from the heat of battle. But ultimately it is the captain's responsibility to make decisions on the field, and neither he nor I would have it any other way.

A prime example of the misconception of me being some sort of Svengali figure pulling those strings came during the Boxing Day Test against India in 2014. On the final day we were trying to work out when it was best to declare, making sure we left ourselves enough time to bowl India out a second time while at the same time ensuring we didn't, in Steve Smith's words, 'give them a sniff' of victory. We were already 2–0 up in the four-match contest and India's only chance of sharing the series and retaining the Border-Gavaskar Trophy was to win in both Melbourne and Sydney. And in order to achieve the first part of that requirement they needed to show some intent on that last day.

Far from it, MS Dhoni set the field back even though we started the day seven wickets down. It meant the match meandered a little in that morning session and I was the one who was eventually seen calling the batsmen in when we decided on a declaration with our last pair, Nathan Lyon and Josh Hazlewood, at the crease.

But that wasn't me taking control; it simply reflected the fact that the viewing room at the MCG is set under the canopy of the Members' Stand and from the middle it can be a very difficult place to see. There were several of us waving our hands, but it was me who was spotted making the signals, so it was assumed it was me, not Steve, who was calling the shots and, in this case, making the closure. Nothing could be further from the truth. It was Steve's declaration and Steve's team. For the record, the match was drawn, meaning we had the series won.

Of course, it is easy to appear wise now I am Australia coach, but when I played the game I was certainly regarded as someone who you might say was old school. I was brought up in the game under Hookes – who, himself, was a young player under Ian Chappell in World Series Cricket in the late 1970s – and so came to regard the gospel according to senior players as the way to go and, in turn, I got plenty of advice from coaches that I ignored or disregarded.

I have no doubt that my approach and my attitude cost me the chance to fulfil my potential at international level. When I was first on the fringes of the Australia team, Simpson said that in order to get selected I needed to go away and work on my fitness and my fielding. I listened, but when I went away my reaction was to do the exact opposite. I thought: 'What does he know? I'm making runs and I have the respect of the South Australian dressing room.' But the reality was that I spent years in the international wilderness because I ignored what I see now to have been perfectly reasonable advice. And although I do not have any regrets – life is too short for them – I know that I should have made far more than the 27 Test appearances I finished my career with, and in all probability I would have done so if I had listened to

Simpson. My failure to do so gave him all the reason he needed to sideline me from his thinking.

For my part, that perception about me being old school has stuck. You know the chat and how it goes: 'Good old Boof, likes a beer and a yarn, likes his players to talk cricket, likes them to enjoy life.' But while that is all true, it is also a simplification of me and my approach and something that I can now put to bed once and for all.

Yes, all the above does apply to me, but in terms of my role as head coach of the Australia cricket team it merely scratches the surface. I am as new age as they come in terms of many of my methods. We use video analysis to dissect opposition batsmen and bowlers as much as any other side at international level and we go into minute detail in preparing for series and the matches within those series with our analyst Dene Hills, the former Tasmania batsman, very much to the fore.

We are always on the lookout for the so-called 'one per-centers', the small yet significant advances that can make the difference, whether it is the use of ice vests or isotonic drinks to keep players cool and hydrated and allow them to bowl that one extra over, or GPS tracking devices that allow us to analyse how much ground players cover during training and playing – and so help us weigh up how they are travelling and whether or not they need a rest.

I believe absolutely in hard work from the players and while you might say that attitude is rich coming from someone who, during his playing career, had a reputation for enjoying a drink and smoke, I believe it actually puts me in a strong position to crack the whip if needs be. Why? Because I can say to the players: 'Look, I didn't put in the hard work during my career and it cost me. It cost me caps and, from a fitness perspective, it probably cost me hundreds too. Don't make the same mistake as me.' And in the dressing room I am fortunate that, having played the game at the highest level, I am able to command respect on that basis, as I have been there and done it.

I give players personal responsibility – just as Simpson did with me – and they have the option to either take that and run with it or ignore it and potentially suffer any consequences that may result from that approach. And at the same time I also give that responsibility to my staff. I cannot tell a player the best running technique, the best way to handle a ticklish question in the media or how best to treat a particular injury; those things are the areas of expertise of the people under me and I leave it to them to manage those situations in the best way they see fit.

In that regard, the head coach is now no longer simply a coach as such. Of course I will offer my expertise and experience on a technical or tactical issue if it is needed; but the role now combines not only coaching but also man management, overseeing the work of both the players and support staff that back me up, along with a dollop of amateur sports psychology and anything else that can make the players tick and get the best of them. I have a host of off-field staff under me and honestly, with the stakes in the modern game, both for individuals and collectively for Cricket Australia, never higher, that development was inevitable.

When I was playing for Australia the team manager – back then it was Steve Bernard, the former NSW seam bowler and now an ICC match referee – was the person in charge of the squad and everyone, even the head coach, answered to him. But that has changed and the buck now stops with me. By going down that path cricket has merely followed other sports like soccer, the rugby codes, Australian Rules football – you name it, every sport I can think of is the same now. Ultimately someone has to be responsible and that is the lot of the head coach.

You might argue that is unfair given I don't set foot on the field throughout any given match, but in this era in which millions and even billions of dollars are invested in the game, someone has to be accountable and that someone is me. And although I might not like it, I would not have it any other way. I have seen the pressure that comes with leading the side on the field, a job that caused John Howard once to observe his role as Prime Minister was second in importance to that of the Australia captain. On that basis my primary job is to take as much of the heat, preparation and organisational responsibility as I can on to my own plate while, at the same time, allowing the captain to be his own man out on the field and also to allow him to perform to the best of his abilities as a player. If I can do that then I say that I have done at least a part of my job.

3

LEARNING FROM THE EXPERTS

I like to think of a coach as something of a cricketing magpie. Of course you have your own style born of your individuality, and you have your own ideas too, but at the same time, whether consciously or unconsciously, you will always find yourself using ideas and adopting approaches picked up from people you have worked with in the past.

In my case, over the course of a 20-year playing career, I worked with some of the best coaches in the business, as well as outstanding mentors and senior players, and I realise now that through all that time I acted as a sort of sponge, sucking up styles and ideas and making mental notes on the way they did things.

You definitely learn from the way others go about their business, there is no doubt about that, and that learning process can cut both ways, at least in my experience. You see how coaches work and if something proves successful and effective – maybe a drill, or a way of dealing with a player or a situation – then you lock it away in your subconscious for future reference. But at the same time you also note when approaches do not work and make that mental note about how not to do things.

Despite my lengthy experience in the game, first as a player and now as a coach, the last thing I would ever claim is that I have all the answers, and even now I can cheerfully admit I am still learning about the game. Some people made fun of me in 2013 when I was pictured on the dressing room balcony at Lord's with an earpiece listening to the Sky Sports commentary of the Test match, but why wouldn't I? The ex-players in that commentary box, people like Sir Ian Botham, David Gower, Michael Atherton, Nasser Hussain and Michael Holding, played a lot more international cricket than me and they knew the conditions far better than me. Why wouldn't I listen in, just in case they had some observations that I could take advantage of? That was a no-brainer to me.

The first person I regard as having coached me is **Wayne Bradbrook** at Salisbury Cricket Club, a place where I spent a decade from my early teens until I moved to Victoria to play club and first-class cricket there for three years in the early 1990s. Wayne really has been instrumental in drumming into me the right and wrong ways to play the game. What he taught me right from the get-go was that cricket was to be enjoyed, it was meant to be fun, and although it was something you wanted to do well at and win, you had far more chance of doing that if you felt good about the sport.

One way to do that was to enjoy the company of your teammates and the camaraderie that comes from doing exactly that, and they are lessons I still carry with me to this day. And in a nice bit of symmetry I can still call Wayne a good friend, as he has continued to stay in touch through his work with my eldest son Jake, who he's coached at East Torrens Cricket Club.

Once I got into the state squad, the first coach I worked with at that level was **Barry Richards**. Barry came to South Australia at the start of my second season as a first-class cricketer and he was superb for me, a magnificent coach. He was already a legend in South Australia thanks to his incredible season with the state in the summer of 1970–71, when he scored a phenomenal 1538 runs in 10 first-class matches, including 325 in a single day against a Western Australia attack that included a young Dennis Lillee, Graham McKenzie, Tony Lock and Tony Mann.

Barry was part of the lost era of South African cricket, whose chance to play at international level was curtailed by the onset of his country's sporting isolation thanks to the evil of apartheid. He played just four Tests, but his first-class record was outstanding – more than 28,000 runs and a first-class average of almost 55 with 80 hundreds, including nine of those achieved before lunch, and 508 runs in his four Tests, against Ian Chappell's side in 1970. And Barry carried an aura about him.

Aside from that aura, the first thing I discovered about him was that he was a very good communicator and had a way of explaining the game that made it easy to understand. Some great players struggle when they have to work with individuals and teams that aren't as gifted as them – just look at the long list of West Indian stars who have tried and failed to lift the team out of its current malaise as prime examples of that – but Barry was not someone who fell into that category. He helped me think about and develop game plans for a match situation: 'If X is bowling and he has this field, how will you look to counter him and where are you looking to score?' And he made sure that all players knew what was required of them.

As you may know, given the way he glided effortlessly into television commentary boxes around the world in the 1990s, Barry read the game brilliantly, and having someone like him work with me was justification, I felt, for passing up the chance to attend the Australian Cricket Academy. I do not believe I could have learnt any more if I had gone there than I did by working with and listening to Barry. I know that Hookesy really valued him as someone to bounce thoughts and ideas off and also as someone whose counsel he respected.

For someone like myself, still a teenager remember, Barry's thinking about the game and his ability to analyse it really challenged me as, up to that point, I had not really gone into a great deal of depth in my own mind about the intricacies of the sport. Before I met Barry cricket had seemed very simple: as a batsman my approach was simply 'see ball, hit ball,' but Barry taught me that there were plenty of times when a bowler would be on top, and if he was then I would have to adopt an approach to counter that. He was exactly the coach I needed at that stage of my career.

Barry was definitely pivotal in my development as a player of spin bowling. During my career I was regarded as someone who dealt very effectively with slow bowlers – the tour of Sri Lanka in 2004 when I scored 375 runs in three Tests against an attack led by Muttiah Muralitharan, including 129 in Galle and 153 at the Sinhalese Sports Club in Colombo, was probably the main reason why I had that reputation – and Barry's guidance was significant in that regard. He had played against some of the world's best, including the likes of Lance Gibbs and Bishan Bedi, during his time in county cricket in England for Hampshire, and much of his career was spent batting on uncovered pitches. His approach to batting against slow bowling was a simple one: 'Try not to let the ball bounce!' He encouraged me to think out of the square to try to counter the threat that spinners posed.

Perhaps the most outlandish way I put that approach into practice was on that tour of Sri Lanka when I showed Muralitharan all my stumps, batting way outside leg-stump to try to counter him. He was bowling over the wicket and my position at the crease allowed me to open up the off side and also negate the threat of his doosra getting me out leg before wicket. If he tried to tuck me up by bowling outside leg stump, he was taking LBW out of the equation and also giving me a free hit because of that. It was a strategy that worked perfectly – my figures in that series bear that out – and I have Barry to thank for encouraging me to think in that manner.

Barry was also a gifted squash player, as I discovered to my cost when I tried to be a smartarse at South Australia. A teenage upstart, I challenged him to a game, saying I would thrash him, without knowing that he was also a champion in the sport, as was his now ex-wife, Anne. He beat me 11–8, 11–8. If that scoreline makes it seem as though I was competitive, I should add that Barry gave me an eight-point head start in each of the two sets! He made me feel like a fool, but did not seek to rub it in; he just beat me and let me realise my mistake for myself.

The contrast between Barry and my next coach at senior level, **Les Stillman**, who was in that role when I moved to Victoria for the start of the 1990–91 season, could not be more pronounced, but then neither could the difference in circumstances.

While at South Australia we had Hookes, Hilditch and Phillips as our stars and then, for the most part, a squad of players who did not really figure on the radar of the national selectors, the opposite was true at Victoria. It really was a team based in the firmament.

The side was captained by all-rounder Simon O'Donnell, a World Cup winner in 1987, who had battled back from cancer. He led from the front with bat and ball.

Alongside him were Dean Jones, Mervyn Hughes, Darren Berry, Jamie Siddons, Tony Dodemaide, Paul Reiffel and Damien Fleming, as well as several other players of class including (another) Wayne Phillips – who played one Test against India in 1992 after Geoff Marsh was dropped – and emerging talent such as Shane Warne. James Sutherland, who went on to become Cricket Australia's Chief Executive Officer, was a new-ball bowler on the fringes of the squad.

International duty meant that not all of these players were available all the time, but it still added up to an impressive collection of talent and I was delighted to become a part of the group, as I thought that mixing with these different players, playing in a different environment, stepping out of my hometown comfort zone and being coached by a different person like Les could only be beneficial to my development as a cricketer.

I made the move to further my international ambitions as, at that time, there was a perception that batting at Adelaide Oval was a straightforward occupation and that runs scored there were worth less than those scored elsewhere, at least in the eyes of the Australia selectors. I thought if I could go to Victoria and make a success of my time there then I would make a compelling case for the chance to earn my baggy green.

Looking back, it was certainly good for my cricketing education, especially seeing the way Les operated. The dressing room was a fiery one, as you might expect with so many experienced players within it, all of them having firm opinions on virtually everything that happened. Managing that and getting everyone to head in the same direction all the time was a challenge, to say the least.

It is fair to say that Les struggled with that challenge at times, and looking back now, I am sure he would be the first to admit that; a lot of coaches would have struggled in the same way. He was a terrific coach when the side was winning, but when things started to go wrong he would struggle to maintain his calm and the degree of equilibrium you need in that position.

I would never criticise him for that, but Victoria at that time probably needed someone who was a little less volatile, especially in pressure situations. And it did not help that during my time at Victoria I noticed Les's relationship with Simon O'Donnell – the pivotal coach–captain relationship that in my opinion is the fulcrum of every successful side – was an increasingly fractious one.

I had three seasons with my adopted state, playing for the Carlton Cricket Club when not turning out for Victoria, and we won the Sheffield Shield for the first time in 11 seasons in my debut summer there. But although my figures over those three seasons were steady – 2176 first-class runs at an average of just under 43 – they were certainly not head-turning and I returned to South Australia still feeling unfulfilled.

My Victoria experience was an interesting time. Ahead of that 1991 Sheffield Shield final against NSW I was hit in the head and suffered a fractured cheekbone, struck in the nets at Princes Park by Carlton fast bowler Stephen Irvine. That was just three weeks before the final, in which I played, scoring 11 in my only innings, and we ended up winning very comfortably by eight wickets, despite being bowled out for just 119 first time around.

The blow to the head haunted me into the following season and Les dropped me after a couple of matches, thinking

I had become a bit gun-shy – and he was probably right. It turned out to be a blessing in disguise, as I went off to the second XI, made a double-hundred and went on to have the best of the three seasons I spent with Victoria.

The key lesson I learnt from my time there to carry forward in my future lives as first a senior player and then a coach was that you should never allow yourself to get distracted by matters you cannot control. The ferment within the dressing room was something that I let occupy too much of my time when realistically there was nothing I could do about it. It certainly opened my eyes to the real world as, prior to that, in South Australia, everyone within the rooms had got along like a house on fire and now, over the course of my three years in Melbourne, I realised that an environment like that was more likely to be the exception rather than the rule.

I can look back now and see that my experience with Victoria shaped my desire to ensure that, in any side I oversaw, getting everyone pulling in the right direction in the dressing room was a key dynamic in making a successful side. With the talent within that Victoria squad it should have enjoyed far more success than it did.

Also, I realised that although I remained driven by my desire to play for Australia, I needed to be a lot clearer in my approach and my motivation for playing the game. Part of that realisation came because of that head injury I suffered in 1991, an injury that could have been avoided or at least lessened to a great extent if I had been wearing the correct headgear – a helmet rather than the floppy sunhat I was batting in. In future I made a mental note that if I was going to practise with proper intensity then I had to replicate what I would do in a match – and against the faster bowlers that was to bat in a helmet.

All the dressing room angst at Victoria certainly made me question why I was playing the game. Of course, I was playing it because I loved it, but there were times during those three years where fun and laughter were definitely off the agenda. Yes, you want to win and yes you are competitive, but that sense of enjoyment and the ability to laugh with each other and relish the battle should also be there and, again, I resolved to ensure that was a perspective I would take forward with me to the next stage of my career.

In that sense, a comment of Barry Richards from the recent past really struck a chord with me. He was reflecting on the loss of his Test career because of South Africa's sporting isolation, something that he was very bitter about at the time, as he wanted to prove himself on the world stage and was denied the chance to do so by factors beyond his control.

But that was cricket and it paled into insignificance compared with the loss of his son Mark, who committed suicide in 2009. In an interview with ESPNCricinfo in 2015 he said: 'I have been blessed with the life that I have had. To put the cricketing things in perspective, nothing is worse than losing my son – that is what I call a tragedy. Losing your cricket career – it happens, it happens to other people who might have done it through injury or other means and lost careers. But losing a son just puts everything into perspective.'

It is important to realise that cricket is a *game*, not life or death. An important one to us, yes, but still just a game.

By the time I arrived in Victoria I had already come into contact with the national team – although not in the way I would have wanted. In early 1990 I was drafted into the Test squad for the final match of the series against Pakistan, following injuries to David Boon and Geoff Marsh, but I was overlooked in the starting XI with Mike Veletta and Tom Moody preferred ahead of me.

I felt more than a little indignant, as I had trumped both of them in the run-scoring stakes that season with close to 700 first-class runs by Christmas, including 228 against NSW in the first Sheffield Shield game of the season.

That said, I still felt my chance would come along shortly although, with hindsight, I should have known better, because during my time with the squad during that week – and the Test was ruined by bad weather – it became apparent that the side's coach **Bobby Simpson** and I were not on the same page.

I've never asked him whether he had an issue with me at the time, but we were just oil and water, fire and ice, complete opposites at that time, and for whatever reason – my body-shape, my attitude, even maybe a perception on his part that I had not fully merited my elevation to the top table – we did not hit it off. And although I was retained in the first couple of matches in the One-Day International series that followed, I did not get a game before being ditched in favour of Mark Waugh – not a bad alternative, I have to admit.

'Simmo' certainly put me and the rest of the players through some punishing fielding drills during my time with the squad during that abortive Test match week and I have to admit I struggled to cope with the intensity he was demanding of me. But it was a shame that he seemed to go away from that week with the view that I was not up to it, while I went away without thinking 'Hey, I need to step up and lift my game when I get back to my state side now.'

I left Sydney thinking, not to put too fine a point on it, that he was a f***wit, but I can see now why he did not rate me: I was a young player, with obvious talent but at the same time I was someone who did not seem to want to go the extra yard to make myself the best I could be. I smoked and I drank and I simply did not comprehend the sacrifices and commitment required to make it to the top. With people like Allan Border around me in the dressing room that week, it was not as if I was short of examples of the way to go about my business, but I was not sharp enough to cotton on to what was required of me at that time.

I think about myself back then and the impression I must have created, and I think of the contrast now with the current generation of players I am working with. I will not say they are monks but they are all wholly dedicated to their careers. Look at David Warner as an example, someone who gave up alcohol for more than a year to realise his goals and who, in the space of less than 12 months, was rewarded with a World Cup winner's medal and the Allan Border Medal as Australian cricket's star man of the year in 2015.

His wake-up call came when he was dropped from the side for disciplinary reasons in 2013, but just look at the way he responded – with runs and a much greater level of maturity, both in his game and his general behaviour. He acted in the way I should have done all those years before. David is now a fantastic role model, not only to all young players who come into the Australian dressing room but also to a whole generation of children who are falling in love with the game.

David is an incredibly generous man too: he did a television advertisement for Woolworths about how he started off as a shelf-stacker there on the understanding that his fee went to charity, and he is a prominent supporter of the cancer charity of his good friend Geoff Goodwin.

Geoff – or 'Popeye' as he is universally known – has been driving Australian touring squads around the United Kingdom for more than a decade and his lovely wife, Suzanne, became ill with cancer in 2013. She fought back and as I write this she is in remission, but the Goodwin family's brush with death prompted them to look to raise money to support those who had played a role in bringing Suzanne back from the brink.

David formed a bond with Geoff during their times together around the motorways of Britain – his seat on the bus was always right behind Popeye – and he not only donated large amounts of gear to be raffled off, but also stayed on the 2015 tour even after he was ruled out with a broken thumb just so he could honour his commitment to attend and speak at a dinner to raise funds.

Yes, it took a few years for the penny to drop with David and he had to hit rock bottom before it did – but contrast his enlightened approach with me back in the early 1990s. I was certainly driven, hence my move to Victoria to try to further my case for Australian selection, but I lacked the necessary focus that you need alongside that sort of aspiration. I had been given an early opportunity to impress or, looked at from another perspective, an early glimpse at the promised land, and I failed to take the chance I was offered. Had I done so then I could be writing this book with at least 100 Test caps and a decorated career rather than the 27 I eventually secured.

Do not get me wrong; I had a great career, in the sense that I made 82 first-class hundreds, got to play in some amazing places with and against some amazing players, and won two World Cups, even being involved in the winning moment both times. But just occasionally I do reflect on the fact it could and should have been better. I do not do regrets – life is too short, as I said – but that does not stop me wondering about 'what ifs'.

The funny thing is that now, all these years after our paths crossed in 1990, Simmo and I get on extremely well and I look forward to chatting with him whenever we get the chance to meet. I failed to heed his advice about improving my fielding and fitness when we first met, but I am happy to admit now that he was right and I was wrong, and so I bear him no grudge.

I cannot change the mistakes I made back then but I can – and do – incorporate his approach to training in my coaching now. It was my fault and no-one else's – certainly not his – that I missed out on Australia selection for another eight years after coming so close in Sydney and I can see now that I really should have viewed that elevation in 1990 as merely base camp in my attempt to scale Everest rather than thinking I had made it as I trailed along behind the likes of star players like Dean Jones and Mervyn Hughes on nights out.

It was ironic on two counts that when my chance to play Test cricket for Australia finally came around, in India in 1998, **Geoff Marsh** was the coach, having replaced Simmo following the side's defeat in the World Cup final two years earlier. Ironic firstly because he was one of the players whose injuries led to my initial call-up eight years earlier and again because he had been very much a player in the Simpson model.

'Swampy' was a country boy who believed there was no substitute for hard work and in that sense he suited Simmo's approach perfectly. He had been one of the poster boys of the successful Ashes tour of 1989 under Allan Border and in one of the Test matches, at Trent Bridge in Nottingham, he batted through the whole of the first day alongside fellow opener Mark Taylor, eventually sharing a stand of 329.

He would be the first to admit that there have been more talented batsmen who have opened the batting for Australia, but I am not sure there have been many who have worked harder to get the absolute most out of themselves.

Swampy's work ethic extended to his life outside cricket, as he ran a newspaper delivery service for a while, but he will always be remembered as the first man to both play and coach in a World Cup winning side, achieving the former in 1987 and the latter with the squad I was a part of, in 1999.

I enjoyed working with him as he brought the best out of me and that was what I needed, as our time together coincided with me getting into the Test and One-Day International sides on a regular basis for the first time. I needed someone to keep me on my toes and Swampy definitely did that.

The fact he was close in age to many of the players, and played with or against quite a few of us, could in some ways have been held up as a reason for him not to get the job, but it turned out to be the right appointment. Because he was familiar with us from before his time as the team's coach, it meant he did not stand on ceremony if something needed to be said. During our successful World Cup campaign in 1999 he absolutely laid in to me for sloppiness during a fielding session and he was spot-on to bawl me out. He knew what he could say to which players to push the right buttons and that public dressing-down achieved its aim.

Swampy was also able to admit when he had made a mistake, something I believe is vital. There are those who think a coach should be infallible, almost like God, and that any admission you have not got all the answers or that you have got something wrong is a sign of weakness. On the contrary, I believe the ability to admit you are wrong shows your human side and can also work as a positive, because it can draw in the playing squad in a collaborative approach. I like to ask my players 'What do you think?', because ultimately they are the ones who have to find the answers to problems on the field.

Swampy, together with Steve Waugh, decided when we arrived in the United Kingdom for the World Cup following a limited-overs series in the West Indies that we would have a drinking ban until we had completed our commitments, either by winning the tournament or getting knocked out. Not many of us were particularly impressed by the decision, but the captain and coach stressed that the event was a relatively short period of time – just over a month – and that the sacrifice in terms of our improved well-being was not too much of a price to pay if it helped us go on and win.

That theory was fine, but it ignored the fact that we liked to have the freedom to have the odd drink now and again, especially after a match, and that we had all got to where we were by doing exactly that. The bottom line was that decisions like that treated players like children rather than adults, removing their personal responsibility.

We started the tournament playing poorly, losing to New Zealand and Pakistan, and were in jeopardy of not qualifying for the second stage. You could not blame our form on a lack of booze, but our performances were a reflection of a wider malaise within the squad. We were not relaxed and therefore not playing our best cricket.

Swampy, along with Steve, took the decision to ditch the ban and the rest is history. We became more of the team we had been in the past, enjoying each other's company, and each other's successes, particularly in the dressing room after the wins as they began to pile up, and by the time we got to the final we were unstoppable. Without Geoff's ability to admit the original decision was flawed, we may not have won that World Cup.

Swampy went on to coach Zimbabwe and Sri Lanka, as well as Pune, in the IPL, but none of those appointments matched his success with Australia, which also included Ashes wins in 1997 and 1999. He made an important contribution to the next generation of Australian cricket by providing us with two of his sons, Shaun and Mitchell, as Test cricketers to follow in their father's footsteps. Only Walter Hadlee of New Zealand and India's Lala Amarnath have done the same thing. It is a remarkable legacy.

Talking of legacies, **John Buchanan**'s is one that will struggle to be matched, with the World Cup successes of 2003 and 2007 both involving sides that went through their respective tournaments without losing a match. The West Indies did that in 1975 and 1979, but back then there were just eight teams involved and three group games before the semi-finals and final; in 2003 the tournament had grown to 14 teams, and four years later that figure became 16, with the Australians playing 11 matches in each event in order to lift the Cup.

There are plenty of people willing to take a pot-shot at John, with the naysayers suggesting anyone could have coached the side of champions he had at his disposal. But my view is that 'Buck' actually did a fine job during his eight years at the helm.

With the top-quality players he had – the Waugh brothers, Justin Langer, Hayden, Damien Martyn, Ponting, Gilchrist,

Glenn McGrath, Jason Gillespie, Warne, Brett Lee, the list goes on and on – there was no need for him to be a technical coach; his role was more as an organiser of training sessions but also, importantly, he challenged both the players and the Australian Cricket Board and I liked that.

His challenge to the players was for them to see if they could get even better than they already were, and push the bar in cricketing terms. He was the first person I heard suggest that players would start to throw with either hand – and I saw Sri Lanka's Kamindu Mendis bowl with his left and right hands during the 2016 ICC Under-19 Cricket World Cup – and his challenge for the squad was to try and score 400 in a One-Day International. Nowadays, with the advent of Twenty20 cricket, a score of 400 is considered very achievable but back then it was thought close to impossible, cricket's equivalent of the four-minute mile before that was achieved. The fact Australia did pass 400, in 2006 at Johannesburg against South Africa, was brilliant; it was just a shame that South Africa scored four more on the same day!

Buck's challenge to the administrators was to try to provide the level of support we now take for granted at international level. He was a big advocate of bringing in experts in specific fields, which has led to where we are now – with the head coach managing a group of specialist coaches below him.

Buck was the man who brought in the American Mike Young, the former baseball player, to act as a fielding consultant. Mike was terrific for the group because he came with no knowledge of cricket. That meant he asked questions that a cricket person might not ask – things like 'Why do you attack the ball in that way? 'Why do you throw in the way you do?' 'Why don't you double-team balls towards the boundary?' 'Why don't you use relay throws from the deep on certain grounds?'

I enjoyed working with Buck. It was under him that I played most of my international cricket and he and **Ricky Ponting**, as well as **Steve Waugh** as Test captain when I returned to the Test side, were happy to use my experience and ask me for my views on tactics. That suited me just fine as, having played first-class cricket for well over a decade by the time I won my spot back, I had plenty of experience to call on.

Both Waugh and Ponting expected the best from their players – their attitude was always that the Australia team sets standards and that others follow – but they, along with Buck, were also happy to hear other views and that was where players like myself came in. Some of the senior players like Shane Warne and Mark Waugh did not always welcome too much talking – and I agree with that – and I remember hearing Mark's reaction to a team meeting that was dragging on discussing bowling tactics. 'Good length, hitting the top of off has worked for 120 years, hasn't it?' he said. And that was the end of the meeting!

People actually forget that Buck came to the Australia job as the top-credentialed coach in the country, having helped Queensland break its Sheffield Shield drought and secure domestic one-day honours too. There was no-one better placed to take on the side than him and his record will stand up to the closest of scrutiny.

The only black spots on his report card were the side's habit of losing matches after series were secured and the India tour of 2001. In terms of the former, try as he might, Buck and Steve Waugh and then Ponting often struggled to lift the players again after the silverware had been won. Examples that stick in my mind were the South Africa Test and One-Day International away series in 2002 and the Ashes series in 2001 and 2002–03. On all those occasions we managed to allow the opposition consolation wins after dominating the series. The players were treated as adults and it is fair to say we did not always respond and switch on to the same extent as when series and titles were on the line. My experience of that time has helped colour my approach that each match for Australia is important no matter when it is played or what the situation is in the series. The players under me have bought into that idea. I never want us to take our foot off the opposition's throat.

As for India in 2001, I joined the tour only for the One-Day International series at the end, but the Test series that preceded it will go down in history as one of the game's most amazing contests and one that will be remembered for an incredible turnaround in fortunes. Australia was without a series win in India since 1969 and Steve Waugh beforehand dubbed it as his team's 'final frontier'.

All went well with a three-day win in the first Test in Mumbai thanks to hundreds by Gilchrist and Hayden and in the second match in Kolkata a Steve Waugh hundred had put the side in command. India failed in its first innings and allowed him to enforce the follow-on, only for

VVS Laxman and Rahul Dravid to bat all through day four and knock the stuffing out of the side.

Still, a draw was very much achievable until the loss of seven wickets after tea on the final day saw the end of Australia's run of 16 consecutive wins. The sides then moved to Chennai for the finale where, despite a Hayden double-hundred, Australia failed to bat India out of the game and when the hosts secured a lead of 110, eight wickets for Harbhajan Singh – as well as 15 in the match – set up the hosts to sneak home by three wickets.

In between the second and third Test Buck said to reporters that Shane Warne had a 're-fuelling' issue – in other words, that he wasn't looking after himself properly. I had sympathy for Warney because he went on that trip underdone after breaking his thumb early in the season. He missed the whole of the home Test series against the West Indies and only returned for the one-day matches that followed against them and Zimbabwe, which meant he had not had enough bowling going into the tour. I also had some sympathy because the truth was, the same sentiment applied equally to me!

The comment was another example of John trying to stimulate a player and although it backfired in the short-term – and Warney probably never forgave him for the public nature of the remarks – you only have to look at the way he transformed his body shape and looked after himself far better over the years that followed, extending his career as a result, to wonder whether Buck's remarks may have struck home after all.

The latter stages of Buck's time as Australia's coach saw **Tim Nielsen** come onboard as his assistant and he would ultimately assume the senior role when John stood down. I spent plenty of time with Tim, both as a player – as he was a longstanding keeper for South Australia – and when he moved onto the coaching staff at the Adelaide Oval. He was always destined to be a coach and a very good one too, because he knew the game inside out and also had a fantastic work ethic, something he looked for in those around him, both players and staff. I was saddened that it didn't work out for him with the Australia job, although it is probably fair to say he got dealt a tough hand. With a host of great players leaving the stage in relatively quick succession, it was an impossible task to maintain the previously achieved levels of success and he suffered because of that, through no real fault of his own. If he had been coach in another era, I believe he would have become a hugely successful operator.

Wayne Clark, who coached me at Yorkshire, was someone I had only previously come into contact with when he filled the same role at Western Australia. He was a very useful fast bowler who played Test cricket during the split between the establishment and Kerry Packer's World Series Cricket, and he and I established the most enjoyable and the closest partnership I experienced with a coach during my playing days.

He realised that in order to overcome Yorkshire's chronic underperformance over many years – the side had last won the county championship in 1968 – the players had to lose their fear of failure. That fear came from the team's terrific history, having won the title more than any other side, but after that previous success the goalposts were moved with the inclusion of overseas players in the county system. Other sides included them but Yorkshire chose not to, instead maintaining its approach of choosing only players born within the county's boundaries. With most sides boasting overseas quick bowlers, it left it fighting missiles with bows and arrows for the 1970s and 1980s, and it was only at the start of the 1990s that Yorkshire relented and recruited foreign stars, starting with India's Sachin Tendulkar – a decision that ultimately paved the way for my arrival.

Clark – or 'Dunny', as he was known – knew the way I liked to play the game, positively, always looking for victory, and so he asked me, through my role as an overseas player, to act as a leader and a mentor to encourage the other players to throw off the shackles and attack to put the opposition on the back foot wherever possible, rather than just simply sitting in a game in the hope of the other side making a mistake.

That suited me fine and I rode a young, technically correct batsman called Michael Vaughan especially hard. Vaughan had all the shots – we saw that in the nets – but when we got to the middle he would make these beautiful looking 20s and 30s that would take a couple of hours, sucking time out of the game.

One day I said to him: 'Mate, you have got to start taking it up to the opposition or I am going to run you out.' He looked shocked, but I added: 'You have got all the shots, all the ability in the world, and you need to start showing it and dominating because that is what a player like you should be doing.'

I am delighted to say the penny dropped very quickly and he came out of his shell and did dominate – although from an Australia perspective, there was an element of regret about giving that advice as he then went on to play superbly in successive Ashes series, in 2002–03 and 2005, leading his country in that latter clash to a victory over Ponting's side of stars.

Dunny played a key role in making me switch on in Yorkshire's championship winning season. I scored four 50s in my first five matches of the season but had failed to go on and make a big score. After making 90 against Kent he took me to one side and said: 'Are you getting bored? You get past 50 and you should go on and make a big one but, instead, you keep getting out. You need to be hungrier, for yourself and the side.' I took his questioning to heart as, in my next match, against Somerset I scored an unbeaten 187, the first of five hundreds I made in that title-winning season.

I managed to play a part in the winning moment in the decisive match that sealed the title, taking the final wicket by dismissing Glamorgan's Simon Jones at Scarborough, the place where Andrea, my future wife and sister of Yorkshire and England all-rounder Craig White, lived. The celebrations lasted a long time, so long that we lost our last two championship matches of the season.

The hangover of those celebrations lasted into the following season and we were relegated, a result that spelt the end for Dunny as the side's coach. That was unfortunate given everything he had brought to the county, but such had been the outpouring of relief after the 2001 success that he proved unable to lift the players to go again. The side was now the hunted rather than the hunter and it was a tag it wore very poorly.

I averaged 83 when we won the title but that slipped to 66 the following season. I was late joining up with the squad in 2002 as I finished a One-Day International series in South Africa and then had to head back to Australia in mid-season for more One-Day Internationals, this time against Pakistan, and that meant I was not as hands-on as I had been in 2001, but I did not perform to the standards I had set myself previously and that cost us dearly.

Thankfully the fact that Dunny did bring that championship success to Yorkshire means his reputation remains pretty much intact at the county and that pleases me, because he deserves that.

Jeff Hammond was coach at South Australia when we won the Sheffield Shield in 1995–96 and he was very similar in temperament to Wayne Clark – quiet and thoughtful.

To give you some context of that time – which will seem light years ago to modern readers – 'Bomber', as he was known, actually combined his role as coach with a job at Telstra. That would not happen today.

His great assets were his experience and knowledge of the game – as a seam bowler he was part of Ian Chappell's squads that drew an Ashes series in 1972 and then went on to win in the Caribbean the following year – and his organisational skills and calmness. The latter was especially relevant on the final day of the 1995–96 season when we somehow held on for a draw to win that Shield title, ending up nine wickets down against Western Australia at the Adelaide Oval, thanks to Shane George and Peter McIntyre batting through the last 40 minutes of the match.

That was a tremendous achievement but, just as with Les Stillman, a criticism of Bomber could be that his side did not have more success beyond a solitary Shield win. After all, if you look at the photograph on the wall in the home dressing room at the Adelaide Oval, of the side celebrating after the presentation ceremony on that April day in 1996, you do tend to wonder why it was not the first of many titles. The side boasted players like Greg Blewett, Jason Gillespie, Tim May, McIntyre, myself, James Brayshaw and Jamie Siddons as captain, yet that was the extent of our success.

Bomber eventually moved to county side Glamorgan, taking over from Duncan Fletcher when he left to coach England, but he was not able to replicate what Fletcher managed, as the Zimbabwean had led the Welsh team to a championship flag in 1997. But from a South Australia perspective any criticism of Jeff's failure to build a new golden era should be tempered, as I believe it gives the players a cop-out we do not deserve.

It is true that Bomber was never a hands-on coach; that was not his style. For me, it was up to us players, especially the senior ones, to take more responsibility in the years that followed our 1996 win, and the truth of the matter is we basked in the glory of that success rather than building on it.

I was a well-established senior player by the time I came into contact with **Greg Chappell** at South Australia, but he showed me that even someone like myself, who thought he knew all there was to know about his game, could still learn more. Greg was a fantastic technical coach and a great thinker on the game, very much in the Barry Richards mould.

During our time together he tended to focus on the senior players like myself and not so much on the up-and-coming members of the squad. Looking back, that in itself was interesting because he later went on to coach the Indian national side and took a completely opposite position, looking to ease out the older players, including Sourav Ganguly, while trusting the younger brigade.

I think that approach came as a result of his reflecting on his time with South Australia where I think, with hindsight, he realised you needed to trust your senior players to do what they needed to do, because if they did that and churned out runs and wickets at an acceptable rate, the key component in a winning combination was always likely to be the youngsters. They can give you freshness, added enthusiasm and an x-factor. It didn't work out for him in India and ended acrimoniously, but now back in Australia he is being given the chance to develop the next generations of our talent in Brisbane. As far as I'm concerned, that means we are in safe hands.

Under Greg my batting went through the roof and I'll always be grateful to him for that. Like Barry, he worked on developing match awareness among his players and he helped simplify my approach at the crease. In one net session he pulled me up for getting too technical. I was spending time trying to get my feet moving and over-analysing what I was doing and he stopped my session. 'What are you doing?' he said. 'Just hit the ball. Forget about where your feet are going. Just focus on hitting the ball and the rest will follow.' He was spot-on too. For all his excellence as a batsman and his know-how, that was an example of someone not over-coaching and, instead, keeping it simple. It is a lesson we can always bear in mind.

Wayne Phillips missed out by five years on being part of that 1996 Shield victory but was coach in my last full season with South Australia in 2007. He had a distinguished career at international and domestic level and his selflessness in taking on the wicketkeeping role for the national side after Rod Marsh retired probably cost him a longer run at international level, as his batting undoubtedly suffered because of it.

'Flipper' came to the South Australia job off the back of a successful time coaching alongside Rodney Marsh at the Australian Cricket Academy, but his time coincided with our performance flat-lining. In 2006–07, which was to be his final season as coach, the team managed just three first-class hundreds across the whole season. We finished bottom of the Pura Cup (as the Sheffield Shield had become), I lost my job as captain and it was the beginning of the end for me as a player.

I was not able to pull my weight in that season because of a hamstring injury. My body packed up at the back-end of my career, as I realised too late I needed to take care of myself and get as fit as I could.

I tried to lift my fitness work from previous levels but my body, not used to that extra load, rebelled, not just with that hamstring issue, but then with an Achilles injury and deep vein thrombosis that developed while I was idle following surgery on that Achilles condition.

Flipper impressed me as a coach because in addition to his technical excellence and the fact he could command instant respect – especially in South Australia where he once shared the state's record partnership with Hookesy, of 462 against Tasmania the summer before I began my first-class career – he was calm and retained a sense of humour.

In fact, Flipper was one of the funniest coaches I ever met and he taught me the value of laughter in the team environment. He was the first coach I met who used a joke of the day, where he would ask any of the players to say something funny ahead of warm-ups. As you can imagine, some joke-tellers were better than others and even that act of telling, never mind the joke itself, provoked enjoyment and created a positive feeling around the group. The joke was something I brought in when I started as Australia coach as, at that stage, the squad was definitely in need of a laugh.

Flipper was very loyal to me, as we were close, having played alongside each other, and his daughter was a nanny to Amy and Ethan. Perhaps that was a blind spot of his, but he showed me the value of fun and enjoyment as a coach. After all, if you are not having fun with what you do for a living, you are not going to enjoy it or get the most out of either yourself or others. And that is something you have to do as a coach.

4

A HAPPY ACCIDENT

Getting into coaching was a natural progression following my playing career, but my first step on the ladder was something of a happy accident.

My first-class career had ended in late 2007 in what were, at the time, rather acrimonious circumstances. I had suffered a bout of deep vein thrombosis in my left calf in the first half of the year, brought on by inactivity thanks to my foot being in a support following an operation on my Achilles tendon, but at the start of that summer of 2007–08 I was determined to play on for as long as I could and enjoy my cricket. I knew I was nearer the end of my career than the beginning, but that actually made me hungrier than ever to succeed and make every post a winner.

When I did get on to the field I actually scored heavily and have the distinction of scoring a hundred in both my final first-class and limited-overs matches for South Australia. However, by the time I had made those centuries, both the state's Chairman of Selectors, my former teammate Paul Nobes, and Rodney Marsh, the ex-Australia wicket-keeper then reviewing the cricketing side of the business at Adelaide Oval, decided it was time to move me on and for them to look at other longer-term prospects as players.

First they stepped me down as captain in the winter of 2007 and then, when I returned to the ranks, it quickly became apparent my face no longer fitted as a player, full-stop.

I won't pretend I wasn't bitter. I was. I wanted to end my career on my terms and it felt like not only was I being denied the chance to do that, I was being shown a great deal of disrespect, given the service I had given to South Australian cricket.

My axing as captain came in a face-to-face encounter with Rodney and Paul. It must have been especially awkward for Paul, given we had plenty of history together as teammates as he had been a gritty top-order batsman for the state alongside me, before moving on to the administrative side of things. I was shown into a room for a meeting and they cut straight to the chase: 'We are going to replace you as captain.'

It actually took me somewhere between six to 12 months to get over that sacking and the subsequent end to my playing career in Australia that came early in the following summer of 2007–08. I had wanted to stick around and continue to prove my worth but I quickly got the message that my views were no longer valued within the team's hierarchy.

I remember the day when it came to a head. We were playing a match in Hobart against Tasmania and I made a series of suggestions to the man who replaced me as captain, Nathan Adcock, none of which were acted upon. That hurt, but it hurt even more when I made another suggestion, this time to wicketkeeper Graham Manou, and asked him to take it to the captain. When he did, and Nathan did act upon it, I knew my face no longer fitted and it was definitely time to go. At the end of the day's play I walked back on my own to the team hotel in the centre of Hobart from Bellerive Oval – about 12 kilometres, I reckon – complete with a pack of beer and pack of cigarettes, reflected on the situation and called Andrea. 'That's it,' I said. 'I'm fed up, not enjoying it and that's me finished.' I played just one more first-class match.

While the issue of me being eased out of the state side was far from perfect, with the benefit of hindsight I can see the wisdom of the decision and that it was the right one, taken for the right reasons. The reality was that I should probably have been relieved of the captaincy a season before I was. We weren't having success, something needed to change and I was a casualty of that generational switch. I actually appreciated Rodney and Paul's tough love and their honesty and that was something I have sought to take into my life as a coach and a manager of players and staff. Honesty and straightforwardness is the best policy.

I made my peace with both Rodney and Paul, and now Rodney and his wife, Roz, are two of the closest friends that Andrea and I have. Rodney is a fantastic confidant and, aside from our close working relationship as members of the National Selection Panel that he chairs, I know I can pick up the phone and call him at any time to sound him out on any subject I have concerns with, cricketing or otherwise. It is a great result following an unhappy episode.

The absence of first-class cricket in my life in the early part of 2008 was a gaping hole. I had played at that level for 20 years, ever since my teenage days and through all my adulthood, so to suddenly have just about the only thing I knew taken away from me was a huge shock. But in my case it really was a case of one door closing and another one opening. That open door took the form of a chance to play in the inaugural IPL.

Shane Warne, who I had been close to for many years as a teammate, smoking companion and card-player, was captain of the little-fancied Rajasthan Royals alongside his good mate Darren Berry, the former Victoria wicketkeeper, who was coaching the side.

They needed some experienced cover at the start of the tournament and thought with my limited-overs know-how that I could do a job for them, so they asked me to join them and I jumped at the chance. It was still in that period where I was having the 'I'll show them' feelings towards the people who had ended my career in South Australia. With the eyes of the cricketing world on the new event, it seemed like the perfect chance to prove my point.

As it turned out I hardly set the tournament alight. I played just two matches, made just 1 and 17, and then sat on the sidelines for the rest of the action while others made the headlines and we lifted the trophy.

The 17 I got against a Kings XI Punjab side including Brett Lee, Irfan Pathan and Shanthakumaran Sreesanth gave me a very clear signal that my career was over – and that it had to end immediately. I went in to bat, Brett was bowling seriously quickly and I couldn't see the ball. I was s****ing myself – there is no other way to describe how I felt. I feel no shame in writing that, because that was the reality. I thought: 'Binga could kill me here'. We may have won a World Cup together, but we were teammates then and here we were opponents. It was the first season of the IPL and all the players were busting a gut to make sure it was a success as, if it was, then it represented a fantastic pay-day.

Shane Watson was at the other end – he finished with an unbeaten 76 from 49 balls, including five fours and five sixes, making batting look ridiculously easy as he steered us home to a potentially tricky target of 167 with 11 balls in hand. I told him when we were out there in the middle under the lights at Jaipur in front of 20,000 rowdy fans: 'I just can't see the ball when Bing is bowling!' I can laugh about it now, but when I faced my first ball from Brett, trying desperately to look cool and in control, I attempted to run it down to third man for a single just to get off strike. The trouble was I somehow hit it too well and the ball went for four. I knew that would mean only one thing: the next ball would be even faster and I would be even less likely to see it. I was right about not picking it up, but somehow I survived, only to fall leg before wicket to Pathan, which was a blessing for the side as it brought Ravindra Jadeja to the crease. He and Watson finished the match in no time at all, whereas had I stayed in then it might have been a close-run thing.

At the end of the match, after those three balls from Brett, I knew I had a decision to make. I went to see Warney and said: 'Mate, it's time for me to give it away – I'm s****ing myself!' It's rare that a cricketer is so decisive when it comes to his retirement, and Warney knew there was no point arguing. He accepted my resignation, but wanted me to stay on as cover for the international players and to work with the young players. So it was there and then that my coaching caper truly began.

It was the perfect gig for me, as it stopped me moping about and feeling sorry for myself. I talked cricket with the youngsters, offered the odd tip here and there and bought in to the team ethic that Warne and Berry were peddling to all the members of the squad.

There was some terrific young talent at the Royals at that time. Jadeja was just emerging, Munaf Patel was an effective and at times distinctly slippery fast bowler and Yusuf Pathan made a significant impact with the bat. Add to that trio overseas stars Graeme Smith, Watson, Sohail Tanvir and Warne himself and it's not difficult now to see why the team was so successful in that first season, even if we had been rank underdogs.

I was not to know it at the time, but my manner around the squad made a positive impression, not just on the players within the group but outside it as well. The jungle drums were beating that I had been an important cog in the Rajasthan machine and that led to me being contacted by my former Australian teammate Adam Gilchrist ahead of the second edition of the IPL.

Gilly and his long-time manager Stephen Atkinson approached me, wondering if I might be interested in throwing my hat in the ring for the role of head coach of the Deccan Chargers, the franchise that Gilly was playing for and the side that ended with the wooden spoon in IPL I, winning just two of 14 games. They told me I was by no means a shoo-in for the position, but that if I was interested then they would arrange an interview for me.

I was flattered by the approach and also excited. There are three levels of coaching certificates that Cricket Australia offers – Community, Representative and High Performance – and I had just finished my High Performance course in Brisbane (a prerequisite for working at an elite level within Australia) and so it was perfect timing for me to go and put into practice what I had learnt in the classroom.

Of course, in order to do that, I had to pass the interview via a video conference, with me in Adelaide and them in India. I was nervous beforehand and dressed in a jacket and tie, on the basis you only get one chance to make a first impression. I found the whole thing, which lasted well over an hour, to be thoroughly nerve-racking. For people in the real world, job interviews are a fact of life, but for cricketers interviews are done on the field with a bat or a ball in your hand.

You have to remember my interview for Deccan took place just a handful of years after I was banned for use of racist language when I shouted out some words I don't want repeated or said again in the home dressing room at The

Gabba after being run out against Sri Lanka in January 2003. And although that was an absolute one-off, an aberration on my part that to this day I cannot explain and an incident I deeply regret and have apologised for, the fact remained that some of the mud I had caused to be thrown at me through my use of those three words continued to stick.

On that basis Deccan's owners ensured I endured a very confrontational interview. It was a case of getting everything out in the open and seeing how I coped and it really was a case of me sinking or swimming. I had to make them believe that I could not only handle a multi-cultural environment but also thrive in it while, at the same time, ensuring the team thrived too. And I would have to do so in South Africa, where the tournament was being played, because with a general election set to take place in India it was impossible for the police and security services to look after that and manage arrangements around the IPL at the same time.

I convinced the owners – and we went on to win the trophy. That is one of my proudest moments as a coach. I can still picture Gilly receiving the trophy from South Africa President Jacob Zuma as if it was yesterday. We had just sneaked into the top four ahead of Kings XI Punjab on net run rate and in the final we won despite scoring only 143. In addition to Gilly, Herschelle Gibbs was outstanding for us and we had a trio of Indian players in Rohit Sharma, RP Singh and Pragyan Ojha who also rose to the challenge.

For someone from Adelaide who had toured extensively but always lived inside the bubble of the Australian team,

I suddenly had to adapt to working within a different culture and with players of different religions. I had to realise that scheduling training at noon on a Friday was not ideal for the Muslims in the squad, while the same was true of a Sunday when it came to the Christians. Some players drank alcohol and for others it was a complete no-no; there were no bacon sandwiches for the Muslims and no beef rolls for the Hindus. It might sound obvious but for someone used to – for the most part – the relaxed atmosphere of an Australian dressing room, it was a great eye-opener.

I was undoubtedly helped in my passage into this new world of coaching by the tournament taking place in South Africa, as it was somewhere that was far more familiar to me than India. But in many ways that also made things harder, as it meant I had to put the Indian players at ease in what were unfamiliar conditions for them.

That victory alongside Adam Gilchrist was a terrific shared achievement, as he led by example as captain. Times like that provide picture-book memories for a coach.

Of course, the other side of the coin is to tell a player he has to make way. That is the hardest conversation of all. And I had to do that to Gilly, of all people.

Five years after that IPL win in Johannesburg, we were both at Kings XI Punjab, again as a captain-coach combination. I went and saw him and told him it was time he was dropped. The side was struggling, he was no longer the force he had once been as a batsman, and the side needed to move forward. I was honest – all you can do is to be honest, because as a player that is all you can ask for – but also did my best to show some empathy for a player who was at the end of the road. I had been there six years earlier and so I knew that was the only way to go about what was a very disagreeable task.

There were only two selectors of that side – me and him – so he could have made it very awkward and dug his heels in, but instead he thought through the situation very quickly and realised he had to step down both as a captain and a player. We moved on and remain the closest of mates.

From an Australian perspective, those types of awkward conversations are now the job of Rodney Marsh, who took over as Chairman of the National Selection Panel from John Inverarity in 2014. I don't envy him the role one bit. Yes, he also has the task of breaking good news to players, that they have been selected in the first place, and that is one of the joys of that role, telling someone that they are about to achieve the ambition of a lifetime and play for their country. But the job of telling players they have been left out is no fun at all and Rodney has to make those telephone calls almost every time a squad or a tour party is named.

The easiest way out for everyone is if a player retires – that he jumps before the selectors have to give him the tap on the shoulder – but that is an option that doesn't always appeal. For starters there is the adrenaline and the enjoyment, feelings that are not easily replaced. If you want an example of that then look no further than Michael Clarke's announcement in January 2016 that he wanted to come back to cricket, having retired just five months earlier. When he made the announcement that he was quitting cricket in

August 2015 he gave the impression that he had had enough and I could understand that.

Michael had spent much of the previous 12 months rehabilitating from injury rather than playing the game, and when he did make it on to the field he struggled to recapture his form of previous years. His outstanding leadership of the players in trying to come to terms with the death of Phillip Hughes had taken a great deal out of him and, having won the World Cup as captain – coming back into the side after a long period out through injury – he could justifiably wonder, once the Ashes series was over, what was left for him to achieve. But, in acting terms, the smell of the greasepaint and the roar of the crowd is addictive – and he missed it. It is as simple as that, I think.

Of course, another disincentive against retiring is the financial rewards the game now offers. Players are now dollar millionaires from just a year's salary and when you are receiving those sorts of rewards, why would you want to stop? The haven of the various Twenty20 leagues around the world do offer a gradual comedown for those players who suddenly fall out of favour at international level, but they, too, can last only so long.

The truth is that many of today's players have known nothing other than cricket and so the prospect of retirement can be a frightening one. And while I fell into my new career thanks to a combination of Warne, Berry and Gilchrist's thoughtfulness, there was still that period after I had been shown the door by South Australia where I genuinely wondered what I would do next with my life. Sure,

I had coaching qualifications, but who would take on an untried and untested person?

For many ex-players the Australian Cricketers' Association provides an invaluable crutch, helping with courses and retraining individuals for life in the real world. Some even start that process while they are still playing. My path, initially at least, saw me do some work for a local brewery in Adelaide and although much of it involved public appearances it was actually far harder than it might sound, as regular rounds of socialising over a few drinks did not represent the ideal recipe for a healthy lifestyle. I married that work with public speaking and I found I was quite good at it but, in truth, I didn't enjoy doing those 'sportys', as they always required you to put on a happy face for public consumption and, like any other person, I was not always happy, something that was especially the case in that year after I ended my playing career in Australia.

The one thing that did make my eventual transition from playing into coaching much easier was that for the previous decade I had filled the role of mentor and senior professional in most of the teams I was involved in. If you like I was a sort of dressing room shop steward, a barometer of the atmosphere among the players, a mentor for many of the younger generation and someone who, particularly in my time at Yorkshire, many of my teammates looked to for guidance, wisdom and advice.

Like many of the best things that have happened in my life, that time at Yorkshire started out as something of an accident. It was early 1997 and I was in serious need of a fresh challenge. I felt like my international career was going nowhere – I was still to make my Test debut at that stage – and, closer to home, my first marriage was failing. I had two terrific children, Jake, born in 1992, and Tori, born two years later, but professionally I needed something to put a smile back on my face.

My then manager Terry Davies, a Welshman who had played county cricket for Glamorgan, put out feelers and it seemed that both Hampshire and Yorkshire were interested. They had both lined up Australians to play for them – Matthew Hayden for Hampshire and Michael Bevan for Yorkshire – but both were expected to be named in the squad for that winter's Ashes series in England, so both counties needed cover for a season.

I made up my mind to go to Yorkshire and Terry and I approached them to seal the deal only to find out they had also been negotiating with Michael Slater, who was their preferred option. But when Slater was included in the Ashes squad and Hayden wasn't – allowing him to go back to Hampshire – it opened the way for me to go to Yorkshire and the rest is history. As mentioned earlier, my time there saw me become part of the first Yorkshire side to win the county championship in 33 years, which perhaps makes me forever welcome in Yorkshire. It helped me secure my place in the Australian squad in both Tests and One-Day Internationals. Most of all, it also introduced me to my second wife, Andrea. On that basis you have to say I did pretty well out of the deal!

I met Andrea through her brother Craig White, who I played alongside at Yorkshire but who had been brought up in Australia. We had played junior cricket against each other but although he attended the Australian Cricket Academy he opted to make his career in England as he had been born there, before his family moved to Australia when he was a small child.

We became firm friends once I went over to play for Yorkshire and after seeing Andrea once before actually meeting her, I asked Craig to introduce me during a match we were playing in the north of the county, at Scarborough, where she was working as a nurse. I'm not sure I made the perfect first impression as before I arrived at the bar where we were due to catch up, I had been out for a few drinks with the ex-Australia batsman David Boon, at that time captaining Durham. And not long after arriving at the bar I moved behind it and started to serve drinks to the customers!

Andrea told me much later that I was spot-on: that first impression was hardly ideal. She thought I was too full of myself and too happy to enjoy a drink. But fortunately, during the evening I managed to get my head together, move over to see her and have a chat and, although she knew I had been married already and had two children, thankfully she gave me the benefit of the doubt. We married in 1999 and I can safely say it has been the best partnership I have ever been involved in.

5

CREATING A PHILOSOPHY

'To provide an exciting and enjoyable environment for players and staff to grow on and off the field.'

Those were the words I came up with when, studying for my Level 2 coaching qualification in Brisbane while I was still playing, I was asked to summarise the philosophy I wanted to have as someone seeking to guide others in the game.

Almost a decade down the track I can still look at those words and feel they remain very much my aim as a coach and that they are something I have sought to live in every role I have filled.

Yes, there is the desire to make that difference that Andrea referred to when we spoke about whether or not I should take the Australia job, and yes, I know a coach is judged by results. It means you can have the greatest ideals in history, but you will still find yourself out the door if the team is not successful.

My rationale is that if you get the basic culture of the side right in the first place, results will hopefully take care of themselves. It is no substitute for having good players, but it is definitely a start. It is a cricketing equivalent of looking after the cents, and the dollars – in this case, the side's performances and, hopefully, its results – will start to look after themselves.

It was a philosophy that took shape in my own mind following the senseless and needless death of my mentor David Hookes in 2004. Hookesy died when he was struck from behind during a night out we were having in Melbourne and his death and its aftermath made me re-evaluate what was important to me.

I realised that while winning is why we are in the game, and there are few better feelings than when we succeed in that aim, at the same time, as I often say to my players and staff, we are not trying to cure cancer; we are playing cricket, a sport we all love, and we should do it in a way that not only brings enjoyment to ourselves but also to others because at the end of the day, in the grand scheme of things, cricket is not that important.

That may sound like a shocking admission from a person in charge of millions of dollars of talent in an industry that generates hundreds of millions of dollars and employs, directly or indirectly, thousands of people in Australia alone. But it is the truth and I believe that truth helps us to play with a freedom that would otherwise be gobbled up by morbid introspection and needless intensity.

In the current era, with the squad on the road either within Australia or overseas for roughly 300 days every year, it is very easy to slip into the trap of believing that cricket is the be-all and end-all, especially if you are a young player coming through the system now. These days, players have rarely been exposed to any sort of life outside the game and that is a fraught situation.

To counter that and to broaden our young players' minds, I am constantly on the lookout for experiences for the players to have outside of their working environment, experiences that make them realise there is a life beyond cricket and that while our legions of supporters want us to win, at the same time they also have far more important priorities.

I encourage players to get involved – and actively embrace – charitable causes, things like the McGrath Foundation, set up by Glenn McGrath to raise funds to battle breast cancer, which claimed the life of his wife, Jane. That charity is actually a special one for me, because my mother died of breast cancer and the good thing from a players' point of view is that they can actually see a tangible result from their support for a charity like that through the money raised during the Sydney Test, where it takes centre stage.

Ahead of the Twenty20 International series against India in early 2016, I arranged a visit for the squad to the Royal Society for the Blind (RSB) in Adelaide. The players were genuinely unsure of what to expect but, to a man, they all came back saying they had found the experience thoroughly uplifting.

During the visit – which sadly I missed as I was hospitalised with deep vein thrombosis in Sydney – they also met up with the Australian visually-impaired cricket team, battling it out with its England equivalent in their version of the Ashes, and afterwards Steve Smith told me of a speech given by Michael Zannis, a member of that team.

Michael first told the story of how he had become blind. Aged six, he was moving around the side of his house and accidentally walked into a wall. He bounced back up with the elasticity of childhood and went inside, but within five minutes he found himself asking his mother: 'Why have you turned the lights out? Why have you turned off the television?'

Sadly, the reality of the situation was far more serious. The retina in one of his eyes had become detached and that, in turn, put too much pressure on his other eye, so that two days later he became completely blind.

Far from feeling sorry for himself, however, Michael set about making the best of his new circumstances and he spoke of how he did it: he rose to the challenge, adapted to circumstances, and a place in the Australian team was his ultimate reward. Michael now works as an RSB staff member – he is a Braille instructor and runs the society's youth mentoring program. He works with children who have either lost their vision or who are losing it through degenerative conditions. As you can see, he is an outstanding example of what a blind person can achieve.

Steve told me Michael's brief speech would not have been out of place on the first morning of a Test match in alien conditions. It made a profound impression on him and the other players and staff present.

Occasions like that are a great reality check as it makes our players realise there is a big, wide world outside the bubble in which they exist. At the same time I also want the players to realise the game does not simply exist for them. They need to know there were players who came before them and that they are merely this generation's custodians of our great sport.

Perhaps the longest-running example of players stepping outside their bubble and embracing the real world exists at my old home, the Adelaide Oval, thanks to Barry 'Nugget' Rees.

Barry is a fixture in the South Australia and Australian dressing rooms and has been for the best part of 50 years. The way he has been embraced by successive generations of players shows the game in its very best light.

Barry was a lad with learning difficulties who loved his sport. One day back in the 1960s his father Ray approached the then South Australia and Australia wicketkeeper Barry Jarman, who co-owned the sporting goods store in Adelaide – which I also worked at – to see if he would take him on within that store.

Jarman asked him who his favourite cricketer was and Barry said 'Keith Miller'. 'Ah,' said Jarman, 'you mean "Nugget" Miller? That will be your nickname from now on.' And so the legend of Barry 'Nugget' Rees was born.

Jarman would take him to South Australia Sheffield Shield matches and very soon on interstate trips too. When Jarman retired Ian Chappell took over responsibility for maintaining Nugget's place within the fabric of South Australian cricket.

And so it has continued ever since. Nugget receives team kit – both Australian and South Australian – and can be seen in the viewing area at the front of the dressing room during every match at the Adelaide Oval. He sits there with his batting gloves on, waiting for his chance to shine in the middle, and although he has long since retired from work he continues to be embraced by the current crop of cricketers. He and his legendary team talks – including his frequently used catchcries 'much much', 'keep your throws up', 'catches win matches' and 'get behind the captain' – are as much a part of an Adelaide Test as the old manual scoreboard or the view of St Peter's Cathedral behind it.

When he retired from work, his friends within the Adelaide sporting community put together a 'Night with Nugget', a celebration of what he means to the people who have come into contact with him. His pulling power was incredible – Steve Waugh was there that night as the keynote speaker, Ian Chappell was there too. It was something of a who's who of Australian cricket, as well as being attended by many of his friends made over many years at Port Adelaide football club.

Nugget has had a profound effect on Port Adelaide too – its players, officials and supporters. Former coach Mark Williams said his players really related to Nugget and he attributed a pick-up in form during the second half of the 2006 season at least in part to the relaxing effect he had on the squad.

Steve Waugh summed things up brilliantly when he said Nugget has the uncanny ability to bring a player back down to earth, whatever the situation. He told ABC Television's *Australian Story* in 2007: 'Having Nugget around I think just gives you perspective, you know. When things aren't going well on the field and you've come off and you've played a bad shot and you've been dismissed, I mean, you feel pretty angry with yourself and then you see Nugget in the corner of the room, sort of waiting there, saying, "Well played, bad luck. It was a terrible decision." All of a sudden he brings you back down to earth and grounds you.'

Nugget doesn't have a bad bone in his body and he has touched so many people for so many years that when he finally pulls up stumps and the final siren goes, I expect Adelaide will grind to a halt. I saw Sir Donald Bradman's funeral on television and attended the service for David Hookes at the Adelaide Oval and I think any tribute to Nugget will be just as big. He has even been the subject of *Australian Story* not once but twice. How many others can say that?

The habit of inviting former players to present caps to newcomers is something that to the best of my knowledge developed under Steve Waugh's leadership and it remains front and centre in my approach. I love getting past players back and enjoy the fact that it's a two-way street: it keeps them connected to the game, making them continue to feel a part of something truly special as only a select few get to represent their country and, at the same time, it brings the past to life for the current players. It makes that business about being a custodian of the game so much more real.

Our dressing room door is always open to those former standard-bearers and for me it was an especially moving day when we had Bruce Reid, the former Western Australian fast bowler, present caps to One-Day International new-comers Scott Boland and Joel Paris at the WACA in Perth in January 2016.

Bruce was one of the outstanding players of his day, a truly terrific left-armer who was good enough to get 13 wickets in a Test against England at the MCG in 1990. He would have become one of the all-time greats had he not been stricken with injury. I still have a vivid recollection of how quick he was, as he smashed me on the helmet and knocked me out in my second season in first-class cricket in 1988–89!

He stayed with us throughout the match against India and it was great to hear the young players chat to him and for him to share his knowledge with them. And just as impor-tant was the fact that it brought home to those players how fortunate they are to be playing in this era; for Bruce there was no multi-million dollar contract and no big sponsor endorsements to make him comfortable in retirement. He now earns his living as an electrician. Nothing wrong with that – but it's hard work.

The connection to our past players was behind the inno-vation we adopted within the One-Day International squad during the World Cup in 1999, when myself, Tom Moody and Steve Waugh came up with the idea of putting our cap numbers on the side of our headwear. It was crude at first, done with a marker pen, but now every new player gets a cap with his number embroidered.

We have also started inviting past players into the dressing room to receive specially embroidered bags for their caps, complete with their names and their cap numbers on the outside. Many of the past players used to receive their caps in a cardboard box in their hotel room or, as Dean Jones told me, from his postman! Those players deserve just as much acknowledgement as the current generation and that is what we are seeking to give them.

During our One-Day International series against India in early 2016 we decided to travel from Canberra to Sydney by road rather than air, which allowed us to stop off at the Bradman Museum at Bowral, the first time an Australian squad had visited the site during its 26 years of existence. It was fascinating to see the players' faces as they handled the equipment used by Bradman and his contemporaries – I reckon three or four of the bats of that era taped together would just about replicate the thickness of one of David Warner's blades! – and to see several of the squad try – and fail – to perform The Don's famous batting drill of hitting a golf ball against a water-tank stand using a stump. The players left with a better appreciation of life as a cricketer in that earlier time and it truly was a living history lesson for them.

What I seek to bring to any side I work with is a sense of enjoyment and also a desire to do things out of the ordinary.

At the IPL in South Africa in 2008 I arranged for surfing lessons for the Deccan Chargers squad in Durban. The sight of a young Rohit Sharma trying to stand on his board and master the waves is something that will live with all of us who witnessed it forever! Rohit won't forget it in a hurry either. During that same tournament the whole squad went on a game drive. For many of the players it was the first time they had ever seen lions and elephants in the flesh.

For one of Queensland's pre-season camps I took the squad to Maroochydore, where we stayed in a distinctly different motel, complete with themed rooms – I remember we had an Elvis room and a Pink room! The players had to cook for themselves, do the team laundry, pick up groceries and do the washing-up, all things that most people have to do all the time, but for cricketers used to having things done for them, it was a valuable lesson and also a way to ensure better time management. It was not simply a case of doing their training and then drifting back to the accommodation to find a meal waiting and their clothes cleaned. They now had to plan and shop before training and ensure they were ready to sort out the food and the laundry duties once they returned. It brought everyone together and the results we enjoyed at Queensland during my time as coach – a Sheffield Shield win in 2012 and Big Bash League and Ryobi Cup successes 12 months later – showed it was a philosophy all the players bought into.

In England on my first tour as Australia's head coach in 2013 we had a night out in Liverpool that included time in the Cavern Club, the nightclub from which the Beatles set about conquering the world. The evening ended up with Shane Watson – who is a keen guitar player – up on stage singing. It was another memorable night!

My approach as a coach is based around three very simple concepts: openness, honesty and hard work, and if we get those things right then we will always be on the right track.

Team meetings are pointless unless people are prepared to say what's on their mind. If they can do that without fear of recrimination, that creates a great environment for proper debate where constructive results can be achieved.

In the United Kingdom in August 2015 we lost a Twenty20 International against England that was ours for the taking. We wanted 28 from the final three overs with seven wickets in hand and one player – Steve Smith – well set with hitters around him. Yet from that position of strength the wheels fell off and we ended up losing by five runs.

Two of those hitters were Mitchell Marsh and newcomer Marcus Stoinis and both found themselves rendered stroke-less through a combination of clever slower balls by the England attack along with the pressure situation.

Afterwards, as we dissected the match in the dressing room, George Bailey spoke up and said to Marsh and Stoinis: 'Lads, you are both great hitters. You've done it consistently at home, which is why you're here, and you've done it consistently in practice. It's up to you to do it for us in situations like that too.'

It was true. The position was made for them to go out and win the game for us and they weren't able to do so, something they both knew and admitted. That is the type of honest feedback we encourage within the team environment. No grudges are held and, if they are, then players within the team ensure that those issues are swiftly resolved. There is no backbiting and it has become self-policing.

Bailey himself struggled in one of the matches of the One-Day International series that followed. Against the spin of Moeen Ali in game three at Old Trafford he kept trying either to run down the pitch or to sweep, achieving little success with either option. The more he tried, the more he struggled. He became frustrated and the scoring rate required – already up above a run a ball at the start of the innings – spiralled out of control.

Afterwards I said to him: 'What was wrong with just sitting on the back foot and easing the ball with the spin through the vacant square leg for one to get off strike? You were struggling, so just turn the strike over, keep the board ticking and reflect on better options from the non-striker's end.'

Bailey thought about what I said, took it on board and then, in the final match of the series, he put what we'd spoken about into practice and helped us to victory.

The squad works hard, but I like to think we work smart as well. When we train we have a group warm-up to start the session, but after that I encourage players to do what they feel they need to do and nothing more. There is no point in hanging around at a net session for three hours just for the sake of it and there are no points from the coach to be gained for doing so; my approach is: 'Get in, get what you need and get away so that you can be fresh for the match.'

The idea is for players to go to a practice session with a clear idea of what they want to work on. It might be a particular shot, it might be a new type of slower ball, but I tell the players not to turn up without any real aims in mind. That is a recipe for a mediocre session that achieves nothing. That is an advantage of having our group of specialist coaches with the squad at all times: those coaches know the players' games and are also in a position to work with them on specific issues; in previous eras that sort of bespoke training simply was not possible, because the squad's support staff usually consisted of one or, at most, two coaches, who were always spread far too thinly among the players.

Another philosophy I am very strong on is that family comes first. They are the people who have looked after us and nurtured our love of the sport and they are the ones we owe our first debt of loyalty to. As Jeff Thomson said during his wonderfully funny and moving acceptance speech after being inducted into the Australian Cricket Hall of Fame in 2016, they are the people who get successful players to the top through their support. If a player has a family commitment then I always encourage them to look to that commitment first, above and beyond cricket.

In England in 2015 I was accused of paying lip service to that philosophy through the treatment of Brad Haddin. Now it is time to put the record straight.

Brad pulled out of the second Test of that Ashes series at Lord's to spend time with his family and with daughter Mia, who was unwell. Peter Nevill came in and performed well in a terrific win for the side before Brad returned to the squad ahead of the next match of the series in Birmingham.

That left us with a decision to make and we opted to retain Peter and leave Brad on the sidelines, a decision that drew criticism. We were asked: 'How can you encourage players like Brad to put family first and then reward that decision by leaving him out when he returns to the fold?'

The whole episode was a great learning curve for me as a coach and a selector – you never stop learning, even when you have been at the top end of the sport for as long as I have – and the thing I learnt most of all is that there are times when you need to grasp the nettle and be as bold as you can in your decision-making.

You see, in the case of Brad Haddin what it boiled down to was, first and foremost, a selection issue, as we should never have taken him to the West Indies and the United Kingdom in the first place, something I think he, too, now acknowledges.

Towards the end of the home Test series against India in the summer of 2014–15, I started to have my doubts about how much longer he could go on for, but I allowed my love for him as a player and a team man to cloud my judgement. I thought he could continue to perform to the required level in the Caribbean and during the Ashes series but, with my experience, I should have known better.

In the Caribbean, during the two-Test series in which Brad made 30 runs in two innings, I said to him – and Shane Watson, who was also searching for form – 'Are you going to get some runs or are you going to retire?' They both said they would get some runs, but I knew in my heart of hearts they had run their race at Test level.

So when Brad dropped England's first innings century-maker Joe Root on the first morning of the Ashes series in Cardiff and then failed twice with the bat, playing a poor shot to be dismissed in the second innings as we slid to defeat, his place in the side was very much on the agenda, even before he missed the Lord's Test. And when Peter stepped in and performed so well in a winning side, there was no way we could drop him and bring back Brad, who had been struggling for form for some time.

What needs to be known is that we had to pick our Test squad for both the West Indies and United Kingdom Test tours together, because the series were back-to-back. Logistically it made sense, but from a selection perspective it locked us in to taking players on the second tour who were either out of form or over the hill. Given my time again, I would try to ensure we never have a repeat of that scenario and that after each tour there is a period, however brief, where we can at least take stock and weigh up our options. We didn't take that time in 2015 and it cost us dearly.

As for dissent in the squad over Brad's situation, I have to say if it did exist then I did not see it. I think the players were all aware of the issue of form and that the biggest voices of protest came from those outside the camp. It is a measure of Brad's character that he remained a fantastic team man throughout the rest of that trip, working his socks off with Peter and very much remaining the conscience and heart-beat of the side, even though he was not on the field.

Hard work is what drives me and impresses me and in that sense you may argue that my position as coach is weakened because of my poor approach to fitness during my time as a player. I would argue it actually strengthens my hand in that regard.

I can say 'Do as I say, don't do as I did' and mean it because I have the record to show that mine was a career of missed opportunities. Yes, I played in two World Cup finals, but I can point to my statistics and say 'I played 27 Tests and if I had looked after myself, I could and should have played 100.' That is a compelling argument in anyone's language.

In any case, the schedule these days means I do not think a player like myself – talented, but not terribly hard working in terms of my fitness; master of the game but not necessarily athletic – would survive. The need for athleticism has never been greater and players of my type are a dying breed. Some may think that is sad, but I prefer to see it as reality. Adapt or perish, that is the modern way and so it should be.

6

DEVELOPING A STYLE

Each coach will have his or her own style; that is a given, born of an individual's personality. It might be primarily hands-off, collaborative or dictatorial but, for me, I think the best coach will always be someone who incorporates a bit of all of the above into their approach.

The coach's own preferred mode of operation will also come into the equation, of course, but the key is to read the group you have in front of you. Once you understand their mood you can react accordingly.

When Bobby Simpson was installed as the first national coach, he focused on hard work and intensely drilling his players, a method that was carried on by one of his former players, Geoff Marsh. By the time John Buchanan took over the reins, the side was well and truly established at the top of the tree. His time at the helm was less technical and more about challenging the players mentally, challenging those greats of the game to go even higher.

During my time with the national side I have found myself alternating between the Simpson/Marsh style on the one hand and the Buchanan style on the other. I began by focusing on hard work and then, as the players became more established and started to win more often, looked to challenge them more. It is always easier to start tough and then wind it back than begin with a loose idea of the boundaries and then try to rein things in if it all goes wrong.

At the start of the One-Day International tri-series against India and England ahead of the World Cup in 2015, I asked the side whether it would be possible to go through the rest of the summer unbeaten. As it turned out, the side did lose one match from that point, the World Cup outing against New Zealand in Auckland. After that loss I challenged them again, to go through the rest of the tournament unbeaten. They succeeded. I always regard a goal like that as important, something for players to focus on, whatever external things may be bothering them, helping them to turn their attentions, at least when on the field, to the game itself. I also viewed it as a way of trying to take the players' minds off the tragic death earlier in the season of their great little mate, Phillip Hughes.

Incidentally, I do not regard goals like that as counter-productive; there is a school of thought that says players should simply focus on one match at a time and by doing so the rest will take care of itself. I believe it is important to always have an end goal in mind. Ask Sir Alex Ferguson when he was manager of Manchester United what his ambition was for the season before a ball was kicked and I am sure he would not have said he just wanted to win the first match and then take it from there; his ambition was always to win the English Premier League title and that desire was what drove him and his players year after year.

The danger for the coach is to just stay in one mode, failing to adapt to the changing needs of the players. As the group changes and develops, so should you, and the coach that does not is going to have a very short shelf life.

I am often asked what I actually *do* as head coach. As I have mentioned already, I see myself primarily as a manager of people and of many aspects of what goes on around the team, with the captain as the Chief Executive Officer. I am across as much as I feel I need to be and my staff will approach me with other matters on a need-to-know basis. The physiotherapist and doctor might let me know that player A is struggling with a tight hamstring, while the bowling coach might tell me that player B bowled his full quota of deliveries at the nets and the strength and conditioning trainer might alert me to the fact that player C covered five kilometres more than anyone else in the field during the previous match and so, combined with lower than normal speed and endurance results during a running drill at a training session that followed, he might need to be rested from the next match. I am a receptacle for information and my job is to decide what is important and what is not and to act upon it in conjunction with my staff, my fellow selectors and the captain.

Strange though it may seem, the matches themselves are actually a time for me to relax. Relaxation is, of course, a relative thing. I am invested in the result, so I still ride the highs and lows of any game in the same way that players and supporters do. But as long as I know the players and I have done our preparation, there is nothing more for me to do. Yes, I might have the odd word here and there if I spot something technical, and the coach's box is a good place to observe from, giving a much better perspective of the ground than a player gets in the thick of the action. Maybe cover-point has been placed too square, maybe third man needs to go a bit finer. I will throw the occasional suggestion to the captain at the appropriate time and he can then choose to take it on board or ignore it, but during play I will often use my time to plough through emails. Anti-corruption regulations do not allow me to connect to the internet in the dressing room, but I still write and reply to outstanding correspondents and once I get back to the hotel I log on and out they all go.

Using my time in that way is vital, because while players are focused on what happens on the field, that is now just one part of the coach's role. I have to be accountable to not only those players but also to the Cricket Australia Board of Directors. I have my hand in schedules, budgets, player availability – especially when the international program coincides with the Big Bash League – and selection, as well as managing my staff, alongside the team manager

Gavin Dovey and Pat Howard, the Executive Director of Team Performance. That is a lot of fingers in a lot of pies.

The key to keeping all the juggled balls in the air simultaneously is to be organised and prepared. Thankfully that is something I have never struggled with. Go to my hotel room the day *before* our departure and you will find me already packed and ready to go. I cannot abide having to rush around at the last minute and I do all I can to avoid it.

I think my desire to be ready stems from my mother. She was terrific in that regard and her approach rubbed off on me. It is fair to say I probably took it too far at times, as I often slept in my whites the night before a junior match for one of the clubs I played for as a youngster – Gawler, Sandy Creek or Lyndoch – and more than once Mum had to come into my room and demand I took off my cricket gear and put on my pyjamas!

David Hookes was another who was meticulously prepared, mirroring my mother's 'always ready' philosophy. Given two of the most important people in my formative years had that approach, I guess it was inevitable I would adopt it too.

One of my key roles is being one of four selectors that pick every senior Australia squad. My view on whether the coach should be part of that inner circle has altered during my time in the hot seat.

When I first took on the role of coach on the Ashes tour of 2013 I was clear in my own mind that I should not have a formal role in selection, as I felt it had the potential to create friction between the players and myself. After all,

I thought, would a player, especially one struggling for form or fitness or both, be entirely honest with me, knowing that I am there to mentor him on the one hand and have a role in potentially dropping him on the other?

Experience, however, has led me to see things differently and I am now more than comfortable alongside Rodney Marsh, Trevor Hohns and Mark Waugh. After all, as a coach I live and die by results, so surely I have to have a say in the players who will help to deliver those results?

Also, having created that culture of honesty within the group, along with open and honest feedback, the reality is that players generally now know exactly where they stand. If any of them are left out then they are told why and also what they have to do to get back in.

In any case, any coach worth his salt should know when one of his players is struggling, whether it is physically, technically or mentally, and, if so, what the issue is. If he doesn't, he is not doing his job properly. Once any issue is established, the coach needs to show some compassion to the player. We are all human beings, after all.

I have already touched upon the larger numbers of support staff around than in previous eras. I know it can draw ridicule in some quarters, but every one of the people has been identified as filling a need, whether it is the doctor, the physiotherapist, the media manager, the strength and conditioning trainer, the dietician or the batting, bowling and fielding coaches. This is now a multi-million dollar business and as coach, along with the likes of Pat Howard and, further up the chain of command James Sutherland,

Cricket Australia's Chief Executive Officer, we would not be doing our jobs if we were not constantly on the lookout for the next one per-center, the next small but significant competitive advantage that could separate us from our rivals. That is the nature of modern-day sport and it applies not only to cricket.

You could argue that the extra support around the squad has the potential to make the players less self-reliant, but that is not my experience. The players are still happy to take personal responsibility as, at the end of the day, it is they who go out and play and not the people behind the scenes. If things go wrong then the players – along with the coach – are the ones who carry the can, as has always been the case.

When I became Australian coach in 2013 I did so with just one stipulation: that all the staff already employed on the tour would stay and that, whatever happened in the future, all of them would have their contracts honoured.

There was a view at the time that I should have come in and swept away everyone from the previous regime and started with a clean slate, but I viewed that as counter-productive. Changing the coach so close to the Ashes series was destabilising in itself, so I wanted to keep any other disruption to a minimum.

I used the series to assess each and every member of the support team and subsequently I brought in Damian Mednis as strength and conditioning coach, someone I had worked with successfully at Queensland, but overall my approach was very much evolution rather than revolution.

It was interesting to see what happened when David Moyes took over as Manchester United manager after Sir Alex Ferguson had occupied that role for 27 years. It was an impossible act to follow, but I think Moyes made things harder for himself by jettisoning Sir Alex's support staff, men such as first-team coach Mike Phelan, and bringing in his own men. It was understandable that he would want to put his own stamp on the place, but by making wholesale changes in the way that he did, he removed any semblance of continuity. The familiar became the unfamiliar for many of the players, with unfortunate results, as Moyes was eventually sacked, without lasting one full season.

It would be far-fetched to compare the Manchester United squad of 2013, English Premier League title winners in Sir Alex's final season, with our Ashes squad touring the United Kingdom that same year – we were anything but serial winners at the stage – but I think the lesson is still applicable: professional players like the familiar, they like continuity and they like a regular routine. They like working with the same coach week-in and week-out, because they know that the coach will then have an understanding of their game and its mechanics and will be more likely to pick up little things and be able to diagnose any adjustments that may need to be made. Players are creatures of habit, and if you offer them certainty in their routines they are more likely to focus on their own techniques rather than worrying about trifles like training times and who is working with them. The relationships between Steve Smith and our former batting coach Michael Di Venuto – who has now moved on to coach English county side Surrey – or between Nathan Lyon and spin bowling coach John Davison are prime examples of men who know a player's game inside-out and can spot subtle little changes in technique before the player himself may be aware they have crept in. Those sorts of relationships, based on technical know-how and trust, take time to build. While there is a valid argument that a fresh pair of eyes can also prove useful in analysing technique, my first instinct is always to trust those who have worked with a player over a prolonged period.

My first address to the players and support staff at Taunton was a nerve-racking affair. I knew several of the players were close to Mickey Arthur, not least the captain Michael Clarke, and I also knew that I was portrayed in sections of the media as some sort of white knight, riding in to save the day, with the impression that all I had to do was wave a magic wand and everything would suddenly be transformed.

I knew that sport does not work like that, particularly at the top level and particularly with a group of players who had become used to losing. In that environment all I sought to do was to tell the squad that everything we did from now on would be governed by one word: care.

I would care for everyone in my charge and we all would care for each other. And while we might have disagreements – what families don't? – the most important thing was how we dealt with them. Agree to disagree if you have to, but do so and then move on.

I knew, too, that whatever I was feeling inside, as a rule of thumb I always had to give the impression I was relaxed. It was a lesson I learnt from my time at Victoria under Les Stillman, who really did wear his heart on his sleeve. I know from speaking to some former England players from my era that David Lloyd was very much like that when he was coach of England. If I can give the impression I am calm – even if, inside, my heart is racing, my stomach is churning and I feel like I am about to explode – then that can have a positive influence on the team; if I race around talking to players throughout a match, throwing advice out left, right and centre or blow my top at a poor shot, a dropped catch or a poor piece of bowling, that has the potential to sour the atmosphere, take away from players' focus and upset the whole applecart.

What I wanted to achieve, first and foremost, in 2013 was to change the atmosphere. What I found was a group of players who were constantly looking over their shoulders, worried about getting the chop. That fostered an atmosphere of self-interest and distrust. Players were looking out for themselves rather than each other. That was something I sought to address by honesty and constant communication. I was determined to let players and staff know where they stood, and slowly but surely an atmosphere of trust rather than mistrust began to prevail.

I made a small but, I felt, significant change in 2013 by stopping the players from having their mobile phones back immediately after the day's play. Phones are taken off players by anti-corruption officials as soon as they arrive at the dressing room at the start of the day. This is a mark of the reality of the threat of corruption in the modern game, as the measure prevents the possibility of anyone within the squad either betting or passing on team information to outsiders who may be looking to profit from the news.

When I started playing the idea of players or officials fixing matches just wasn't on the radar, but the rise of the internet and global broadcast coverage of cricket has opened up the chance for more and more people not only to watch the sport but also to bet on it. It is an extremely lucrative business and if someone can get the inside track on an issue, they have the potential to make a fortune.

Under the anti-corruption regulations the players are free to get their phones back once the last ball has been bowled, but my approach from day one was to tell them they could have them back only when they went to the team bus. That meant that rather than checking emails or updating their social media profiles, they actually had to have conversations with each other. I had no problem with players having a beer after play, as anything that helps an individual relax is okay by me. I would obviously draw the line at someone getting drunk, but the self-policing element – together with the incident earlier on the tour involving David Warner – ensured that no-one stepped out of line. All I asked of the players in everything they did was to answer a couple of straightforward questions: 'will this be detrimental to what the side is trying to achieve?' and 'what would my team-mates think?' If the answer to either of those questions were negatives, the player would know he was in the wrong.

My desire to show the players that I cared for them did not mean I did not read them the riot act from time to time. Our performance in the Lord's Test match on that tour was lamentable and I told them so, but other than that I think it is fair to say that although we lost the series 3–0, things could quite easily have been very different.

Yes, a combination of Phillip Hughes, Ashton Agar, Brad Haddin and James Pattinson took us to the brink of victory in the opening Test of the series, but the truth was we were outplayed in that match, and although we fought hard and ended up with the rough end of the odd decision we got what we deserved. And the less said about the Lord's debacle the better.

But thereafter I do not think anyone could say we were not extremely competitive and we had the better of large chunks of the last three Tests. We would have won at Old Trafford but for rain, and we should have won at Durham but for a superb spell of bowling from Stuart Broad that brought about a batting collapse from a position of strength. We were in complete control of the final match at The Oval before rain forced us to try to manufacture a result through a generous declaration, which was the only way England was going to get back into contention. Things were heading in the right direction and that view was borne out by both the One-Day International series that followed the Tests and the subsequent home series against the same opposition in 2013–14.

There is no doubt that the role of the coach does differ from franchise and state cricket to international level. When

I took over at the Deccan Chargers I had to deal with not only working with players, many of whom I had not met or seen before, but also with owners who were very demanding. Of course, having invested a great deal of money in the team, they had every right to be demanding and as a first assignment it was ideal for me. I felt if I could get through the rough and tumble and pressure that created, then I would be able to cope with anything.

My answer to that level of expectation was to plan and also to encourage the players – and the owners – never to get too high following a victory and never to get too low after a defeat. No-one means to lose, after all; the key is whether you learn from defeat so that you can be better next time.

Deccan's owners were not only demanding, they were also extremely superstitious. Each time we won they wanted to ensure we did the same things ahead of the next match and they actually asked me to pick the same side even though we might be playing on a different type of pitch that demanded the selection of different players. We had prayer sessions and when we won we had to do them again by way of a thank you to the powers-that-be that had looked favourably upon us. As a new coach it was a fascinating insight into another way of working and living.

As a player I had my own superstitions: I never ate duck at a Chinese restaurant during a game, I would wear the same gear the next morning if I was not out overnight, and when batting I would wear the same old socks my mother had patched up thousands of times. It was always a great reminder of her and everything she did to get me to a place where I could make cricket my chosen career.

I would mark the crease twice for the first ball I faced, then four times thereafter, each over. Talk about superstitious! So I understood why my bosses at the Deccan Chargers behaved that way. I reckon you can go through any side and find players full of traits like that.

Deccan's owners were demanding but also fair and the same could be said of my bosses at Queensland Cricket. In many ways I was faced with the same challenge I had encountered with Deccan, in that the Bulls were rock bottom and so the only way was up.

When I linked up with Queensland my only stipulation was a three-year contract, because I wanted some security, as the role would involve moving my family lock, stock and barrel up to Brisbane. Queensland Cricket agreed to that and threw in an incentive off the back of our agreement: every time we won a competition I would have my deal extended by a year. That suited me fine as it gave me something to work towards.

The advantage of coaching Deccan and Queensland, and later Kings XI Punjab, was that the seasons of all three teams took place over a set period of time. You knew when the matches would be played and you knew when the off-season was, and that was the time when you were able to get your planning done. I would maintain that one of the key reasons I enjoyed success with Deccan and Queensland was that I was able to prepare for each campaign. The international environment has nonstop demands, which makes it far more challenging. That is another reason why you need the numbers of back-up staff and support to help you navigate through the challenges.

One question that often seems to get tossed around is whether a good coach can make a modest team better and, conversely, whether a poor coach can drag a good team down. I think the answer to both questions is yes as, on the one hand, a culture with planning, organisation, honesty and openness of the type we have developed in the Australian system is always more likely to help players to grow. On the other hand, a set-up without those disciplines, at least in my opinion, greatly reduces the chance of the best talent flourishing.

Do I coach differently depending on the match? For example, do I coach differently in a World Cup final from, say, a Matador Cup match for Queensland or a match for Deccan Chargers or Kings XI Punjab in the IPL? The answer to that is yes and no.

At domestic or franchise level, because some of the players may not be world-class, you can tend to be more technical. You might not boil it down to basics like how to play a cover-drive but you might, for example, discuss how to handle various bowlers or which scoring areas to target. At international level you tend to keep things simpler. Once players get to that level they tend to know what to do – although, as I mentioned earlier, sometimes match awareness is something you need to drill into them if they have been promoted at a young age – and so the messages are clear and concise.

As a rule of thumb though, no team meeting, no matter how impressive or revelatory the content, should run for more than 30 minutes. If your meeting lasts longer than that, you haven't prepared properly and you are liable to lose the players through an overload of information.

The team meetings we had before the 1999 and 2003 World Cup finals when I was a player and the 2015 edition when I was a coach were all pretty similar. The players were ready, they had performed outstandingly to get to the ultimate match and now it was a case of going out and executing so that we came out on top. The advantage we had on each of those occasions was that we had already met our final opponents – Pakistan in 1999, India in 2003 and New Zealand in 2015 – earlier in those tournaments, so we knew more or less everything about them and how they would play. It was up to our batsmen and bowlers to have their own plans to combat those opponents and that came back to the personal responsibility I have always preached. In 2015 if any player needed help in working things out they could come and kick around ideas with myself or one of my coaches, but that was something that tended to happen at practice when players refined their approaches rather than before or after a team meeting.

What did vary from the times I was a player in 1999 and 2003 to my time as a coach in 2015 was that the players' intake of alcohol throughout the tournament was significantly less. As mentioned earlier, in 1999 we started the tournament with a blanket ban on alcohol, but we found bcing so prescriptive turned out to be counter-productive and the ban was lifted by the coach and captain midway through the tournament, after which we began to win as the players became more relaxed. In 2003 we certainly celebrated, especially after our semi-final win against Sri Lanka in Port Elizabeth. I can still remember the flight to Johannesburg the following afternoon: it was like someone had sprayed the plane with sleeping gas as we snoozed off our night out.

That was an illustration of the relaxed culture we had under John Buchanan and Ricky Ponting with a side full of stars. Again, there was a huge emphasis on personal responsibility and while no-one was banned from enjoyed themselves, woe betide anyone who turned up for training or a match the worse for wear, as Andrew Symonds found out to his cost on the tour of the United Kingdom in 2005.

In the decade or more that followed that World Cup win of 2003 the goalposts in terms of consumption of alcohol have definitely shifted. Part of that has been brought on by a far more hectic playing schedule, which means players can no longer overindulge and expect to remain at peak fitness. In that 2015 World Cup, for example, we flew further than any other side and there was no way our players could have coped with that had they been the worse for wear every time they boarded a plane.

Another part of that change has been the advent of social media. Everyone now seems to have a camera in their phone and every move of every player if they are out in public is liable to be captured, uploaded and re-Tweeted in a matter of seconds. Mitchell Marsh told me during the summer of 2015–16 that he has not been out socially to a bar in his home city of Perth in two years because of the concern of being in the wrong place in the wrong time. That is a sad state of affairs.

You might think I am therefore against social media, but the truth is quite the opposite. As a coach, the likes of Facebook, Twitter and Snapchat are an absolute must for me, because they are ways in which I can stay in touch with my players and staff. I can find out when birthdays are and how families are getting on and I find it an invaluable tool to stay connected.

This generation lives on the phone and we have to adapt to that. It is something Cricket Australia has embraced. It has an app that is a diary of activities for players, updated by the team manager, the media manager and various support staff. It is the ideal way of informing players of everything they need to know, from training times to what the dress code is for a certain event. There are no more notes under hotel room doors, a practice that often seemed to go wrong during John Buchanan's tenure. I still remember, in 2001, the media trying to work out the significance of Sun Tzu's book *The Art of War* and its relevance to a Test match between England and Australia at Trent Bridge!

My routine in the lead-up to a match tends not to involve reading Sun Tzu; instead, the night before a game usually sees me relax with a beer. By then I know I have done all my preparation and it is now in the hands of the players. If I am not relaxed, it means I have not done my job.

I will always go to the ground early on match days – I like to be the first there – and just get a feel for the place, the atmosphere and conditions. In Melbourne, Perth and Canberra we usually stay quite close to the venue, which allows me to walk. I call that walk my time, my chance to switch off and just let my mind wander. I might call my wife as I am strolling along or I might listen to some music (my playlist is sorted out by Amy and Ethan).

Once the players' warm-ups are done and dusted I tend to float between them, assisting any that may need my help – a chat with the captain about the toss here, a few throw-downs for a player there, and maybe taking a few deliveries from the quick bowlers using the catcher's glove or giving some catches to a fielder or the wicketkeeper. Once that is done it is time to head for the coach's box and let the match take its course.

I am less superstitious than I was as a player, although I will tend to try to use the same pen, the same notepad and even wear the same running shoes if we are winning.

I do love a joke, but over the years I have learnt when to play them and when not to do so. I remember someone once cut the laces of Peter Siddle's shoes and he absolutely blew up, so it is a case of picking your target and your time. Half an hour before the start of a match is not one of those times, but at the same time humour is often a great way to defuse tension. I once put a Queensland player's car up for sale by placing its details, along with a very competitive price and his mobile number, in the 'for sale' section of the local newspaper. Just hearing his voice as he answered his phone for the umpteenth time – 'NO! My car is NOT for sale!' – was priceless. It was payback for him spiking my drink with Tabasco sauce. I waited three months before I got my revenge. As with batting, timing is the key.

7

MAN MANAGEMENT

The modern coach, at least at international level, is first and foremost a man-manager, and the ability to do that success- fully means you cannot adopt a one-size-fits-all approach.

Players – and support staff – are individuals, so it is all about quickly sizing up newcomers to the group and then working out what buttons to push to get the best out of each person.

It may be an arm around the shoulder with one, a kick up the backside with another and a few words of praise or encouragement with yet another.

The ability to interact well with individuals in the team environment certainly requires that you have the respect of those individuals and thankfully I was able to achieve that through a combination of my reputation as a player and also my desire for plain speaking and honesty. People very quickly know where they stand with me, and that is something I find most appreciate very much.

Of course, I also have to manage the squad as a group too – as opposed to any individual interactions I have – and how hard I work them depends on two things: our travel schedule and the experience within the line-up. The modern play-pack-travel existence can be demanding on bodies and minds, and so my challenge is always to know when to push the players a little harder and when to ease off them work-wise. It is a delicate balance.

I will often allow myself to be guided by the medical and performance staff I have around me, particularly as I have found the modern player is far less inclined than those from my generation to take time off. With the players I have worked with since 2013 I can say, almost without exception, that if you give them the option to work, they will take it. So there have been times, like for example ahead of the final, decisive One-Day International of the tour of the United Kingdom in 2015 and the last One-Day International of the home series against India in January 2016, where I have had to *order* a complete day off.

Players might not always realise it, but a day away from cricket is sometimes a must just to recharge, more mentally than anything else, allowing them to get out of bed without having to think about when the next training session or meeting is. I am strongly of the view that once players reach the elite level, missing one net session is not suddenly going to make them terrible players.

On top of that, breaks also give the support staff time away too. They are the unsung foot soldiers of the squad. Whenever there is a practice session, even if it is an optional one and only a handful of players choose to attend, there will still be strapping to be done, balls to be thrown, techniques to be fine-tuned and medical issues to be dealt with.

The backroom boys are the ones who spend the hours getting the players on the field in the best condition possible, but are often the ones who, in the past, have not had a break themselves. On that basis I have made a conscious effort, alongside Pat Howard, to try to rotate those people so that some may work in Tests only during a home summer rather than across all three formats, and others, on especially long tours like 2015 when we bounced from the Caribbean to the United Kingdom, may miss blocks of that schedule. We sent virtually the whole backroom team home after the Ashes series, and replaced them with another for the limited-overs matches at the end of that trip. That was important, as it not only gave those who left a break after a relentless period, but it also brought fresh people – and therefore fresh energy and enthusiasm – into the group, something I believed helped get those of us on the whole trip across the line.

Rotation! Now that has become a dirty word in Australian cricket when it comes to players – and that annoys me. What I, together, with my medical and support team, try to do in assessing whether or not we need to give breaks to players is to assess their fitness ahead of every match. Are they absolutely right to go, have they thought about their game plans and prepared their bodies? And if a series has already been won, we also take that into account in reaching a decision on whether or not to give someone a chance to freshen up on the sidelines. In an ideal world you would obviously like to pick your best available XI for every match, but when players spend up to 300 days each year on the road that is simply not possible. Ever since my era we have created a climate where rotation does not happen with Tests, as that format has become untouchable – and fair enough too. Earning a baggy green cap is no mean feat and cheapening that honour is not something we would ever want to do. But we have felt able to be a little more flexible when it comes to One-Day Internationals and Twenty20 Internationals, because neither of those two formats have quite the same history as the longest form of the game.

That flexibility gives us the opportunity to look at players in the international environment and allows us to form an opinion on whether or not they might be ready to make the jump up to Test level. Think of Adam Gilchrist, Brad Haddin and Michael Hussey as three examples of players who have gone down that route to Test stardom. Even Michael Clarke first played for Australia in a One-Day International in 2003, replacing me when I was suspended. Without that approach we would never have got a first glimpse at those players in international colours and been able to see they were ready to go to the next level.

I sympathise with the argument that the public may sometimes feel short-changed when they buy a ticket for a match months in advance hoping to see a certain player, only to find that the player has been given a break. But that, for better or worse, is the reality of the modern game. Players simply cannot play every game. Just imagine trying to do your job day after day, either training for the job or actually doing it, without a weekend off. Eventually you would become stale, your performance would suffer and it would be of no benefit to you or your employer. The same is true of the modern international cricketer.

Of course, we try to tinker less with our One-Day International squad in the build-up to a World Cup year. The vast majority of the 1999 and 2003 squads that I played in were together for the best part of a year or 18 months before the main events, with just the odd addition here and there, like Tom Moody's inclusion just ahead of that 1999 success. In 2015 the core of the team was also pretty much set in stone a long way out from the event, although the same was not true before the ICC World Twenty20 in 2016. That was due to scheduling and nothing more, as we have so little Twenty20 International cricket on which to base our selection. The earlier you can set out the roles for players within a set-up the better, and our success, especially in the one-day format, is testament to that. Even when we do rotate players – or give them managed rest, or a break or whatever term you want to use – the make-up of the side remains the same, in that whoever comes in does so on a like-for-like basis so as to minimise any change to the dynamic of the team.

I mentioned my treatment of the group depends on the level of experience within it and there was a great example of that during the limited-overs series in the United Kingdom.

We had won the first two matches of a five-game One-Day International series against England and done so convincingly, but in game three played very poorly indeed, first to allow England to reach 8-300 and then to be bowled out for 207 with six overs left unused. The batsmen played poor shots and did not produce decent game-plans, especially against England's spinners on a pitch offering increasing amounts of turn.

Had our group been made up of the World Cup winners earlier that year I would have laid into them post-play and told them exactly how poor I thought they were; but this was a different, inexperienced group, with not one of them having reached 100 career matches. So I opted instead for a more understated post-match debrief in which they did plenty of talking themselves. The proof of the pudding turned out to be an improved batting display in game four – albeit with another loss – and then victory in the last match of the series to lift the trophy.

I have learnt from experience that the best time to get angry with players is when we win. Following defeat they are already feeling flat and that is the time you really need to lift them up, remind them of the quality they have and also of the plans that need to be adhered to in order to give ourselves the maximum chance of success.

I made the mistake of losing my temper during the lunch break on the second day of the Lord's Test of 2013. England had begun the day at 7-289 and we had high hopes of rolling the last three wickets over quickly.

We did take those last three wickets in a little more than 11 overs, but they cost us 72 runs, as England's lower order made merry against some very average bowling and fielding. Our response saw us 1-42 at lunch, during which I tore into the players, saying how disappointed I was with our effort in the field.

It certainly did not help the mood ahead of the second session and although there was no direct tie-in between my comments and the hapless batting that followed – we were rolled for just 128 – I realised I had not helped matters. It is not something I will repeat again in a hurry. Any comments I have for the group nowadays are reserved for the post-day wrap-up.

If I have something to say to a player, especially if it is critical, then I will usually reserve it for a one-to-one discussion. The last thing I ever want to do is belittle a player in front of his peers.

And if you ever see me being critical of a player in the media, you can be absolutely sure of two things: that I will have had the conversation with the player first and that I ensure I sugar any criticism with an explanation of what I am looking for by way of an improvement.

Take Glenn Maxwell, for example. During the Matador Cup domestic one-day series against Queensland in October 2015, Glenn got out playing a reckless shot and contributed to a Victoria batting collapse that saw it lose when chasing a very gettable total of 210.

'He's exciting, but we have to see him be really hungry to make big runs,' I said on radio. 'Take the example of his performance [against Queensland] . . . He was out caught at deep third man, where the wicket was low and slow. He really could have played a technical innings, which we know he can do.

'We want to see him perform on all types of wickets,' I added. 'He's got the whole game to play all the shots, but it's a case of him staying in.'

I said in that interview that I had 'harsh words' with Glenn in the past and would not hesitate to do it again but then I added: 'He's been brilliant for us over the last 12 months in the one-day format. But again, it's a case of him taking his game to the next level.'

The truth of the matter is that no-one likes to be criticised, but if it can be done in a way that emphasises the positives and what a player has to do in order to get better, that is probably the best result for everyone.

If a player does make a mistake on the field my approach to dealing with it is in three stages: firstly I cut them some slack as they, more than anyone else, will know they have mucked up and it is up to them to learn from that and get better.

If they do it again then we talk about it and they are left in no doubt that it is not something they should be repeating. If they do it a third time, they will get a rocket from me. Again, it comes down to the player being personally responsible for their actions. My staff and I, and also their teammates, can guide them, but ultimately it is about individuals finding a way to work things out for themselves, because no-one else can hold that bat or ball or go for that catch apart from them.

Maxwell got out twice in successive innings in England in the one-day series of 2015 playing the reverse sweep, but that was never something that I would have a go at him about. It had been a shot that had brought him success in both innings before his departure and although it looked, to an outsider, to be reckless, I knew that he was as comfortable playing the shot as he would be playing a cover-drive. Also, when I spoke with him afterwards about his second dismissal, against Moeen Ali at Headingley, he explained his thinking and I was very comfortable with his thought process.

He had helped us out of a tricky situation of 3-30 and with the introduction of Moeen he thought that if he could hit him out of the attack then we were maybe five overs away from breaking open the game completely and setting up a target that England would struggle to chase. Maxi had already played the stroke to good effect against both Moeen and Adil Rashid, but then chose the wrong ball to try to repeat the stroke and got bowled.

It looked horrible and also a terrible waste of a wicket, as he had raced to 85 from 64 balls, but given that he was clear in his thought processes and that it was a natural stroke for him, there was no need to be critical.

Of all the relationships a coach has within the squad, the most important one is with the captain. As I have already said, that relationship is pivotal, the fulcrum of the team, and I am quite clear on who is in charge.

I am a strong believer that it is the captain that runs the ship on the ground. He is the man in charge, and he should have a big influence off it as well. He is the one in the firing line if it all goes wrong during a match. The role of the coach is simply to make the captain's life easier, both as a player and as a leader, so that he can focus on the things that matter most, especially once he and his players cross the boundary rope.

During my time as Australia's coach I have been fortunate to have Michael Clarke and Steve Smith at the helm. Both are forward thinkers who know and read the game well. That ability to do what needs to be done on the field means I cannot recall an occasion when I have found myself thinking 'What on earth is he doing?' or 'Why on earth hasn't he done that?' I have been equally lucky with my other coaching assignments, as captains like Adam Gilchrist and James Hopes have made things just as straightforward for me.

Of course, that dynamic will vary depending on circumstances and individuals. I am sure that, in his early days, Allan Border was very grateful for the tactical input provided by Bobby Simpson who had, after all, much more experience than AB or anyone else in that side in the mid-1980s, but by the time you get to the Buchanan-Waugh or Buchanan-Ponting relationships there was less need for that hands-on approach, as the captain had vast experience and was also surrounded by equally experienced heads out on the ground too.

When I say that the captain runs the ship, I really do mean it, right down to a decision on what time players meet up on the ground for a group warm-up before a day's play or a limited-overs match. If players want a bat in the nets on game-day, then they go to the venue and do that before that warm-up, which involves a few stretches, some running, some catching and also, in the case of the bowlers, the chance to mark out their runs and roll their arms over on a pitch adjacent to the 22 yards to be used for the match – and many take the opportunity to do that.

When Michael Clarke was captain he usually wanted that warm-up to be maybe an hour before the start of play – perhaps because, with his injury problems, he wanted more time to get loose – but with Steve Smith, in limited-overs matches for example, the warm-up is closer to the start – sometimes just 20 minutes before the toss. I can see sense in both approaches. Some players like to spend time on the morning of the match ensuring everything is in the right place, while others dislike being at the venue for a long period before actually getting into the thick of the action. My role is simply to ensure that whichever approach the captain wants, my staff and I are there to help ensure it runs smoothly. In both instances, the responsibility is on the individuals, especially the batsmen, to have completed their personal work beforehand, and then everything flows on from there.

One of the big debates – which seems to be never-ending – within Australian cricket is the one about whether or not the captain should be a selector. My view would be that if you get the right selectors the captain should not need that additional burden on his already crowded plate.

If that blend is right everyone should be on the same page and given that, as coach, I try to be in touch with the captain on most days during a summer, either face-to-face or via Skype, phone or email when we are not together, then the lines of communication should be sufficient to ensure we do not diverge too greatly.

So why do I think that the coach should be on the National Selection Panel (NSP) while the captain misses out? After all, as we are on the road together most of the time neither of us get that much chance to watch potential newcomers in action. And the captain, in the not-too-distant past, has been a selector. Michael Clarke filled that role following the Argus Review that was undertaken after the Ashes series loss of 2010–11, before relinquishing the position a couple of years later.

I think the coach needs to be on the NSP as, although there is always a selector on duty at every international match, that person can vary from game to game and, as such, I am the only one with a live view of every match we take part in. I can, in theory at least, be someone looking on from the sidelines, without the potential to be swayed by being too close to a player through any on-field contact, something a captain cannot avoid.

That is the theory, although in the cases of players like Haddin and Watson ahead of the 2015 Ashes series I admit I did allow myself to be blinded a little through sentiment and a belief they could turn around their declining form. In that sense, the issues surrounding the selection of those players on that trip have proved a great help to me, making me realise the potential for that conflict in my roles and so hopefully that will assist me in avoiding that error of judgement again in the future.

Of course, I need plenty of input – as does the captain – from the other members of the NSP about players who are liable to come in from outside our group due to my limited exposure to cricket at state level. An example of how that plays out came with the selection of Adam Voges for the West Indies and Ashes tours in 2015. One panel member said: 'We have got to get him in, he is batting like Bradman!' His statistics could certainly not be ignored and his hundred on debut, as well as excellent form through the 12 months that followed, was a reward for making that call.

It is also worth pointing out that although the captain is not a formal member of the NSP, he will still have a decent, non-voting, say in what we decide. After all, he is the man who will take the players out on to the park and so he needs to have the people around him that he has faith in. And, in any case, on tour that set-up alters, as he does become part of the selection group, along with an on-tour selector and me.

We will have discussions around individuals and the balance of sides, but ultimately the aim is always the same: to pick a side that we feel, in the conditions, has the best chance of delivering us 20 wickets and sufficient runs to allow us to boss the game. Most of the time we get it right, but just occasionally we get it wrong. Selection is not an exact science.

The dynamic between captain and coach during a match is pretty straightforward, in keeping with the idea that he is in charge. If I or any of my coaches see something during the course of play, I will usually seek him out at the interval to chat, but as a rule of thumb – helped by the fact all my captains have read the game so well – I try to stay out of their hair and avoid saying 'We saw this' or 'We saw that' during a match.

We will, players and coaching staff, always look to have a debrief after a day's play or after a limited-overs match, as I tend to prefer to get things off the chest relatively quickly, say what needs to be said and then move on. I have never been one to allow things to fester overnight or over a day or two if I can help it, and the players I have worked with seem to have appreciated that approach.

The players of the current era are undoubtedly the best-paid cricketers in the history of the game in Australia and there will be several in our dressing room, and plenty more in the dressing rooms of India and England in particular, that are millionaires, some of them several times over. In soccer, at least from the outside, that appears to be a cause of friction, with popular, big-name players appearing to call the shots and egos ruling the roost. Whether that is true or not in soccer, it is not true in cricket.

Yes, the current players are wealthy and they have endorsements and managers, but at least in my experience I have found this generation to be a pleasure to work with. Egos have been the least of my concerns.

Their managers appear to have drilled in to them the fact they, whether we like it or not, are a brand and that they have a duty to the public. I cannot recall too many occasions over the last couple of years of the Australian team's media manager coming to me and saying 'Such-and-such a player is refusing to speak with the media,' or 'Such-and-such a player is up himself and out of control'.

When I played for Australia in the late 1990s and early 2000s we had some big-name players in the dressing room and many of them enjoyed being front and centre of attention. Shane Warne was always saying he did not want to speak with the media, but once he was in front of a camera he lit up the room and invariably had the media eating out of his hand. And all the players of that era knew that while personal success was important, it did not mean very much without team success. Shane was our standout player in the losing Ashes series of 2005, but I am certain he enjoyed the winning series far more, even if he did not feature quite so prominently.

As I mentioned earlier, the team is made up of individuals and as a coach you deal with each person slightly differently. But in terms of team rules, it is very much a case of one size fits all.

Time-keeping, in my book, is something that is a non-negotiable and I made the Australian players realise that pretty quickly after I took over in 2013. We had a team meeting during the one-day series and Mitchell Johnson was a couple of minutes late and, as a result, was excluded. He understood and apologised, but it made it clear, not only to him but to the whole squad, that failing to be punctual was not something I would tolerate. It was also an illustration to the whole group that it was not a case of one rule for one and one for another: Mitchell may have been a senior player but he got no latitude because of that.

The issue of David Warner was near the top of my in-tray when I started as Australia coach, as he had been suspended leading into the Ashes series and then sent to South Africa to play with the A side, which meant he would miss the first two Tests, which were back to back.

The first conversation I had with him was what you might call honest and adult. I stressed that the incident that saw him suspended, when he punched Joe Root, was a line in the sand. I said that any more such misadventures would leave him at risk of throwing away his career – 'You'll be flying home straight away if you step out of line again' was one thing I recall saying – but also that, at his best, he was a fantastic asset to the side and I wanted him to be part of what I planned for the future, which was a winning, successful line-up playing entertaining cricket.

After my chat with David in June 2013 the ball was very much in his court – he could either knuckle down and mend his ways or continue to drift along from mistake to mistake, with the public and the authorities above my pay-grade eventually losing patience with him. I saw it happen with my great mate Shane Warne when he was removed from the vice-captaincy in 2000 and I did not want to see it happen to David. In my experience, putting the onus on a player to sort himself out is usually a decent way of dealing with an issue, as if things do continue to go wrong then they have no-one to blame but themselves. It was certainly an approach that worked with David, as his stellar form – and his decision not to drink – in 2015 proved.

I guess you could say I had a head start when it came to conversations like that, because I was regarded as a maverick throughout my career. I could relate to the sorts of things David was going through. On that basis, when I say 'Do as I say, don't do as I did,' I make that statement with experience behind me. Players, so far at least, have taken on board what I have said.

And David, in all fairness, was outstanding after that. Before he was sent to South Africa he threw himself into training and the same was true when he returned ahead of the third Test of that 2013 Ashes series. Even he admitted at the time he needed what he called a 'kick up the bum' and it has helped him produce the best form of his career, assisted, too, by the stabilising influence of his wife, Candice, and fatherhood.

Of course it is one thing to deal with disciplinary issues when things are not going well – there is an expectation on you to take action (although people will still judge whether your response is too soft or too harsh or about right). The other side of the coin is ensuring you impose the same standards when things are going well, as was the case when we fined Chris Rogers for oversleeping and missing a function at the Prime Minister's residence in Sydney after our Ashes triumph in 2013–14. You could argue that any punishment was harsh. After all, we had won the series 5–0, avenged the earlier loss in England and done something few people, if any, expected us to do at the outset of that series. It was a truly spectacular success.

On that basis, of course the players wanted to enjoy themselves, have a few drinks and sleep it off. So why not cut 'Bucky' some slack? Well, in my eyes at least, that was not possible for a couple of reasons: one, it was a case of once a team always a team and if the other players – no matter how ropey they may have been feeling – were able to get themselves together, then there was no excuse for one of them to fail to make the grade. And going out as a team that day, and meeting the fans too as well as being seen with the most important person in the country, was as much a part of what is expected of the modern player as scoring runs and taking wickets. The players' primary role is obviously to produce on the field, but it is also to promote the game at a time when the rivalry for the loyalty of fans among competing sports has never been greater. Whether we like it or not we are role models on and off the ground and need to behave as such. That might not have always been the case when I played, but it is now. The players get rewarded handsomely for doing something they love – but sometimes it also means doing things that might not be at the top of their own agendas. And in all fairness, Chris understood why he needed to be punished, took it on the chin and moved on, just like the rest of us, with no more needing to be said.

In 2015, while we were still in England for the back-end of our One-Day International series, I read with interest about how Wayne Rooney and Michael Carrick, two senior players at Manchester United, approached their manager, Louis van Gaal. 'Rooney and Michael Carrick came to me and said, "The dressing room is flat,"' said van Gaal to the media after the meeting took place.

'In my career as a manager I did not have so many who come to say something about the atmosphere in the dressing room or the way we train or something like that. But it is very positive that they are coming to you and that they trust you,' he added.

I was especially interested because it mirrored the way we like to operate in Australian cricket, with a leadership group that can act as a barometer for the players, providing feedback to the coaches. After all, although as coach I like to believe I am the heart and soul of the dressing room, I am not a player and when players chat they tend to chat to each other first.

That is one function of a leadership group, to distil the feelings of the squad outside of a meeting environment and pass it on to me. It may be 'Coach, we feel as though we are training too hard,' or 'Coach, we are not training enough,' but it can be as simple as that.

A group like that can help ensure young players are properly integrated from day one and it can also serve as a means of internally regulating a side without a coach even knowing. For example, if someone is not pulling his weight at training, a member of the leadership group may pull that player back into line before it escalates up to the coach and into a potential disciplinary issue. It means that players policing themselves and setting their own standards can have a hugely beneficial effect, pouring oil on troubled waters long before a flashpoint develops.

When I played and even through to the time I took over as Australia coach, players like Haddin and Watson were invaluable in filling this sort of role. They had contact with the previous, hugely successful era of Australian cricket and so knew the standards that needed to be set. In addition to that duo, over the last couple of years, individuals such as George Bailey, Ryan Harris, Mitchell Johnson and Peter Siddle have been equally valuable to me in assessing the mood of the playing group.

I remember Adam Gilchrist, when we were working together as captain and coach in the IPL, came to me on one occasion and asked whether we were working too hard, and he did so because we had such a great and open line of communication. But as a rule of thumb I believe that the captain and coach should not be in any leadership group. It is a case of the players taking ownership of their own dressing room and I guess you could also call it cricket's own 360-degree appraisal system: I assess the players, both in my role as coach and as a member of the NSP, and the leadership group allows those players to assess me, albeit in a slightly more informal way.

Playing for your country is the pinnacle that a player can achieve in a career and to get there you have to have worked incredibly hard – that goes without saying. When you finally reach that point you are a role model and a high achiever.

You are someone who will inspire others through your story and, hopefully, someone who will also inspire through your deeds on the field. But once you are in that position, should you require someone else to inspire you?

For me the answer is a simple 'yes' and that is where my staff and I come in. Our role is to set goals for the players – goals that are testing, certainly, but also achievable – and continue to monitor them.

We set broad goals for the squad every 12 months, from the New Year's Test match through to the Boxing Day Test, and Christmas is our time for a final assessment of what we have achieved and what would be realistic for the following year. The goals obviously change from year to year as we have different assignments in front of us and those goals, for example, can be as simple as achieving a certain win percentage across the 12 months in all formats, winning a series in certain conditions or winning against a particular opposition.

Beyond that, we boil things down to certain key performance indicators that let us know whether we are on track in a particular series, reminding players what their personal bests are so they can set out to beat them.

At match level it can get down to a particular statistic, which if achieved usually coincides with victory. Bobby Simpson was one of the first coaches who looked into this sort of detail. I remember that he worked out that in one-day cricket, the side that scored the most singles invariably won the match. Hence he was always big on rotation of the strike and high-quality running between the wickets.

Examples for the current side of those indicators within a game may be, in our batting innings, how many players we have scoring hundreds or 50s, how many 100-plus partnerships we are achieving, how few balls we are failing to score off and how many fours and sixes we are hitting. With the ball, we will look at how many maidens we bowl, how few extras we concede and so on. And our fielding coach will look at how many mistakes we make in the field, or taking it in the other direction and naming a fielder of the day for excellence. It is something the players have become quite competitive about, which is good, as that type of competition breeds the maintenance of high standards.

I have already mentioned team meetings and how I do not like them to drag on. They are important as they allow everyone to get together to toss around ideas, but by the time we get to them the idea is that the vast majority of the preparation work should already have been done.

Dene Hills, our performance analyst, will have emailed video clips of opposition strengths and weaknesses to the players and it is their responsibility to go through them and formulate their own thoughts and plans. Then, when the team assembles, the batsmen will get together to discuss what they have seen of the opposition bowlers' strengths and weaknesses and the same will be true of the bowlers too. That means that the final team meeting, when everyone gets together, should simply be a case of dotting the i's and crossing the t's.

I will have my own observations in those meetings and maybe remind the players of our goals for the year, the series and the match we are about to play, but the key is not to overload players with too much information at this stage. Keeping it simple, clear and concise is the key.

My preference is always for the players to do the vast majority of the talking as they are the ones who will be out in the middle trying to put our plans into action. To achieve this I may look to plant some seeds with a player before the meeting, perhaps over a coffee. 'What do you think about this plan against so-and-so?' It is a case of me loading the gun, but it is up to the player to fire the bullets. It is another way of ensuring the players take ownership of any plan or situation.

Something that does not feature in any side of mine is the idea of curfews. I do not agree with them and actually regard them as counter-productive.

We saw at the start of 2016 what a mess the Queensland Rugby League set-up got into over the imposition of a curfew, which resulted in a whole host of players being banned from representing the Maroons in State of Origin for 12 months. It was all so unnecessary and I know rugby league coaching legend Wayne Bennett, someone I was lucky enough to meet during my time coaching Queensland Cricket, shares my view.

'When they [the players] do get on it [and start drinking] there is this mindset that it has to be all the way or no way – binge drinking,' he told reporters in the wake of the controversy. 'That is when they do the stupid things. Our challenge is to try and teach them to drink in moderation, not for them not to have a drink.'

Queensland Rugby League Chairman Peter Betros agreed when he said: 'Booze bans do not work. You would expect a player to behave at a certain standard, that is all we ask.'

I find curfews a hindrance as, when all is said and done, we are dealing with adults. If you impose them then, as was the case in Queensland Rugby League, you normally find they are broken by some and then more are implicated along the way, and some players who were only dropping people off and not going out themselves are called into the scenario as well. And it is not only a problem for the players but it also puts you as a coach and your staff in a corner too as, having set down the rules, you have to either impose them, which will almost certainly be to the detriment of the side, or you let the issue slide, in which case you leave yourself open to the possibility of what you might call 'disciplinary creep'. Someone else might legitimately think: 'Well, so-and-so got away with his breach of discipline, so how can the coach pull me up if I am five minutes late for the bus?'

We have never had curfews on my watch, but if someone was the worse for wear after drinking the night before, non-selection would be the response.

That is the easy part of the scenario, but most of the time it is far more subtle than that. If the curfew is 12 midnight, a player has gone to the movies and the film finishes at five minutes past midnight, is that breaking curfew? Yes it is, and then you have to punish that player as well. Curfews are fine in theory, but in the real world they only create problems; they do not fix them.

I really do wonder how many matches I would have missed had I been playing in teams where curfews operated. There have been occasions, however, when a curfew might have helped me out. I got back to the hotel far too late after a night out during the Melbourne Test against Pakistan in 2004, made just 11 the next day and never played a Test for Australia again (although that was down to form rather than someone reporting me for being out late). I knew my career was nearer the end than the beginning, which undoubtedly prompted my relaxed – far too relaxed – attitude, but my failure and resultant departure from the side was the fault of no-one else except me.

If you create a good environment then you don't need a curfew. I am pleased to say we certainly do not.

The same tendency to micro-manage was behind the so-called 'Homework-gate' saga in India just before I took over as Australia coach in 2013. I was critical of the way that played out and said so on Twitter, which landed me in hot water with Cricket Australia, but I think everyone knows it should never have come to that in the first place.

The team was struggling and Mickey Arthur, who I have got a lot of time and respect for, tried to do the right thing and put the onus on the players to come up with solutions. When four players – Mitchell Johnson, Usman Khawaja, James Pattinson and Shane Watson – failed to come up with a written response they were unceremoniously dropped.

Taken in isolation it looks incredibly harsh, but the context was that the failure was the latest in a line of breaches of team discipline, from being late for meetings and not filing wellness reports to dress code violations – disciplinary creep. It was a line in the sand; a big, thick unmistakable line in the sand. It drew a great deal of criticism, not least from the public back home.

The question was, quite rightly, 'How have things been allowed to reach this point?' The management of the team felt something had to be done, but had that something been done right at the start then almost certainly it would never have come to such an ugly pass.

The one thing I made clear when I began my role with the Australia team in 2013 was that everyone was starting with a clean slate. I did not want to know what had happened previously; all I wanted the players and staff to know was that I would judge them as I found them and if they did the right thing by me then I would do the right thing by them. Rightly or wrongly, that was my approach and in the first couple of years of my time with the side it has not worked out too badly.

Celebrating reaching a hundred in my final limited-overs match for South Australia, at my beloved Adelaide Oval in November 2007. I knew I was on the way out and that allowed me to play with a freedom I hadn't experienced since childhood.

One of my proudest moments as a coach was securing the IPL title with the Deccan Chargers in South Africa in 2009. A squad of easy-beats became winners in what were, for many of the players, utterly alien conditions.

Happy days at The Gabba with Alister McDermott during my time as Queensland coach. A step out of my comfort zone of South Australia, it was a job and a period in my life I loved and it also proved to be a springboard to the role with Australia.

My first state captain as well as a friend, mentor, a huge influence on my career and someone I still miss every day – with David Hookes after a successful day at Adelaide Oval.

Barry Richards was my first state coach at South Australia and helped me realise there was more to batting than just 'see ball, hit ball'. He helped develop my play against spin.

ABOVE LEFT: I failed to listen to Bobby Simpson's advice to get fitter and improve my fielding when I got my first taste of the international scene and it cost me countless caps; only later did I realise he was right.

ABOVE RIGHT: Geoff Marsh (right), seen here with Mark Taylor, followed Bobby Simpson as national coach and brought me in from the cold at international level.

John Buchanan wasn't everyone's cup of tea but I loved working with him, as he and Ricky Ponting gave me responsibility as a senior professional, something I thrived on.

All smiles with captain Michael Clarke as we meet the media after my appointment as Australia's new head coach ahead of the 2013 Ashes series. Bringing in a sense of enjoyment was a key aim of mine following a traumatic few months on and off the field for the team.

There were a few voices that questioned why an international head coach should be listening to the television commentary at Lord's during the 2013 Ashes series. My reply was 'Why not?' as I certainly would never pretend to have all the answers.

Images of my key day-to-day relationships: (top) with national selector Rodney Marsh and captain Michael Clarke (watching Steve Smith bat) at a training session during the 2013 Ashes series; (middle) with Clarke and team manager Gavin Dovey after defeat at Trent Bridge confirmed a lost Ashes series in 2015; and (bottom) with Clarke's replacement as captain, Steve Smith, in Dharamsala ahead of the 2016 ICC World Twenty20.

ABOVE LEFT: Pat Howard, Cricket Australia's Executive General Manager – Team Performance, the man who offered me a shot at the best job in the world outside of playing the game.

ABOVE RIGHT: I'm proud that during my time as coach we have given prominence to the importance of the mental side of the game through our use of sports psychologist Michael Lloyd. Here he is talking with Brad Haddin during the 2015 Ashes series.

When a Mitchell Johnson short ball struck India's Virat Kohli in the match following the death of Phillip Hughes it shook everyone up, revealed our players' humanity and illustrated how raw emotions were so soon after one of cricket's worst tragedies.

It felt like not only Macksville but also the whole cricketing world came to a standstill to farewell our little champion Phillip Hughes in December 2014.

This remains one of my favourite images of a wonderful young man taken from us far too soon and one that typified Phillip Hughes. In Abu Dhabi during a Test against Pakistan in October 2014, and even though he was 12th man he still could not help smiling.

Robert Cianflone-IPL 2010/IPL via Getty Images

Adam Gilchrist – a terrific friend, a game-changer with the bat and, as captain of Indian Premier League side the Deccan Chargers, the man who was key to my move into big-time coaching. I have a lot to thank him for.

Indranil Mukherjee/AFP/Getty Images

After a frank first conversation, David Warner has been a joy to work with and has matured into an outstanding player and human being. He plays the game exactly as it should be – always looking to be positive – and has not given me a moment's trouble.

Alexander Joe/AFP/Getty Images

Steve Smith, seen here celebrating his hundred against South Africa at Centurion in 2014, single-mindedly improved his physical, technical and mental approach and has reaped a fantastic dividend.

Ian Kington/AFP/Getty Images

Steve Smith's decision to pursue the appeal against Ben Stokes for handling the ball during a One-Day International against England at Lord's in September 2015 was a prime example of his strength of character – doing what was right rather than what was popular.

Mark Kolbe/Getty Images

Shane Watson and Glenn Maxwell's partnership against Sri Lanka during the ICC Cricket World Cup in 2015 was a tournament highlight as two top players at the height of their powers gave us a glimpse of brutal batting perfection.

I teamed up with Rohit Sharma at the Deccan Chargers and he is, without doubt, one of the most naturally talented players I have ever worked with.

Hamish Blair-IPL 2010/IPL via Getty Images

I cannot believe there has been a better spell of fast bowling than the one delivered by Mitchell Johnson on the third afternoon of the Adelaide Test against England in December 2013. It was brutal, beautiful and compelling all at once.

My old mate Ryan Harris, seen here celebrating taking the series-clinching wicket against South Africa in Cape Town, was fundamental to the side's successes in 2013–14 and would have been an all-time great but for injuries that plagued his career.

New Zealand spinner Daniel Vettori demonstrated a great temperament allied to skill, determination and an astute cricket brain when we worked together at Queensland. It would not surprise me to see him become a top coach.

What I loved about working with Dale Steyn at the Deccan Chargers was that, as a senior player, he wanted to set the standard for others to follow and that made him a dream to coach.

Keeping it simple and giving him licence to play without inhibitions were the keys to getting the best out of Andrew Symonds, and his best really was exceptional for Australia – and for me at the Deccan Chargers.

MATT KING/GETTY IMAGES

A reward for the outstanding efforts of the players, as well as our planning and hard work: I get my turn in taking the cheers, handshakes and applause of our fans at the Sydney Opera House after our triumphant 5–0 series whitewash of England to regain The Ashes in the summer of 2013–14.

PHIL HILLYARD/NEWSPIX

Unforgettable: captain and coach drink in the atmosphere of the Melbourne Cricket Ground after victory against New Zealand in the World Cup final of 2015, the climax of an incredible journey during that summer.

A special memory, celebrating with the players as the sun came up over Melbourne following our World Cup final success. It doesn't get any better than this.

Farewell to a champion: as players and support staff we relished the chance to spend one final post-play evening with Mitchell Johnson in the dressing room in Perth after he announced his retirement from international cricket in November 2015.

Catching up with old mates from school is always a pleasure. At the Prince Albert Hotel in Gawler are (left to right): Nathan Marsden, me, Jason Smith, Damian Brook, Luke Chammings, Andrew Warland and Johnny Giannitto. Johnny was the one who nicknamed me 'Boof' all those years ago, much to my mother's disgust.

Doing what I do would not be possible without the love and support of my family. Here's Andrea, together with my boys, Jake and Ethan – my daughters Tori and Amy went missing for this shot – relishing the World Cup win in the dressing room at the Melbourne Cricket Ground.

Missing the limited-overs series in the Caribbean in June 2016 meant I was in Australia to say goodbye to my father, Trevor, who died following a heart attack. It was one of my toughest days but with support from family – including here Andrea's mum, Anne White, Andrea and Ethan – we made it through. Dad would have been so proud.

With all my children – Jake, Amy, Tori and Ethan – together in Melbourne for Christmas. Spending important times of the year like this in a hotel rather than at home is a price that comes with the territory, so it is wonderful to be able to have them with me. The Australian squad spends so much time on the road that family time is vital to keep us all grounded.

8

THE MENTAL GAME

If you are expecting me to tell you that the role the mind plays in top-level cricket is all a load of mumbo-jumbo, you are in for a shock.

I am sure some of you – maybe many of you – who think of me as 'Good old Boof' (a nickname given to me as a youngster by my old friend Johnny Giannitto thanks to my wild hair, something you might laugh at now, given I am bald) will imagine that when I see a player who seems a bit preoccupied or is struggling I simply thrust a beer into his hand, have a bit of a friendly chat and, at the end of it, pat him on the back and say: 'Come on mate, pull yourself together.'

Well, the reality is somewhat different, and although I do believe in ongoing communication between a coach and his players as an invaluable and essential means of assessing how they are feeling, I also know that in order to ensure a player is at the top of his game he needs to be feeling comfortable.

I think my light-bulb moment came – although I did not realise it at the time – during the Ashes series of 1998–99. I was recalled for the Boxing Day Test in place of Ricky Ponting but, presented with a chance to finally secure my spot in the Test side, I failed the examination, and after scoring just 49 runs in four innings I spent the next four years once again on the outer.

At the end of the series and for weeks and months that followed I tried to work out what had gone so wrong. I had already played with or against the members of the England attack in county cricket, so I knew I should have been able to cope with whatever they sent down at me. I was familiar with conditions in both Melbourne and Sydney, and England was 2–0 down in the series, so it was not as if its bowlers had been setting the world on fire to that point either. There was the odd poor shot from me, the odd marginal decision that went against me and maybe the odd good ball too. But why should I have failed so badly when everything seemed set fair for me to succeed?

I knew the issue was not a technical one. Admittedly I was never the prettiest of players, but my technique had served me pretty well and it was not as if I had been dismissed the same way in each of my innings, highlighting some glaring fault. And in the limited-overs series against England and Sri Lanka that followed the Tests I scored four 50s and averaged 44. The more I thought about it, the more I realised that

I had put too much pressure on myself. I was not relaxed, I was not in the right frame of mind and that, surely, was a contributory factor in why I failed to live up to my – and others' – expectations.

Fast-forward to my coaching career and, thanks to my experience as a player, I know that more often than not success or failure at the higher echelons of the game is very rarely down to some major technical flaw. Once you reach a certain level everyone can play a forward defensive shot or a cover-drive. A key aspect in the success of the individual is to get players feeling good about themselves.

During my most productive playing years with the Australia squad, in the early 2000s, I was aware of the presence of Phil Jauncey around the group, a sports psychologist John Buchanan had used at Queensland Cricket, who he brought into the national set-up during his time as the Australian coach. I did not spend a lot of time with Phil – it was not mandatory to meet with him – but was aware of why he was there and was happy to have an open mind on the subject. By that stage of my career I knew my game pretty well, knew that both John and captain Ricky Ponting backed me and I revelled in my role as a sort of senior professional within the set-up. I was relaxed, felt valued by the team's hierarchy and it showed in my output as a batsman and a member of a successful team.

When I became head coach myself, I was introduced to Michael Lloyd – 'Lloydy', or 'Psycho', as I like to call him.

Michael had been working with Cricket Australia since 2008, initially with scholarship and pathway players at the

National Cricket Centre in Brisbane, as well as with the national under-19 squad, the women's senior and age-group squads – the Commonwealth Bank Southern Stars and Shooting Stars – and Australia A.

He had been drafted in to assist the senior men's team from early 2013 as Pat Howard looked to provide back-up to Mickey Arthur, and went along on the ill-fated tour of India and also the Champions Trophy. He was due to rejoin the group at the start of the Ashes tour, in time for a warm-up match in Worcester and the first two Tests of that series.

Michael told me later that he watched the sacking of Mickey and my instalment as coach play out from his lounge room in Brisbane. Before he travelled he checked with team manager Gavin Dovey about whether he should make the trip. He was conscious that a new coach might want to be surrounded by his own people and wish to do things his own way.

As I have already mentioned, I was happy to stick with the staff in place at the start of my tenure, aware that the switch from Mickey to myself was more than enough change for the players to put up with on the eve of the series, without further upheavals. On that basis Michael joined the squad as scheduled and that was where our association began.

We hit it off pretty much straight away, but the nature of the start of that tour, with the first two Tests in Nottingham and at Lord's in London being back-to-back, meant it was not until we got home after the series that we got a chance to go through in detail what he envisaged his role to be and how he would go about it. He made a presentation to me and I was so impressed – I felt we were singing off the same hymn sheet – that I asked him to give the same talk to the players ahead of the start of our return Ashes campaign.

What Lloydy advocated was a strong team culture with senior players and staff leading by example. There was no room in either of our minds for a 'not my fault' culture, with individuals not taking responsibility for their actions, and what I wanted was an increased level of trust and honesty within the group. It was all about people being willing to admit mistakes without recriminations and for all players to set their own standards. As coach I expect everyone – including me – to be their own role models, as I have found that sort of behaviour becomes self-perpetuating across the squad: you turn up on time for the bus and for team meetings, you do your work at training, you wear the correct team uniform, and so on. It sounds simple, but somewhere along the way before I took over it had become lost.

If you get the culture right, which means honest feedback across the board with no recriminations and a relaxed environment (players can have a beer, for example), that is the start of getting the players all pulling in the same direction, of putting them in the right mental state to perform. If the players weigh in with their perspectives, that can help the group improve their game awareness.

I want players to build trust in themselves and their game by having trust in me – trust what I have to say and trust my judgement. As I have said elsewhere, I am not infallible, but the fact I have been there and done it should give the players the confidence to rely on my opinion if they either ask for it or I give it. They can never say to me: 'What do you know? You have never been in that situation in a Test or One-Day International.' If they feel someone who actually knows what he is doing is guiding them they are more likely to be relaxed – that is the theory, anyway.

I remember a conversation I had with Lloydy in Johannesburg ahead of the first Test against South Africa in early 2014. We were chatting and he asked me how I would describe the relationship I had with my players and staff. 'I love them,' I replied. It might seem like a strange thing to say and also to write but, to me, the word 'love' in this context reflects the mix of care, support and empathy I have for everyone within the group. At the end of the tour Lloydy came to me and said, 'You know what? I can see what you mean – lots of coaches talk about loving their players, but I can see how you actually do it, and how the players feel it.'

I like to think I keep an eye out for every member of the squad, and I also like to let each person know that I am doing that. It may be a quiet word here, a pat on the shoulder there or a text or an email, but no matter how it is delivered the intention is to make people feel more secure, and if they get that feeling then hopefully they are more at ease and therefore better able to deliver a top performance. The idea is that that atmosphere of trust and security helps foster greater honesty and greater levels of accountability when it comes to performance too.

The dynamic within a cricket dressing room reminds me of the movie *Con Air*. In that film, starring Nicolas Cage and John Malkovich, a prisoner transport plane is taken over by the inmates, leading to all sorts of fun and games. The plane is full of disparate characters and although all of them want the same thing – freedom – they all have their own ideas too. It makes for a dysfunctional and edgy environment to say the least.

It might seem like an odd analogy, but in many ways it mirrors the situation we, as an international cricket team, find ourselves in. A cricket dressing room is an edgy place too – and, talking to Lloydy, so are most elite environments in other sports too – full of strong personalities who all want success, but who may have different ideas of how to achieve it. Add to that the fact that we are on the road for long periods, away from family and friends, often under pressure and heavily scrutinised, and you have a potentially volatile mix. In that landscape issues are more likely than not to crop up and so it means we all need to support each other to ensure we remain focused and pulling in the same direction. And from my perspective having someone like Lloydy on board, alongside me and team manager Gavin Dovey, to assist in trying to manage any issues that do crop up, is an important aspect of trying to help us stay on track.

There is no longer any stigma attached to the mental aspect of performance, at least within the Australian set-up. If a player is now seen around the team hotel or at the ground speaking with Lloydy, it is not a cause for everyone else within the squad to wonder 'What's up with him?' I think of it in exactly the same way as I would if that same player was sitting down with our batting or bowling coach. The players have certainly entered into that spirit too and, far from going to a quiet room with Lloydy away from curious onlookers, you will see them, quite often during our training sessions, walking around the ground with him, in plain sight, chatting away. He is not with the squad full-time; instead we work out a schedule between ourselves, alongside Gavin Dovey and the captain, identifying times when we think he may be of most use. For example, Lloydy had regular involvement with the limited-overs squad for the periods both before and during the 2015 World Cup, but in the summer that followed his time was focused less around the One-Day Internationals and more with the Twenty20 International squad in the build-up to the World Twenty20 in India.

The truth of the matter is that the higher the level you perform at, the more likely you are to suffer from performance anxiety, at least in my experience. At first-class and international level, cricket is no longer a sport that is a bit of fun with no consequences; it is a career and a very lucrative one too. That means that while the rewards are high, so are the penalties for failure.

Distracting thoughts can impede performance out in the middle. You do not want to be thinking about your child's school fees or the mortgage when you walk out to bat, are at your bowling mark or waiting for a catch at slip. But, by the same token, that is just what people not playing for Australia think about when they are at work, so why should cricketers be any different? And, following on from that, why should we not look to find a way to help them get through those thoughts so they can focus on the matter at hand?

On that basis, one of the things Lloydy tries to do is highlight what he calls dysfunctional thinking patterns – in other words, the ways in which your mind wanders away from what is important when you are out in the middle. By highlighting those patterns and making players aware of the traps they can fall into, the hope is they are better equipped to get out of those mental states more easily, so they can focus on their jobs of scoring runs, taking wickets or holding catches.

And it is not just the players who can use Lloydy as a sounding board. I have what I call my regular 'on the couch' sessions with him, where I am able to get things off my chest, and I find that to be an invaluable stress-buster for me. In a results-driven environment where you are surrounded by work at all times, minor things can take on major proportions. In those circumstances it can be easy to let things get on top of you. A chat with him helps me to put things in perspective and focus on what is important.

What Lloydy spoke with the players about ahead of our home Ashes series in late 2013, and what he continues to point out, is that a fundamental route to success is to understand what pressure is. Cricket, as is often said, is a mental game, and if you can understand what pressure looks like and feels like for you, then you have a much better chance of dealing with it.

When you play for Australia, pressure is not about ensuring your front elbow is nice and high when you drive the ball down the ground; it is actually about the execution of your skill in a competitive environment. Getting players to relax and be effective in that environment is the key to top performance.

How to do that is the $64 million question. If it was a simple thing easy to define and quantify with a one-size-fits-all solution for every player, then plenty of others would have cracked the code by now and found the way to succeed at all times. But it's not. Each player will have his own individual methods of finding that way to relax, but Lloydy's view – and it is one I subscribe to completely – is that it is all about mental toughness. What you have to realise is that mental toughness is not about running around snarling or sledging the opposition and having balls bounce off your chest; it is actually about clarity, ensuring your mind is clear and focused on what is important, no matter what is going on around you.

The best performances come from a clear mind and what Lloydy preaches in that regard is very simple, what he calls the 3 Rs: Reflecting, Relaxing and Refocusing.

Reflection is honestly appraising your performance – if you cannot be honest with yourself then who can you be honest with? It requires you to consider what you did well and what you could do more effectively, and figuring that out should leave you well placed to know how you can improve next time.

Some of the best reflection can come when you have failed as, if you pinpoint the reason why, you can avoid the situation recurring. But reflection can also take the form of examining your own success, watching footage of yourself when you have done well, to see how you did it then.

I remember when we played Pakistan in the United Arab Emirates in late 2014. At a media conference ahead of the series Shahid Afridi was asked if he remembered his first innings in international cricket, a 37-ball century against Sri Lanka. 'Of course, yes,' he said – and revealed that whenever he was not performing well he would look up that innings on YouTube. Even the best players use positive reinforcement to boost their confidence.

The relaxation part of the 3 Rs comes from the ability to switch off at the right time. It is impossible to concentrate for every moment of every day's play. You will be exhausted if you even attempt it. I remember when I was a boy, watching England's Chris Tavare on television, I was amazed at what he did between balls, trooping away from the pitch, wandering off towards square leg. Looking back, I can understand exactly what he was doing. He was dealing with the previous ball in his mind's eye, consigning it to history and then, once he had done that, he was ready to go again.

The final R is the ability to refocus, to get into a state where you are switched on to face the next ball. Different players have different ways of doing this. For me, when I played, my signal to get back into game mode after my break between deliveries was to scratch my guard again with the front stud in my left batting shoe. I did that then resumed my stance and I was ready to go, focused on the bowler running towards me with the ball in his hand. I have seen some players talk to themselves as the bowler runs in, saying, 'Watch the ball, watch the ball.' Lawrence Rowe, the elegant West Indies right-hander, used to hum tunes in order to help himself focus. Another West Indies batsman, Carlisle Best, even resorted to commentating to himself as he played each delivery.

If you can master those 3 Rs there is a very good chance that you will be 'in the zone', a term that describes a player having that happy balance between relaxation and focus.

A prime example of a player being in that state was Adam Gilchrist during the first Test against India in Mumbai in February 2001.

He went to the crease with the Australia innings in tatters at 5-99, on a pitch where the ball was spinning sharply, and with the prospect of the side conceding a first-innings lead after India scored 176, not an ideal situation on a surface that was only set to get worse as the match wore on.

Gilly's response was to take the attack to the Indian bowlers. He scored 122 from 112 balls with 15 fours and four sixes. Along with Matthew Hayden at the other end, the pair added 197 for the sixth wicket in only 33 overs. By the time they were separated, when 'Haydos' was dismissed for an equally outstanding 119, Australia was in the driving seat and went on to win the Test by 10 wickets.

How had Gilly done it? As he explained in his auto-biography *True Colours*: 'I tried to imagine that when I went in to bat, I wasn't actually going to face my first ball. The hardest time in batting is that first period – from bang!, you're in!, afraid of getting out first ball, afraid of not making a run, fearing failure, until you start to grow in confidence and settle down. Once you've made 15 or 20 runs, you're comfortable out there and not afraid any more.

'So this time I thought I would pretend I had already been out there for a while and was 15 or 20 not out, already comfortable. If there were fielders around the bat, I wouldn't be intimidated by them. I would shut them out, as you do when you have some runs on the board and nothing worries you. I would place myself in the "zone", with tunnel vision.

'The end result was a century in 84 balls . . . hitting slog sweeps against the spin, all sorts of outrageous shots – everything came off. It was the closest to being in the absolutely ideal state, completely insulated from my surroundings, that I had ever felt.'

Gilly's innings was so brilliant and so out of keeping with everyone else's struggles on the surface up to the time he arrived – Haydos caught his mood, having struggled manfully before that point – that after the squad had a day off following the victory, Gilly later told me that at the next team meeting he was asked to speak about how he had managed to play such a phenomenal innings.

It was John Buchanan's way of trying to find out a bit more about being 'in the zone' and hoping, perhaps, that there may have been something the rest of the squad could take away from Gilly's experience. He did his best to come up with reasons why he did what he did, but one of the keys to Gilly's batting was always the fact it was so instinctive and that made anything he did very difficult to put a label on. Saying it was a case for him of 'see ball, hit ball' was too simplistic, as he worked exceptionally hard in the nets, usually knew where he was hitting it and always thought about what the opposition were trying to do. But there is no denying that his instinctive element was a major reason for his success. The first part of *True Colours* is actually called 'JUST HIT THE BALL'.

Most of the time it worked for him, but there were times, particularly on that tour in the two Tests that followed, where it did not. He got a pair in the next Test in Kolkata and scores of one and one in the final match in Chennai. In the second innings of that Kolkata Test he was out leg before wicket first ball to Sachin Tendulkar's leg-spin as the side spiralled to defeat. As he recalled in his autobiography: 'There were so many men around the bat, and all I can remember thinking is, "Don't sweep, don't sweep, don't sweep." So the first ball, I swept. It hit me on the pad, and [I] . . . was plumb.' It goes to show the importance of a clear head and also that even the best players can sometimes get their minds in a muddle.

For me personally as a player, being in the zone meant being in a position of just playing naturally and almost not thinking of the consequences. My best innings came from finding the relaxation that came from having clear plans. The hundreds I scored in Galle and Colombo on the 2004 tour of Sri Lanka were examples of that where, having devised a strategy to counter master spinner Muttiah Muralitharan and found that it worked, I almost switched on to autopilot. When you are playing well in those sorts of circumstances it is almost like you have a sixth sense of where the bowler is going to bowl. Your feet are moving well, you always seem to middle the ball and your shots hit the gaps at regular intervals.

That relaxed state a batsman seeks constantly also came to me in my last season as a professional cricketer, when I knew I was on the way out. It had been made pretty clear to me that my services were going to be dispensed with at South Australia, so I suddenly realised there was no longer any pressure on me to perform. I went out and played just like a 14-year-old again, simply for the joy of being out in the middle, and made 126 not out in my last domestic one-day innings and 167 in my final first-class effort without a care in the world.

As a coach, my challenge is always to try to get players into that state of carefree relaxation. The key element of that is to make sure they have done all their preparation. You remind them to look at the video clips they have of the bowlers they are likely to face or the batsmen they will be operating against, you ask them to be clear on how they are going to approach the challenges that will come their way – making yourself available to assist in that process, as required – and you give them the opportunity to hone their skills at practice beforehand, working on any shots or types of deliveries they may wish to use. If they can tick off all those elements they are a long way towards being as ready for match action as they can be.

The most important thing to stress as a coach is to ensure the players are trying to keep their thought processes simple. If they have done their work beforehand they should be able to cope with whatever is thrown at them and the autopilot I mentioned earlier has the chance to kick in.

Players at the highest level have a high degree of expertise, and expertise lies in two places: one is physical, the muscle memory you have created through all the training you have done, so that if you get a half-volley you can put it away for four; the other is subconscious, the knowledge about the game, the things you think about when you perform at your best and the knowledge you have of the opposition, what they are looking to do against you and how you are going to counter the threats they pose. The skill of the very best players is to marry that physical and subconscious expertise to create the complete player in any given situation.

It may seem like a cliché, but the phrase 'train hard, win easy' really does have a truth to it, as if you get things right before you enter the arena then you give yourself the very best chance of succeeding.

Haydos was a good example in this regard. He would be in the nets for hours, often with his brother Gary, who would backpack around and join the squad on tour just to bowl to his brother. Haydos would drill himself technically so that he mastered all the shots he thought he needed. Once he was satisfied with that side of his preparation he would go out onto the ground, sit at either end of the pitch to be used for the match and visualise the bowlers he was going to face, what they were looking to do and how he would combat them.

That might sound an extreme way of doing things and it is hardly going to work for a club cricketer who turns up at a venue an hour before the start, but that was the level he would go to to ensure that, by the time he walked out to bat, he was absolutely ready for everything the opposition could throw at him.

I even remember hearing how, before that India tour of 2001, Haydos took his preparation to the next level. He was regarded up to that point in his career as a player who was very much on the fringe of the squad, a player who got runs by the bucket-load at first-class level but who struggled to replicate that success at international level.

He was certainly not someone who was highly regarded as a player of spin, partly because it was not all that common for slow bowlers to get through heaps of overs at The Gabba in Brisbane, his home ground. His response was to go to the nearby Allan Border Field – now the home of the Bupa National Cricket Centre – and ask the curator to rough up some old wickets for him so he could practise batting, and especially sweeping, on surfaces like the ones he would face on the subcontinent.

He swept and swept to such an extent that when he got to India, and in situations like the one he found himself in when Gilly came to the crease in the opening Test in Mumbai, he was able to use his preparation to perfect effect. He knew the sweep would be an effective shot to help him score runs, and having practised it so extensively it was a shot he was comfortable with, so that helped him relax. The result was that he dominated that series, which was his breakthrough as a top-class international batsman.

Haydos, along with many of the players of his era, was never short of a word or two out in the middle and Australia certainly has a reputation for chat on the field. Its detractors call it sledging. For the record, I do not think we do it any more or less than several other sides around the world, but in any case I have no problem with it, as long as it does not get personal.

I guess my attitude has developed as a result of being the way I am – fat and bald. Because of that I always attracted plenty of comments from the opposition, but part of your skill as a player is your ability to switch off from it and only focus on what is important – the little red thing coming at you. A word or two in your direction is never responsible for dismissing you; that is down to the bowler or fielder, and once you realise that and, just as importantly, have your game plan sorted in your own mind, then it really should be a case of 'sticks and stones may break my bones but names – or comments – can never dismiss me'.

Chat out on the field can take many forms, but usually it is subtler than a player simply rubbishing an opponent to his face. If that happens umpires tend to jump all over it and lay a Code of Conduct charge, and rightly so as there is no room for personal abuse as far as I am concerned. Steve Waugh got it right when he renamed sledging 'mental disintegration'. That is exactly what it is, making the person you are focusing on question whether they are up to it.

There is plenty of chat that is not directed at the batsman at all; it is between fielders and said loudly enough for the batsman to hear. Something like 'He's just not picking the leg-break,' or 'If he keeps playing like that then we are in business in the slip cordon,' are designed to sow seeds of doubt in a batsman's mind. His ability to overcome that doubt is often the difference between being a good player and a great one.

I think of Rahul Dravid, for example. In the early stages of his career I think we regarded him as vulnerable to that sort of chat around the bat; however, later in his career – after a chat with Steve Waugh, ironically enough – he realised that he should simply shut out all the background noise and get on with his job. He did it to great effect.

Preparation is one thing, but something else the very best players do is to operate in the present, not the past or the future. Think of someone like Sachin Tendulkar, who was a master at that. To Sachin it did not matter if he had been beaten by the previous delivery; and it did not matter if the new ball was due in five overs' time. All he was interested in was the next delivery, as that was the only thing he could control. It is a simple approach but a mightily effective one.

It's called compartmentalising and it's something my contemporaries within the Australia team were absolutely brilliant at. Shane Warne always seemed to be the centre of attention and it was rare when there was not some issue swirling around him, while Steve Waugh was incredibly in demand, with everyone wanting his opinion on something or other. Their lives, with young families too, seemed to be happening at a million miles an hour and yet, when they crossed the boundary rope, they always seemed, at least to me, to be completely focused on the job at hand.

It was and is a very special skill to have. I sometimes wondered whether Warney's ability to switch on in the way he did on the field owed something to the fact that the ground was the one place where the numerous controversies that dogged him could not get at him. In that sense it almost seemed like a bit of a relief to be playing cricket. Whatever it was, he almost always seemed to respond in exactly the right way when he got out to the middle.

9

MAINTAINING THE HUNGER
AND DEALING WITH PRESSURE

If you are winning and everything is going along nicely the question you have to answer as a coach is how to maintain that momentum and keep the players wanting more. Then there's the question of how to succeed in all conditions, especially away conditions. Very few sides have ever managed to crack the code by having sustained success over a prolonged period of time.

The West Indies team that enjoyed close to 20 years at the top from its series win in England in 1976 through to eventual defeat at the hands of Australia in 1995, and then that Australian side from that 2–1 win in the Caribbean until maybe 2009, are the only international teams to have sustained success at Test level in my lifetime. That illustrates just how tough it is.

Teams that were expected to go on and take the world by storm, like England in 2005 after it beat Australia 2–1 in that epic Ashes series, simply could not keep up that standard, despite being full of top-class players.

And in the modern era you could argue that enjoying a continuous streak of success is becoming tougher as sides excel at exploiting home conditions to their advantage. It means winning overseas is becoming exceptionally hard, a fact that statistics back up.

India's home record in this regard has been remarkable: in 18 Test series it played at home after losing to Australia in 2004 it lost only once, to a Kevin Pietersen-inspired England in 2012.

Even Pakistan, having to use the United Arab Emirates as its base because of opposition reluctance to travel to Pakistan in the wake of the terror attack on the Sri Lanka squad and match officials in 2009, did not suffer a series loss in its adopted home for eight series through to late 2015.

Australia, at least in my experience over the past few years, has gone out of its way to produce surfaces that are fair to both sides rather than provide the home line-up with a particular advantage, but even on that basis our record on our own turf has been spectacular. We went 15 years without losing a home series, from 1993 to 2008, and more recently, despite the loss of a host of world-class players, we still lost just two more series following a dam-breaking defeat to South Africa, against England in 2010–11 and South Africa again in late 2012.

The great sides, like those West Indies and Australia line-ups that held sway over international cricket for the best part of 35 years between them, always made light of conditions and invariably won on whatever was put before them.

The key for any coach (and leadership group) is to convince the players that any success is just the start of something. That was what England patently failed to do in 2005. Its series win against Australia, the first it had achieved since 1987, was the subject of national rejoicing, to the extent that the players were all given honours by the Queen. The team had achieved something no England side had managed for a generation, but the players were unable to build on it. When you have experienced a high like that, what can be higher? That was the question placed in front of those players and it was one they were unable to answer.

To have sustained success you need four things: superstars, an absence of major injuries, players of quality to act as cover if you happen to get those injuries, and also a production line of talent down to age-group level. It sounds simple, but the reality is far harder.

Having that core of outstanding players is the obvious prerequisite and when you look at the names in those West Indies and Australia squads, they read like a who's-who of cricket's Hall of Fame.

When you have players like Clive Lloyd, Vivian Richards, Gordon Greenidge, Desmond Haynes, Jeff Dujon, Malcolm Marshall, Michael Holding, Joel Garner, Curtly Ambrose, Courtney Walsh and Brian Lara, you are going to win more matches than you lose. And the same is true of any side that can boast the likes of the Waugh brothers, Mark Taylor, David Boon, Matthew Hayden, Justin Langer, Ricky

Ponting, Michael Hussey, Adam Gilchrist, Glenn McGrath, Shane Warne and Jason Gillespie.

In both cases, the supply line of great players eventually dried up and those teams came back to the field – so the Holy Grail for all countries around the world is not only to find a way of creating that supply line but sustaining it.

In the wake of Australia's decline following the years of plenty that climaxed with the 5–0 Ashes series win of 2006–07 and a third consecutive World Cup win in the Caribbean, we have dabbled with a range of ideas to prime the pump to produce another golden era.

One of those ideas was to artificially alter the conditions around the state second XI competition, the Futures League, with, in 2009, a restriction on the number of players aged over 23 who could take part. Only three senior players were allowed to be involved and matches took place over three days rather than four.

The idea was to give more young players a chance to push their case for selection at first-class level. By reducing the duration of matches they were encouraged to play positive cricket.

The theory was great, but in practice it meant the standard of the competition actually declined because of a lack of quality senior players taking part and educating the young up-and-comers. It was actually forcing players out of the game early when they may still have been finding their feet – remember Michael Hussey was 30 when he made his Test debut, while Chris Rogers and Adam Voges did not become international regulars until well into their 30s.

Those changes were shelved after a couple of years, which I was in complete agreement with.

You need senior players around to set the benchmark for the younger guys and the changes, while made with the best of intentions, simply did not work.

Our first-class game is healthy now, but not as healthy as it was in the mid-1990s when there was more time in the schedule for established internationals to play the odd Sheffield Shield game, at a time when we were blessed with a perhaps never-to-be-repeated array of talent that was coming through the Australian Cricket Academy. While theories abound about why the likes of Ponting, McGrath, Warne, Michael Bevan and a whole host of other stars all emerged at that time, there seems no definitive reason for it.

The challenge for Australian cricket's administrators is to repeat that era by maintaining, along with the state associations, development pathways, but even with the best planning in the world it is still like trying to turn base metal into gold, especially as young people today have a range of sports that are all trying to get their hands on them. All we can do is make cricket an attractive career path for youngsters and I think we are doing that, but it is a long road and the initiatives being worked on at Cricket Australia's offices in Jolimont and at the National Cricket Centre, things like the One Game initiative, are not likely to bear significant fruit for some time.

The KFC Big Bash League is something that has taken summer by storm and produced record figures across the board in 2015–16, including a total attendance of more than one million supporters. One match alone, the Melbourne derby between the Stars and the Renegades, saw an attendance of more than 80,000 at the MCG. The average number of fans per game watching at home on television reached 1.1 million. Again though, it is too early to know whether any of this very encouraging news will translate into that longed-for conveyor belt of talent.

For the time being – and almost certainly for the duration of my time as the national men's head coach – I have several means at my disposal that can be used to try to get the current team to maintain that winning hunger.

One of those is to use history to put the achievements of this generation into context. One way I like to do that is by inviting in former players as a means of illustrating why it is so important to keep winning.

It was something that started in Steve Waugh's era, bringing in the past greats to be around the players, and I thought it worked very well. In the summer of 1999–2000 players like Ian Meckiff, Bill Johnston and Bill Brown travelled with the squad to matches. It was a two-way street: they got to experience again what it was like to be around the national side and the current players got to pick their brains about how things were back in the day.

In my time as coach I have sought to use some more recently retired players and get them talking about their experiences. I mentioned previously Bruce Reid coming into the rooms for a day, but any former Australia player is welcome and we have thrown open the doors, as I believe you can never have too much knowledge. I noticed the

England squad followed suit during our Ashes series in 2015 – perhaps through the influence of the side's Australian coach, Trevor Bayliss – inviting in the likes of Sir Ian Botham and Bob Willis to their rooms for a beer and a chat. I gather from what I heard that it worked well.

I am very keen for the current group to be aware that they are not the first ones to wear the baggy green and I actively encourage them to research players from previous eras. I remember chatting to Nathan Lyon about the spin bowlers who were around for Australia at the start of my career and was surprised to learn he did not know who Peter Sleep was. Peter was a terrific leg-spinner from South Australia who represented his country in the mid-1980s and then went on to enjoy success in the Lancashire League in England before becoming a respected coach. This led me to ask players if they knew about a particular former Australia player, to speak about them for two minutes to the group, and Nathan was one of the first to do this, talking about Peter Sleep. I was keen for this to happen, not only to make players aware of our history but also to encourage them to improve their public speaking, something that will be invaluable for them after cricket.

Even heading into the 2015 World Cup, I wanted them to know the tournament was not happening in a historical vacuum, so our team doctor, Peter Brukner, regularly presented to the squad about previous World Cups, starting with the 1975 edition.

By the end of those presentations I hope the players were aware of what the World Cup – and winning it – really meant. Although it was not a big thing in the overall scheme of things, I still like to think it helped them realise what they were playing for.

Peer pressure is another means we use for maintaining standards and that has taken several forms. I have written already about the leadership group within the dressing room and the role it plays in maintaining standards. In my era there was also the pressure each individual put on himself to perform – players like Steve Waugh, Ponting, McGrath and Warne to name just four. Those top players set their own standards, led by example, and theirs was a baton that was handed down to the likes of Brad Haddin, Michael Clarke and Steve Smith. Smith, I know, was a huge disciple of the way Ricky went about things, observing him and picking up whatever he could. His results in following that approach speak for themselves.

There is also pressure from within the squad, and not just from that leadership group. New players come in and see how the established stars go about their business. They can then react in one of two ways: they can either settle for continuing to do what got them to the Australian squad in the first place or they can raise the bar again and try to match the standards of the squad. That is a reason why it is good for us to be able to blood young players in the Twenty20 or One-Day International environment, as it gives them a taste of what is expected. They will either rise to the challenge or fail to do so.

In the summer of 2016 Western Australia fast bowler Joel Paris came in to the group for the start of the limited-overs series against India. He was given his chance after a host of retirements and injuries left our fast bowling stocks depleted and he performed really well without performing miracles, largely because the surfaces he was bowling on were completely batsman-friendly and the players he was up against, like Rohit Sharma, Virat Kohli and Shikhar Dhawan, were in red-hot form.

Joel was released from the squad after the first three matches, but left with a message from Chairman of Selectors Rodney Marsh: 'Well done for stepping up. You have had a taste of what it is like at this level and you have not let anyone down. Now go back to your state and make it impossible for us to leave you out again.' He now knows all about the standard he has to achieve and the ball is in his court if he wants more of cricket's top table, which is how it should be.

What you want as a coach is that when a top player retires or is out injured, a replacement is all set to take his place, so the team machine cruises along with barely a blip. From the early-1990s, as Craig McDermott was forced into retirement through injury, up popped Mervyn Hughes as a new enforcer, to be followed by Glenn McGrath. Similarly, whenever Shane Warne was absent there was Stuart MacGill all ready to roll. Adam Gilchrist took the role of the wicketkeeper-batsman to a new level when Ian Healy stepped down, Damien Martyn and Michael Clarke succeeded Mark Waugh, and Justin Langer eased in alongside Matthew Hayden as Michael Slater's replacement at the top of the order.

Things have not been as smooth as that during my time as coach, with six players dropping out of the Test side either during or soon after the Ashes series of 2015. For Brad Haddin and Shane Watson it was primarily about form, with Mitchell Johnson there was a waning in desire and the same was true of Michael Clarke too, coupled with the seemingly constant battle he had waged to fight back from injury over the previous two years, while Ryan Harris was forced out through a chronic knee injury and Chris Rogers made the decision to retire on his terms rather than wait to receive the tap on the shoulder.

That is a substantial amount of talent all walking away within a relatively short period of time and I challenge any side to cope with it and move forward without at least some disruption. That we did so during the summer of 2015–16 was due, at least in part, to the fact we had players like Usman Khawaja and Joe Burns who we had already blooded on the sidelines, together with some others, like Shaun Marsh and Peter Siddle, who stepped back into senior roles.

Should we have seen the mass exodus coming? Maybe we should have, especially as an Ashes series can often mark a jumping-off point for players in their Test careers. As I mentioned earlier, given my time again my preference as just one member of the NSP would have been to look beyond Watson and Haddin for that Ashes series, but circumstances dictated otherwise. Hindsight is a wonderful thing.

Clarke had fought so hard to get back to full fitness and in his public comments he seemed to be indicating a renewed desire for the fight, but the stress of leading another losing series in England simply wore him down. We did everything we could to get Harris on the park, even resting him from the back-end of the domestic season, but he still could not get past the fitness issues that had plagued his career. Johnson's decision was very sudden, not helped I think by how flat the pitches were after the squad returned from the Ashes series. We left him out of the squad for the Bangladesh series – which was subsequently cancelled anyway – to ensure he was fresh for the series against New Zealand and the West Indies, but in the end he just lost that eye of the tiger. Rogers' decision to depart was made easier, no doubt, by the advent of day-night Test cricket as, being colour blind, he said he could simply not pick up the pink ball.

Did I try to talk any of the retiring players out of their decisions? After all, as I and plenty of other past players know, you are a long time retired. Clarke's desire to get back into action, stated at the back-end of the summer of 2016, was a reflection of that fact. But aside from Johnson, who I asked to keep playing One-Day Internationals, I felt they had made their decisions and I had no right to try to change their minds.

My thinking on Johnson was that I knew the One-Day International side was in transition following the 2015 World Cup and I wanted to keep a senior bowler while some of the younger ones found their feet. Johnson declined and I was fine with that. As I chatted with him in the dressing room at Perth on the night it all ended I could see in his eyes he had had enough. I was not going to labour the point.

Our age profile as a squad, especially in One-Day International cricket, has now gone down considerably, as has our experience, but I am confident we will not see the dip the side experienced from the highs of the 2007 World Cup when we did not lose a match (and the Champions Trophy success in South Africa two years later) through to the disappointing attempt to defend the title in the Indian subcontinent in 2011 and the embarrassing exit from the Champions Trophy at the group stage two years after that.

The current group of players has still got quality and experience and that is only going to grow as those dates with destiny – a Champions Trophy in 2017 and the World Cup in 2019, both in the United Kingdom – get closer. All we need to be among the favourites is a little bit of fortune to get our first-choice attack on the park following a host of injuries in 2015–16 that robbed us of Pat Cummins, Mitchell Starc, James Pattinson, Nathan Coulter-Nile and Peter Siddle, among others, for part or all of the summer and beyond.

We will not be at what I like to think of as the ideal age profile come 2019 – I reckon that is around 33 or 34. By that age players know their games inside out, have been around the block and know how to cope with pressure, and the proof of the pudding in 2015 was how the likes of Clarke, Johnson, Watson and Haddin, all of them around that age or, in Haddin's case, a little older, led by example. In the Test side Adam Voges has defied the hands of time by making his Test debut – and starring – at the age of 35, but I think his ability to make that leap had a great deal to do with him keeping himself in great shape and also by having a great hunger, having waited for so long for his opportunity.

I have heard it said that there is such a thing as 'good' pressure – that feeling your spot is under threat helps you concentrate. Well, as someone who has been at that sharp end, I can tell you that pressure is pressure no matter how many ways you like to slice the cake, and there is no such thing as 'good' pressure.

It is true, however, as I always say to the players, there are far more serious things in life than cricket. In that regard I always hark back to the line of the great all-rounder Keith Miller, who flew as a fighter pilot in World War Two before becoming part of Don Bradman's Invincibles on the 1948 tour of the United Kingdom. 'Pressure,' he is reported to have said, 'is a Messerschmitt up your arse.'

But whether we like it or not, we are earning our livelihood in an industry where results are everything, so we have to deliver and there are times when pressure can do strange things to your thought processes.

Even Bradman himself failed in his final Test innings. Who can forget Allan Donald and Lance Klusener being unable to handle the situation in the final over of that pulsating World Cup semi-final against us in 1999? Although if you think back to that latter occasion you might also recall that the ball before Donald was run out, a dismissal that saw the match end in a tie with us going through to the final as a result, I failed to run out Donald from mid-on.

I had a shot at the stumps from close range with Donald in no-man's land at the non-striker's end. It was a throw

I would have expected to get on target 99 times out of 100. I missed and that miss was down to one thing: pressure. I was thinking about the situation and the context rather than simply focusing on throwing the ball at the stumps. Thankfully we got another chance next ball, so I was spared a lifetime of being reminded about it.

Another example of pressure and the way it affects the mind came in my penultimate game for Australia, a One-Day International against Pakistan at the MCG in February 2005. I had already lost my place in the Test side a month earlier and now my spot in the limited-overs line-up was under threat too. I went in to bat with 10 overs left and for a reason that I still cannot fathom I played a reverse sweep to Shahid Afridi first ball – and was caught behind.

When I got back to the dressing room Ricky Ponting came up to me and asked: 'What on earth were you thinking?' I simply did not have an answer for him. It was a shot I seldom played at the best of times, so it was fraught with danger, especially as I had just walked to the crease. Add the fact I had an established batsman in Andrew Symonds going well at the other end.

There was no logic at all to my decision to play that shot other than the fact that I felt under pressure to deliver some-thing special to maintain my spot. Rather than thinking clearly, I succumbed to pressure and allowed my mind to become clouded. I played one more match and then never played for Australia again.

I like to think we have handled the pressure of inter-national cricket pretty well during my time as coach, a view that is backed up by the relatively few times we have been found guilty of violations of the ICC's Code of Conduct.

In two-and-a-half years after I took over in late June 2013 we transgressed nine times – the first of which was me, for my ill-advised comments about Stuart Broad failing to walk when he edged to slip during the Trent Bridge Test match. I made a tongue-in-cheek comment on radio. Taken out of context, it looked like I was inciting the crowds to mischief when the return series was played in Australia. That was a good lesson early in my tenure to put my brain in gear before opening my mouth.

All the guilty verdicts we were handed down during that period up to the start of the New Zealand tour of February 2016 were for Level One offences, the lowest rung of the disciplinary ladder, and while that in no way excuses any mistakes we make out on the field – we are role models, after all, and everyone accepts that – it is a record that certainly compares favourably to virtually all of the other Test-playing teams.

During that same period from mid-2013 to early 2016 only New Zealand, with five offences – three of them by under-19 players – and Zimbabwe with eight (although they play nowhere near as much cricket as us) had fewer transgressions, while we were level with England.

Ahead of us were the West Indies (10), South Africa (13), Pakistan and India (15 each), Bangladesh (18) and Sri Lanka topped the list of offenders with 20 violations.

Whenever there is some spice on the field we always seem to get the 'Ugly Aussies' tag thrown at us, but those figures suggest it is misplaced. I certainly believe that to be the case and I am proud of the way we have played our cricket while I have been coach. Hard, undoubtedly, but for the vast majority of the time fair too, and where we have crossed the line we have been punished. It's true we lost our cool over a third umpire decision during that New Zealand tour and Steve Smith copped a fine for that, but I like to think that was the exception rather than the rule for my players.

Pressure can be your enemy, but so too can complacency, the tendency to cruise and take your foot off the pedal, either individually or collectively, consciously or unconsciously, when things are going well.

As a coach it is something you are constantly on the lookout for and you like to believe you know your players well enough to spot the telltale signs – things like batsmen going in to the nets and playing shots galore from ball one rather than looking to build an innings as they would out in the middle.

We certainly failed to spot a hint of it in the summer of 2015–16 when our bowlers were guilty of overstepping against the West Indies during the Melbourne Test, costing us two wickets. I am not saying that James Pattinson was in cruise control when he transgressed, but that is something that we as coaches – and he as the bowler – should have been more aware of. The West Indies was a young side very much in transition, but that was no excuse for a failure to prepare properly. Thankfully it did not cost us dear.

Complacency was certainly a constant parrot on the shoulder in our World Cup campaign of 2003 as we steamrolled team after team. It almost caused us to come unstuck in our final group match of the first stage, against England in Port Elizabeth.

We had restricted Nasser Hussain's team, a side we had just thumped during our home summer, to 8-204 in a match it had to win to secure a spot in the next stage, and we felt utterly assured of knocking off the runs for fun, without allowing for the fact that the pitch was an awkward one. It was slow and offered some turn, making it very difficult to play aggressively without taking significant risks.

Undaunted, however, we came out and played a shot a ball and soon found ourselves at 4-48. It was a long way back from there and we owed almost everything to another piece of nerveless batting from Bevan, 74 not out, aided by Andy Bichel, who followed up an amazing haul of 7-20 by scoring an unbeaten 34.

In the end we won with two wickets to spare in the final over. It was just the wake-up call we needed and we did not allow anything like that level of casualness to invade our thoughts for the rest of the event.

Losing is the ultimate antidote for complacency and in that sense you could argue that sometimes the bitter taste of defeat is something that can actually serve a purpose if you can learn from it, realise what you did wrong and put it right.

That theory was a long way off the mark when Australia lost the seemingly unlosable Test against India in Kolkata in 2001. Having asked India to follow on 274 runs behind, VVS Laxman and Rahul Dravid pummelled the side into submission before Steve Waugh's line-up lost seven wickets in the final session. Coach John Buchanan tried to put a positive spin on things – the loss followed a run of 16 successive Test wins – but the fact is a loss in the next match in Chennai cost Australia the series.

On the other hand, when we lost against New Zealand in the 2015 World Cup in Auckland, a match that actually meant little in the overall scheme of things as both sides were already certain to get through to the next stage, you could say that it taught us some good lessons.

Michael Clarke certainly seemed to think so, as he said after that match that he felt our batting preparation had been all wrong with too many players looking to play too many big shots in the nets in readiness for Auckland's notoriously short straight boundaries. As it was, the match turned out to be a low-scoring thriller, with New Zealand edging home by just one wicket.

Call me old school if you like, but I just hate losing. Although I am always keen to learn the lessons of defeat, I do not subscribe to the view that it can be a positive experience. The only exception might be that if you remember the feeling you get from losing, it should make you determined not to have that feeling again any time soon.

An ideal way to avoid losing is to ensure you prepare properly, which is becoming harder and harder in the modern era. The days of long lead times ahead of tours is long gone and, in fact, we have had a couple of occasions since I have been Australia coach where we have actually started getting ready for one series while still being involved in the previous one.

In late 2014 we had some players return to Australia in preparation for a Twenty20 International series against South Africa while we were still playing a Test against Pakistan in Abu Dhabi. Again, in early 2016 some of our players left Australia to get ready for a limited-overs series in New Zealand before the end of a three-match Twenty20 International clash against India. The program these days is relentless, but there is no point in complaining; you just get on with it and make the best of the hand you are dealt.

On my first tour as Australia coach, the 2013 Ashes, I was obviously not involved in the planning of the schedule, although since then I have worked actively with Pat Howard and team manager Gavin Dovey to get in as much quality lead-time, including matches against decent opposition, as is possible. I am no great fan of practice matches with umpteen players batting and bowling and nothing riding on the result, and I liked the way England approached its Ashes tour of 2010–11, when it set out to win its warm-up matches ahead of the first Test. Of course, if we have limited preparation time then those glorified net sessions masquerading as matches have to do, but they are far from ideal.

On our 2013 Ashes tour what disappointed me a little was that when we played matches outside the Tests we did not always find ourselves up against the strongest sides that the counties were capable of putting out. It has long been a custom of county sides to rest key players during tour games to ensure they are fresh for domestic action – I saw that first-hand at Yorkshire and benefited from the occasional rest myself in such circumstances – but that sort of decision does not help a touring side get the best preparation possible.

I remember at the end of the tour, following a limited-overs match at Southampton, seeing a very smug-looking senior England administrator, delighted his side had won the Test series. 'Don't worry, you'll enjoy Australia when you get there,' I said. Sure enough we got our revenge with that 5–0 series success – and I enjoyed seeing him looking slightly less smug at the presentation ceremony that followed our final win in Sydney.

10

DEALING WITH THE HYPE

'We were lucky in our day, we could play it [cricket] for fun. I admire these guys that play now. They've got to work their arses off, there's so much cricket, [and] all the stuff they've got to put up with, all the press, all the media, everything like that. We didn't have to put up with any of that stuff. It would be hard work; we flew under the radar. I played football in the off-season so I could get away from cricket. I didn't have to do it 12 months a year; I don't know how they do it 12 months a year, these blokes. You wonder why they break down? Well, why wouldn't they break down?'

The opening to Jeff Thomson's speech when he was inducted into the Australian Cricket Hall of Fame at the Allan Border Medal night in January 2016 sums up the life of a current-day Australian cricketer pretty well, I think. Their lives are lived in a goldfish bowl of scrutiny with little time to themselves. Dealing with that scrutiny – and dealing with the hype – is now part and parcel of what they do. They are public property and the opportunity to fly under the radar, as 'Thommo' put it, simply does not exist.

That is why one of the key things I have to do, alongside my coaching staff, is keep the players grounded.

If you experience the type of highs the players have, like winning a home Ashes series 5–0 or winning a World Cup, it is all too easy to get an inflated opinion of yourself and your abilities. That is especially true when almost everyone you see is telling you how great you are, and when the same applies to much of what you read, much of what you see on television and hear on radio and much of what appears on social media.

Praise like that, of course, is fleeting and the next low score or the next struggle with the ball or in the field is only a game away. And when that happens, the criticism can feel even more crushing if you have allowed yourself to be pumped up too much by all the backslapping beforehand.

The key message I always give my players is never to get too high when we win and never to get too low when we lose. Trying to maintain that equilibrium is the closest you can come to managing the hype.

One thing I never say to the players is 'don't read the papers and don't watch the news'. In this modern age of people living on their phones with 24-hour internet that is impossible and, in any case, they have to understand that, whatever people might say on Twitter or Facebook or in newspaper columns, it is what happens on the field that counts.

When I played for Australia we were a very successful side, but that did not exempt us from criticism. We won the vast majority of our matches comfortably and that meant there were times when the media had precious little cut-and-thrust action to write about. Quite often our match-ups were one-way traffic.

On that basis, and needing to fill column inches, reporters would understandably often home in on what was perceived to be a weak link in the side, a player who, despite the fact we were winning, was not performing to the best of his ability.

Mark Waugh and Damien Martyn, who both experienced life under that particular magnifying glass during their otherwise highly decorated careers, used to have a name for it. They called it 'the blowtorch', and the only way to turn it off was to perform well.

That blowtorch has intensified almost beyond measure in the past decade thanks to social media. It means that what we have to do as leaders of the team, more than ever before, is to show a fair degree of compassion and care for the players. Although they are public figures, they are still as liable as anyone else to be hurt by criticism.

That care may take the form of defending a player in the media but behind closed doors it may also involve not only an arm around the shoulder but open and honest feedback too – if a player *is* doing something wrong then they need to be told, as that is the best way to make sure they are able to rectify the error.

I would be the last person to preach to the players on how to deal with the media – we have a media manager, Kate Hutchison, whose job it is to know more about that than me, and the players' own representatives will also often have a hotline to various media contacts too and will be able to provide their own guidance on that matter.

A prerequisite for any time spent in front of the cameras or before the dictaphones is obviously a chat with Kate beforehand, to find out what the likely line of questioning may be, as the last thing you want is to be caught like a rabbit in the headlights if someone asks you something you are not expecting. From conversations with her will come possible approaches to deal with those likely questions. My preference is also to try to inject a little bit of humour into my media interactions, whenever I can. The reporters have a job to do and so do you as the person before them, but there is no reason why it cannot be done, wherever possible, with a smile on the face.

That sense of humour did start to fail me towards the end of our marathon stint on the road in 2015 that featured the Caribbean and then the United Kingdom. I did not realise it at the time, only later, when speaking with Andrea. 'I could tell you were tired,' she said to me when I had returned home. 'Whenever you were interviewed, you had stopped smiling.'

From my experience I have invariably found that the best way to deal with the media is to be as open and honest as possible. Yes, there may occasionally be things you will want to hold back, news of a player's injury for example or the result of a selection puzzle (which allows you to keep the opposition guessing for just a little bit longer), but being straight down the line is the best way of dealing with the people who write and broadcast the stories about you and your team. It might also cut you a bit of slack when you need it.

That approach probably benefited me most during one of the most harrowing times of my career, the occasion I have already alluded to earlier when I uttered a racist remark after being dismissed against Sri Lanka in Brisbane in 2003. The incident happened late in the evening as the match was reaching its conclusion and did not actually emerge as a story until the following morning when I was preparing to fly to my home town of Adelaide.

It certainly helped me that I was arriving to meet a group of reporters I already knew – and if I was ever going to get anything even close to a comfortable ride in terms of questioning given the circumstances, Adelaide was the place. The story was all over the airwaves already, so there was no point in playing dumb or denying something that had already come out. So I simply fronted up when the flight touched down, admitted what I had done and made my apologies as best I could.

By doing that I actually inadvertently invited the International Cricket Council's Chief Executive Officer at the time, Malcolm Speed, to charge me with an offence under the Code of Conduct, and that was exactly what he did.

But while I was banned and had to sit out the first match of the World Cup as a result – and was also late for Amy and Ethan's christening because of the hearing in Adelaide – I am relieved to say the episode did not have as damaging an effect on my career as it might have done.

I later found out what I had done in fronting the media in the way I did amounted to a strategy known in public relations circles as 'confess and avoid' or, put another way, 'tell the truth and tell it quickly'. The idea behind the approach is to get all the bad news out into the open as quickly as possible so that the story, with no new angles to feed off, runs out of legs. This one did develop new legs thanks to Malcolm Speed's intervention, the resultant hearing and my subsequent five-match ban, but in this instance, where I made a horrible mistake, it worked out as well as it could have done for me in the circumstances.

Fast forward more than a decade and it is amazing that in this age of instant communication there is still the very real possibility that messages get mucked up. One such idea is that I am wedded to the view that we must have seam bowlers operating at speeds in excess of 140 kilometres per hour.

It is true that I like pace and I like to see opposition batsmen disconcerted. We saw that to perfect effect with Mitchell Johnson's efforts against England in the summer of 2013–14: there could be no better illustration of the effectiveness of pace than the bowling that he produced in that series.

Pace like that is especially important in Australia as the ball tends to swing less than in some other parts of the world.

If you do not have pace as an arrow in your quiver, you are liable to be facing long periods in the field.

Yet pace is not the be-all and end-all. There have been plenty of bowlers in the recent past who have demonstrated that very effectively, such as Glenn McGrath, Shaun Pollock and Sir Richard Hadlee.

All three of those began their careers able to nudge the speed gun up towards that 140 kilometres per hour mark and beyond – I remember Pollock, when he first came on the scene at international level in 1995–96, had a reputation for a fearsome bouncer and he regularly hit players on the head with it. As their experience grew and their bodies aged, they found they were able to get by through other skills they learnt along the way, allied with unerring accuracy.

I will always want a bowler in my side who can shake things up speed-wise, but if they are not available or if conditions dictate that other options are more appropriate, I am comfortable to go down a different route. As the saying goes, there is more than one way to skin a cat.

The best way to explain the stresses and strains of a major tournament to the players, and how best to cope with them, is through the mouths of those who have done it. That was something I looked to do in the build-up to the World Cup by inviting in members of the 1992 squad to talk about their experiences.

Allan Border's line-up went into that tournament – which, like the 2015 edition, took place in Australia and

New Zealand – as the defending champion having lifted the crown for the first time in India in 1987. The side wore the tag of favourites and when you look at the list of stars on the roster, players like the Waugh brothers, Craig McDermott, David Boon and Dean Jones to name just a few, it was no wonder. But things did not go to plan, the campaign opened with a defeat at the hands of the co-hosts in Auckland and although there was a late rally in the group stages, Australia failed to reach the semi-finals.

McDermott, by now our bowling coach, as well as opening batsman Geoff Marsh, wicketkeeper Ian Healy and ex-captain Steve Waugh, all met up with the squad at various stages in the build-up to and during the 2015 edition. Between them they distilled just what it felt like to play a World Cup on home soil and also what they thought had gone wrong 23 years earlier.

The message was the same from all of them: 'We thought we'd cruise through.' The side was full of experience and they were in action in conditions the players were familiar with, but the wheels came off, almost from the get-go. Too many losses piled up at the front-end of the tournament, leaving them playing catch-up. It was a mountain that proved too high to get over.

The loss against New Zealand saw Australia's batsmen fail to deal with a new tactic employed against them – spinner Dipak Patel opening the bowling – while victory over India in a rain-affected game at The Gabba in Brisbane came at the cost of wicketkeeper Healy injuring his hamstring. Further crushing losses to England – a side Australia had beaten from pillar to post the previous summer – and eventual champion Pakistan just about put the final nails in the coffin. The latter stages of the event took place with Australia's players looking on forlornly from the sidelines.

I did not want the talks to be sombre affairs – my plan was for them to be about learning lessons and taking those lessons with us into the action – and Healy entered into the spirit I was hoping to achieve by digging out his playing jersey from the garage and bringing it in for the players, some of whom were not born when the tournament was played, to have a look at.

From the chats we distilled four important factors that helped us in our pursuit of the trophy: focus on starting well to set up the rest of our tournament; be prepared to think about and adapt to whatever challenges are thrown in front of us; embrace the fact we are at home as this is a once-in-a-generation experience; and enjoy the occasion, as for some it will be their last World Cup and for others it may be their only one.

I have no doubt that those lessons stood us in good stead for the journey we set out on against England at the MCG on 14 February and they were still with us when Michael Clarke eventually lifted the trophy a month and a half later on 29 March.

As the coach of the team and also a selector, I know that I am also liable to be the subject of criticism. That is not a pleasant experience, but you do develop a thick skin over the years and I have learnt to deal with it.

I work with the team psychologist Michael Lloyd – the 'time on the couch' I referred to earlier – and also have my select group of people I confide in, mainly family and very close friends. When I am on the road I will Skype with Andrea, Ethan and Amy whenever we can find the time, and also keep in touch with my two children from my first marriage, Tori and Jake, but I also have to be mindful that they have schedules too and the world does not revolve around me.

Maintaining a degree of normality and calm in what is a very artificial life is vital, as we move from hotel room to hotel room, airport to airport and cricket ground to cricket ground, and over the years I have developed a couple of coping mechanisms that I find help me unwind and also allow me to gather my thoughts.

You might not think it to look at me, but I do go to the gym at the start of every day. Wherever we are staying you will almost certainly find me in the hotel gym at around 6.30 am for about 45 minutes. It is nothing too strenuous – a walk on the treadmill, some time on the exercise bike and a few free weights – but I find it gets me going and allows me to focus on the day ahead.

I mentioned earlier about how, depending on where the team is playing or training, I will often walk to the venue, but I will also walk back to the hotel after a training session too, another chance for me to just switch off for a while and have some thinking time. There might be an issue over selection to consider or another issue that needs my attention. Whatever it is, I find quiet time like that often helps to crystallise my thoughts.

When I am on the road with the team I probably average around six hours of sleep per night. I would like more, of course, but switching off is always a challenge, especially when you live your life in what is a pretty artificial environment. You are surrounded by the people you work with almost constantly and the fact the schedule is so packed means there is always an issue to be dealt with, whether it relates to your current assignment or one that may be 12 months in the future.

Do not be under any misapprehension – I love my job and I love the challenges it presents me with and in the absence of playing the game there is nothing I would rather be doing professionally. But there are times where you find yourself yearning for a little bit of normality and to take your foot off the throttle every now and again.

When I get home after a tour it is not unusual for me to sleep for large tracts of two or three days that follow. I am liable to wake up for the school run, but otherwise I will do my best to do as little as possible as I try to unwind, while at the same time trying to fit back into the lives of Andrea, Ethan and Amy without ruining their routines. After a week or so I am back to my normal self, but I realise it can make me tough to live with at times and I never cease to be amazed at how tolerant my family is of the nomadic life I live.

They know of course, as I do, that it is not something that will last forever, but at the same time I am also acutely conscious of the fact I have missed a great deal of the lives of all four of my children and that is time we will never get back. That is the price you pay for being involved in cricket.

I do watch the news, mainly on the ABC when I have that rare time at home with the family, and when I am on the road I will often tune in to Channel 7's *Sunrise* first thing in the morning. I like to catch up on what is going on in the world and I like to hear what is being said about the team too, as I think that is important. Over the years my skin has become thick enough to handle most things, but I do worry for my players. That is my first thought whenever criticism comes our way.

I have to admit I am not a good watcher of the game, although I have become better over the years at putting on a mask for the reasons I have already outlined – that a coach who is liable to react in a volatile way is not the right person to have in a dressing room.

I chew gum and lots of it too – there is usually a plentiful supply of the stuff nearby – and that helps avoid the temptation for picking at the large amounts of food that are usually found in dressing rooms to help the players replace all the calories they burn up out on the field.

Smoking has also been a crutch for me over the years in terms of stress relief, even though I know it is far from ideal. I started when I was in my late teens on the production line at Holden as it seemed like the fashionable and cool thing to do at the time. Although I don't smoke anywhere near as much as I used to – helped by the fact that many stadiums around the world are becoming smoke-free venues – you are still liable to find me out the back of the dressing room at drinks breaks having a puff to collect my thoughts.

I don't think it counted against me during the years I was in the international wilderness – although it wouldn't have helped my image with Bobby Simpson, I guess – but it is not something I rail against among my players now I'm coach. There are some players within the squad that smoke but I'm not going to call them out, and from my perspective it comes down to treating players like adults. They need to make their own choices in matters like that.

The problem for any coach is that although you play a pivotal role in the planning for a match, once the action is underway you are no longer in control. You cannot bat, bowl or catch for the players and that is just about the worst tension of all.

I say 'just about' as during the 2015–16 season I discovered something even harder to deal with – following the performances of your own son. Jake's maiden first-class hundred for South Australia, against Tasmania in Hobart, coincided with the opening day of the first ever day-night Test match when we played New Zealand in Adelaide in November. I have to confess that during that opening session I did spend quite a bit of time trying to get news of what was going on at the Blundstone Arena. The pride I felt when Jake reached three figures was immense, as was the feeling I got when he hit the one ball he faced for six to win a match for the Adelaide Strikers in the KFC Big Bash League later in the season.

You cannot compare the tension and pressure you feel as a parent with what you go through in your job of work – the former is far worse, I believe – but the pressure exists in the latter, all the same. My predecessors, Tim Nielsen and Mickey Arthur, both lost their jobs because the team was unable to win regularly and no coach can ever be under any illusions about his or her fate if results do not go their way. In that sense you could say – only half-joking – that there are only two types of coach: one who has been sacked and one who is about to be sacked. That is the reality of the job I have undertaken. I had a honeymoon period in 2013 that is no longer even in the rear-view mirror. The side that goes out on to the field is now the one I have a large hand in selecting as well as preparing, so I live and die by the results it achieves.

I did feel the heat of the blowtorch after the failure of the Ashes campaign of 2015. We had arrived favourites after our comprehensive success in the previous encounter and, although we lost the opening Test in Cardiff, we bounced back so spectacularly at Lord's that we looked odds-on to once more go on and take the series.

That did not happen. We got thumped in the two matches that followed, at Edgbaston and Trent Bridge, but I can honestly say that despite those two spectacular losses – we came close to losing inside two days on both occasions – the thought of resigning did not ever cross my mind. It may well have done had we been rolled over on good pitches.

Still, defeats like that can have a withering effect on even the strongest constitutions. It is times like that you need the support of family and friends around you. That is why we have a family-friendly policy around the team and have done for as long as I can remember.

Before the 1999 World Cup there was a short period between the end of a One-Day International series we played against the West Indies and the time when we were required to assemble in the United Kingdom for the start of the tournament. Rather than fly us all the way home for just a handful of days only to then have to turn around and fly back across the globe, the Australian Cricket Board (ACB), as it was then, flew the wives and partners of the players and support staff out to the Caribbean and everyone had some much-needed rest and relaxation before the serious business began.

These days the hotels where we stay, especially in Australia, tend to be apartment-style and that makes it easier for families to stay with the players during the season. There is a school of thought that says a development like that has the potential to eat into team spirit by keeping players away from each other, but when you spend days on end in each other's company I believe the best way to maintain a good spirit is to give the players the chance to have a bit of family time – and therefore some normality in their lives – too.

When I was playing at the start of the century what often happened was that those players with young children would be the ones to wake up and provide the youngsters with breakfast before they headed off to the match, while the wives would use that time first thing in the morning to get together and go out for a jog or even just have their own breakfasts. Then, once the action began on the field, the wives and children would assemble together at the cricket and be looked after by the ACB.

Since then the demographic of the side has altered, especially since the end of the Ashes series, and as the average age of the side has gone down then so has the number of wives and partners with children. Those families are still encouraged to be around whenever they want and it really does help create a great atmosphere, one that is essential to help players cope.

The idea of family – whether it is blood relatives or the cricketing family we develop by dint of spending so much time in each other's pockets – is absolutely central to all that I believe in as coach of the Australian cricket team. Thommo was spot-on at the end of his Hall of Fame speech.

'What I'm happy about is all the parents,' he said. 'It's all about the people who help you as kids. [It's] the ones who don't come in this room tonight, the ones who do all the s*** when you're a kid, taking you to the games.

'They'll never be here [at the Allan Border Medal dinner], they'll never be the recognised ones, but they're the ones who took you to those games, and they sit back, and they're the ones who ring you up and say, "Well done."

'It's for those people.'

11

COPING WITH ADVERSITY

The afternoon of Tuesday 25 November 2014 is not one that anyone within cricket will ever remember with any fondness.

It was the first day of the final round of Sheffield Shield matches before the opening Test of that summer, against India at The Gabba, a match set to get underway just over a week later.

I was making my preparations, sending and receiving emails and taking and making phone calls, enjoying the fact that I did not have to think about packing as Brisbane was a home Test for me, the city having been my home since 2011 when I became Queensland coach.

Then, in mid-afternoon, I took a call from my old friend and teammate Darren Berry.

'Chuck', the former South Australia and Victoria wicket-keeper, was the coach of South Australia and he was at the SCG for his side's match against NSW. I had checked the score a little earlier and seen that my old side was going well, led by some positive batting from Phillip Hughes, who had moved there from NSW.

That was good news to me. Michael Clarke was struggling with injury and we needed someone to step into the line-up in his place. Phillip looked the ideal replacement, as he had been in our squads for a recent One-Day International tri-series in Zimbabwe against the hosts and South Africa, and the tour of the United Arab Emirates to face Pakistan that followed.

Before that he had been in sparkling form for Australia A in matches in Townsville and Brisbane against South Africa A and India A, with two double hundreds – one of them in a one-day match, the first Australian batsman to achieve the feat – and a further three-figure score. He was unlucky to miss out on selection for the Test against India in the first place, but was undoubtedly the first pick in the event of an injury to any of the batsmen chosen.

Welcoming Phillip back to the Test side was just what I had wanted to do, for a couple of reasons. Back in 2013, in my first series as coach, he had been dropped when David Warner returned from suspension, just one Test after scoring an unbeaten 81 as part of a record tenth-wicket stand of 163 with Ashton Agar. His next three scores had been 0, 1 and 1, but it had still been a tough call – having struggled to cement my own place in the Test team for more than a decade I had great sympathy for him. Phillip was stuck on the sidelines for the rest of that 2013 Test tour, but he had filled that role with his customary good humour and ready smile, even though he was burning with desire to return to the starting line-up.

I got a first-hand illustration of that desire the following summer when we met up after the Allan Border Medal awards ceremony. After the prizes were handed out a few of us went out for a drink, and during the course of that night he asked if he could have a word with me away from the others. We went into a quiet corner and he poured out his heart, full of passion, expressing how much he wanted to get another chance. Phillip spoke with such earnestness that we both ended up in tears. He showed me then how desperate he was to succeed, and now, through sheer weight of runs and with the captain struggling, this seemed like the perfect opportunity for him to get back into the team.

Chuck, though, had some bad news. Phillip had been struck on the left-hand side of the neck, just below his helmet, by a short ball and gone down, clearly in trouble. He had been treated at the scene by medical staff and taken to the nearby St Vincent's Hospital. It did not look good.

I felt sick. And then I thought back to the time a decade earlier, to 18 January 2004, when Chuck and I were out together with my great mentor David Hookes.

Hookesy was Victoria's coach and that day his side had beaten South Australia – including me, as captain – in a domestic one-day fixture at the MCG. The three of us and some other friends and acquaintances had decided to go out for a drink after play in St Kilda, about 20 minutes' drive from the city centre.

That night ended tragically. Hookesy suffered a blow to the head that ultimately proved fatal and now, here we were again, with another dreadful situation unfolding. 'Surely, not again?' I thought. It did not seem real.

All of a sudden the upcoming Test shrunk away in my mind and I thought about not just Phillip but also his family – his parents Greg and Virginia, his brother Jason and sister Megan – and those players and support staff I knew who had been present at the SCG, as well as his many friends. I could only guess what each and every one of them was going through.

The situation, as I discovered next day when I arrived in Sydney, was desperate. Phillip had undergone surgery soon after arriving at St Vincent's to relieve pressure on his brain caused by bleeding following the blow, but he remained critical, in an induced coma.

Players, staff and friends were allowed in to see him in twos and threes and I went in alongside Phil Jaques, his former NSW teammate, and Simon Katich, who had opened the batting with Phillip in his first Test, against South Africa in Johannesburg in 2009.

It was tough for all three of us to see our little mate in the state he was in. It was déjà vu of the worst kind for me, as it brought back memories of the identical situation with Hookesy in 2004. In both instances the person lying in the hospital bed looked so calm and so peaceful. It was hard to believe that the person in front of you was actually fighting for his life, but that was exactly the scenario that confronted everyone.

There was no happy ending in either case. The life-support machines were switched off and the people we knew and loved were replaced, on both occasions, with horrible voids and one question: why?

Trying to explain either death was and is futile. It is possible to say that the scenarios were one-billion-to-one chances, but that does not make them any easier to take or to understand. All everyone was left with was the chance to say goodbye through funeral services.

Both occasions were beautifully done. Hookesy was farewelled at his beloved Adelaide Oval, complete with an old bat and cap of his leaning against a set of stumps in the middle – just the way he always left them when there was a drinks break or he went off the field not out at tea time. And in Macksville, in northern NSW, the whole town – and thousands more – turned out to provide a moving send-off for Phillip.

In both instances, in the days, weeks and months that followed, I found myself trying to make sense of what had happened – and, in both instances, I failed.

The loss of Hookesy hit me very hard, not least because I was one of the people out with him on that fateful evening. 'What if we had gone somewhere else for a drink?' 'What if we had left 10 minutes earlier?' There were so many questions rolling around in my mind that for months afterwards I found sleep hard to come by.

Very soon after the incident on that night in St Kilda, the doctor in attendance at the Alfred Hospital, where

Hookesy was taken, told those of us who had followed the ambulance, along with Robyn, his wife, who joined us there, that he would not survive. That was a crushing thing to hear. It left me numb. I was able to make myself useful in the aftermath of that devastating news by calling Hookesy's step-children Kristofer and Caprice, as well as his brother Terry Cranage and his old mate Ian Chappell, to let them know the situation, but pretty soon after that I hit the wall and was unable to deal with the situation any more.

I went back to the South Australia team hotel and attempted to rest, but sleep just would not come, through a mixture of a racing mind and a telephone that never seemed to stop ringing. In the end I had to pass on the duties of team spokesman to vice-captain Greg Blewett, who handled the whole situation with real class and dignity.

Hookesy had been the person who welcomed me to the South Australia side when I made my first-class debut still two months short of my 18th birthday and as far as I was concerned he was 'the man'. He was hard as nails on the field and was always looking to find a way to win – and he always backed his players, which was a terrific feeling for a teenager starting out in the game. When, as an 18-year-old in just my third first-class game, I was run out following a mix-up that saw me collide with Geoff Lawson, Hookesy, together with coach Barry Richards, tore into the NSW players, accusing them of cheating me out. It did not change the decision, but it showed me how passionate he was in supporting his teammates.

Hookesy was impulsive and by no means infallible. I remember when I wore a helmet for the first time, on my first-class debut against Victoria at the MCG, he criticised me, saying that if I had been used to playing without one it was foolish to suddenly change tack. I was glad I ignored his advice – just for once – as the following season, when I was hit by a Bruce Reid bouncer at the WACA Ground in Perth, I would surely have been killed if I had not been wearing one.

He was always someone who believed in looking after young players when they came into the team and one instance of that from very early in my career sticks in my mind. In just my second season, in February 1989, we were playing Victoria in a Sheffield Shield match at the MCG and I went out to join him at the back-end of day two. Victoria had scored 284 and we were 3-144 in reply, so the match was very much in the balance.

At one end was fast bowler Mervyn Hughes, absolutely in his prime and steaming in, and it is no exaggeration to say that I was terrified at the prospect of facing him. Meanwhile, at the other end was an off-spinner called Mark Osborne who did not play for Victoria again after that season.

The first thing Hookesy said when I arrived in the middle was that he would take Hughes and that I should go after Osborne. He was as good as his word and saw off the big quick while I made hay against the slow bowler, and I ended the day 50 not out, feeling pretty pleased with myself.

Then, next morning, the new ball was due after the first hour of play. Hookesy decided to cut loose. We added a further

113 in no time at all, of which just 37 were mine, before I was dismissed, and he scored his second 50, to go to three figures, in just 35 balls. It showed me what a great reader of the game he was and how he made sure that he always looked to take advantage of any situation he found himself in. It was a great lesson for a young player like me and it was something I still talk about with players today, as it shows the art of knowing when to defend and when to attack.

Just before the life-support machine was turned off, a few of Hookesy's close friends were given the chance to go and say goodbye to him. I went along with Wayne Phillips and I think we both struggled to come to terms with the reality of the situation. Hookesy had a bruise around his eye, but otherwise looked his normal self.

I stayed with him for about 20 minutes, although it may have been longer, and sat there just talking as I had done countless times over the years. When the time came to leave, I kissed him on the forehead, said goodbye, told him I would miss him and squeezed his hand. Then I walked out of the room. I felt absolutely shattered.

In the weeks that followed I underwent counselling to try to come to terms with what had happened. For the rest of the season and for a long time after that I found myself thinking of him whenever I went out to bat and when, later that year, Australia beat Sri Lanka in a Test match at Kandy to seal the series, I sat quietly outside the dressing room and just wept – our victory had come at the same venue that saw Hookesy score his one and only Test hundred, 143 not out, in April 1983.

*

The death of David Hookes certainly changed me as a person and made me realise that although cricket may be my career, in the grand scheme of things it pales beside health, friends and family. I think many players who played with and against Phillip Hughes or who worked with or even knew him went through the same feelings when he passed away in 2014.

His was a death that, helped by social media, really did touch the whole of the cricketing world, not least in the #putoutyourbats campaign, which saw people all around the country, and indeed the world, put their bats out overnight. It seemed to resonate with everyone, whether they were international players, club cricketers or just fans of the game. Elton John dedicated his song *Candle in the Wind* to Phillip during a concert in Munich, which was a remarkable gesture, reflecting the impact his death had on the wider community beyond the sport.

While Hookesy's death had happened away from the field of play, here was someone dying while playing the game we all love, so suddenly it brought everything that happened on the field, right across the globe, into sharp focus. As he battled for life, messages came from across the cricketing world, and they were repeated when that battle was lost.

In the immediate aftermath, no-one really had any stomach to play. The whole of the ongoing round of Sheffield Shield matches, not just the NSW–South Australia match, was abandoned, the Test at The Gabba was postponed and

Cricket Australia and the Board of Control for Cricket in India got together to rework the schedule. That decision to go for a postponement followed a meeting between a group of Australian players that I attended at the SCG on Friday 28 November, the day after Phillip's life support was switched off. There was a unanimous feeling that we all wanted to say goodbye to the little fella by paying our respects and attending his funeral before anyone could even start to think about playing the game again.

The Test match taking place in Sharjah in the United Arab Emirates between Pakistan and New Zealand was delayed by a day while the players of both sides sought to come to terms with what happened. And when play there did resume, New Zealand's response was remarkable, as they played with a freedom and a lack of inhibitions that was not only a terrific tribute to their colleague from across the Tasman, but also showed that they saw cricket for what it was and what it really is – an entertainment.

Looking back, I am still not sure how our players not only managed to take the field for that rearranged first Test in Adelaide, but also found the ability to secure a thrilling win that was a fitting tribute to a terrific young man.

The funeral took place on 3 December in Macksville and I have a host of memories from the day, not least how hot it was. I remember John Hastings, the big Victoria fast bowler, actually had to take his shirt off and wring it out before putting it back on again. But that heat did not stop people turning out in their thousands to pay their tributes.

Those tributes included a moving speech from Australia captain Michael Clarke, who showed himself to be a magnificent leader, not only on that day in Macksville but also throughout what was a very dark time for Australian cricket. It began when he raced to the hospital to be with Phillip and his mother and sister – who had both been at the SCG watching him bat – and went right through to his brilliant century battling pain and injuries in that Adelaide Test.

Before Phillip suffered that fatal injury, the lead-up to the India series had been dominated by talk of a rift between Michael on the one hand and the selectors on the other, as we wanted him to prove his fitness by playing for the Cricket Australia XI in a two-day tour match against the Indians in Adelaide, while he felt he could show he was ready to play in a Test by turning out for his grade side, Western Suburbs. The battle lines were drawn, but greater events meant the issue simply melted away.

You could argue that when the on-field action finally resumed as the Adelaide Test match got underway on 9 December, Michael should not have been playing, given the fact he had not even had that grade game to show he was up to the task and the fact he broke down during the Test backs up that view. But I am entirely comfortable with the decision to select him for the match, even in hindsight. He had been such a focal point for the players, support staff and Australian cricket as a whole during that traumatic period that it just felt right to have him leading the team. In any case, I think even being left out by the selectors would not have been enough to keep him from the field for that match. He was determined to be there, whatever it took, to pay his own tribute to his great mate Phillip, and his first-innings century, even though he was handicapped by back and hamstring injuries, was an inspiration to the rest of the squad.

On 1 December, before Phillip's funeral took place and before the decision had been made to rejig the schedule by staging the first Test in Adelaide, I decided I had to write to all the players and staff. I think it is worth reproducing excerpts from that email here.

It is hard to email this to you all the day after Huey's birthday and admit whilst writing this, like all of you, there have been tears in this. Let them roll always lads. Firstly let me say that I/we have never been so proud of the way you handled everything at this time.

From players/support staff/ACA [Australian Crick-eters' Association]/CA [Cricket Australia], all have been fantastic at handling every aspect of a shit situ-ation. The emotions will keep rolling on and we just have to deal with it the best we can. As we embark on another tough week and work towards trying to play again, we must, as everyone has said all the time, make sure we are doing everything for Hughesy's family first and foremost.

Then we worry about our own families and then get the cricket family back on track.

It is not going to be [as] easy as that, we know, but we need to try and get some things moving in the direction of playing again if possible. We all know it is going to be small steps and please take them with care.

If someone is struggling, as I'm sure there will be a few, let someone know and make sure we have the best possible communication at this time as we have ever had before.

Whilst no decision has been made about the first Test yet, we need to start to think about preparing for cricket once more. How do we get there and how do we get our thoughts in the best possible space is going to be the question.

We need to take with us player #408 and make sure we do things for him, his family and ourselves. He would want us to look after each other and come up with a way to play and wear the Baggy Green again and do it proud.

The whole world is behind you as we search for answers within and the cricket world has been unbelievable.

The little fella would have been so proud of what has happened and also a little embarrassed, knowing him.

With regard to getting back on the horse, what I would like each player and staff member to do is . . . take your time with each step, it is important.

One example of this, and what we need, is from Huey himself, which was brought to my attention this year.

[Huey] had to return home from the Darwin A Series to mourn the death of a dearly loved family member [his grandfather] but then found a way to return to his team and steel himself for one of the performances of his life, becoming the first Aussie to score a double-hundred in an international 50 over game – offering the performance up to the memory of his grandfather.

[It was] a true testament to the amazing bloke that Hughesy was and his determination to overcome adversity, and do what he loved doing [playing cricket with his mates] to honour the memory of his pop.

As for batting [again], I believe it is as simple as a few throw downs to start the process, with a mate or a state squad system. It took me a while to get to this process so don't rush it.

It is always going to be hard at this time as we have funerals to think of and celebrate a great life as well as spending some quality time together with the family in the grieving process. Wednesday will be tough, but take it all in and lean on anyone you need. We are all here for each other and will be for years to come.

Understand, as we spoke about on Friday, we can't go on as a group until we have worked through the funeral and had some time to grieve with family members. It rings true, that we speak about it all the time that we are only playing a game and life is more important.

I just want to thank you all and send my love to you as we try our best to move forward each and every step. Hughesy would have been so proud of you all and now it is our chance to make him proud of us as well as get back to doing what you do best and that is our great game.

I understand some of you won't be ready and that is OK, all we are all asking is start to try some things if and when you can . . . Again, if at any time you can't do what is required, let's chat and make a plan. If you need to talk with anyone on staff or the chairman of selectors please do, as there is so many wise people out here willing to help all of us.

Take care. Love you with all my heart and want to protect you all as best as we all can. Coach.

Right up until the morning of the match I had no idea who was going to be able to play. We had assembled in Adelaide three days before the Test – and two days after the funeral – but there was recognition that there was no point in everyone just heading for the nets as if nothing had happened. The players and staff still needed to grieve for their little mate. Initially it was a case of taking those very small steps I mentioned in my email in order to try to eventually get everyone thinking about playing cricket once more.

We got together as a group first of all at Park 25, a club ground that was formerly used by the Australian Cricket Academy when it was based in the city – and there were tears. But I was also keen to foster some smiles too and we managed to achieve that through some lighthearted dancing that I asked our strength and conditioning coach Damian Mednis to lead, as well as through the presence of Barry 'Nugget' Rees.

As I mentioned earlier, Nugget has the ability to get everyone feeling good. He was moved to tears as he addressed the players – but he also got everyone smiling too, as he always seems to do, and that was a breakthrough at a desperately sad time.

Different players coped in different ways. David Warner, for example, just did not feel able to go into the nets for a hit and spent most of his time in the lead-up to the match with our sports psychologist Michael Lloyd. 'Lloydy' was in high demand from the time of the incident right through the rest of the summer and did a terrific job, often just being there to listen to the players. He was part of a tremendous support network around the squad. Cricket Australia and the Australian Cricketers' Association played their parts in finding the right balance between, on the one hand, being respectful and caring and, on the other, recognising that at some point cricket had to resume. David eventually found the strength of mind to play and paid his own tribute to Phillip with twin hundreds.

That support system had to include looking after Sean Abbott too, of course, the bowler who had delivered the ball that struck Phillip. Sean had been part of the limited-overs squad that toured the United Arab Emirates to play against Pakistan in October and actually made his Twenty20 International debut alongside Phillip at the Dubai International Stadium on that tour, less than two months earlier. He knew Phillip well – Phillip was in the NSW side when Sean made his first-class debut in 2011 – and so that made things even harder for him to deal with.

Sean was devastated by what had happened, as you would expect, and I made a point of speaking with him whenever I could. Finding the right words to say in such circumstances is just about as challenging a situation as I have ever faced. I felt it was important to stress to him that it was not his fault. Short balls have been a part of the game for as long as anyone can recall, NSW had made a decision to bowl short at Phillip to try to force an error and Sean was merely carrying out that plan.

My message was a simple one along the lines of 'I hope you are doing okay but if you are not then please make sure you get some help, as there are plenty of people around and available to help you'. I am sure there is not a day that goes by when Sean does not think about what happened that day at the SCG, but I know he is a well-grounded young man. His strength of character was shown in his next match, two weeks later, when he took 6-14 to secure an innings win for NSW against Queensland at the same venue.

In the wake of the death of Hookesy, and certainly following Phillip's death, I have become a lot calmer around the game. I was never a big one for ranting and raving, but occasionally I was prone to losing my cool, as players who have worked under me would testify. Now I tend to be more tolerant towards players' mistakes than I may have been in the past. That is not to say that I do not pull them up if they keep making those mistakes, but I really do feel that I do not blow my top as much as I did. The two incidents have made me realise that getting angry is pointless, providing everyone is trying their hardest, as invariably players are.

I think that the players in the dressing room, those who knew and played with or against Phillip, have grown as people too and it is a pleasure to be among some really terrific young men. Phillip's death has given every one of them perspective on what is important and what is not, and the way the players now embrace their extra-curricular activities, trying to give pleasure to people outside of our circle with charity visits or social functions that we attend, is a testament to that. I attended functions with teammates where we tended to stick together in groups and not really mingle, but nowadays the opposite is true and I have actually encouraged the lads, when they go to such events, to pick up two or three business cards of the people they speak to. Such things are preparation for the next phase of their lives, when they will no longer be the centre of attention. I am pleased to say they have embraced that idea.

The maturity the players showed in the aftermath of Phillip's death was terrific. Think, for example, of someone like Brad Haddin, who after the Adelaide Test appeared to be in line to captain the side following Michael Clarke's injury. As vice-captain, a senior player who everyone within the dressing room looked up to and someone who I always had a tremendous amount of time and respect for, he would have been an ideal fit to steer the squad through a difficult summer. To be chosen as Australia captain would have been a wonderful honour for him at the back-end of his career but, instead, he said he felt it would be better to blood a younger player who was likely to be with the side for the long term, and so Steve Smith stepped up. It was a wonderful gesture by

Brad, typical of him as a terrific team man and a great illustration of the feeling within the squad during that summer.

I was proud of the way the players dealt with the series against India, as the Indian players were actually quite aggressive towards us during the summer. Whether that was their deliberate attempt to get under our skins or whether it was simply a reflection of the characters of the players they had on the tour, I do not know. By and large I think we handled potential flashpoints pretty well. There was the odd blow-up, like David Warner's confrontation with Rohit Sharma when he urged Sharma to 'speak English', but that was just the tail-end of some chat that had been going on for a while, where David felt he was being abused in Rohit's native language. David's attitude was basically: 'If you are going to have a go at me, then at least do it so I can understand you'.

Our players have continued to play it hard on the field, as they always should, but whenever a member of the opposition gets hit in the head then they have shown their caring sides and also their sensitive sides too. When Mitchell Johnson struck Virat Kohli in Adelaide and then, in the limited-overs series against England in late 2015, when Mitchell Starc hit Eoin Morgan, our players were around those batsmen like wasps around jam, making sure they were okay. But, at the same time, those incidents also affected our bowlers too, as they were acutely aware, following Phillip's death, of the potential damage they could cause. In those instances it was always a case of making sure both Mitchells were okay too, as the blows actually caused them to get upset as well.

There was chat within sections of the media and on social media following what happened to Phillip that the bouncer should be banned, but that was never a view I took. Yes, it was and is a dangerous ball, but it is also part of the fabric of the game. Implementing such a suggestion would be tricky, as you cannot simply draw a line across the middle of the pitch and say that all balls must land beyond that line, as the length a bowler has to bowl in order to get a ball up to head height will vary depending on the nature of a pitch. And the idea of giving batsmen the licence to just prop forward without any worry that they might receive a short ball would not only detract from the game – seeing someone hook a fast bowler is one of the most thrilling sights there is – but also detract from players' techniques.

The better answer is to ensure that safety equipment is improved, so that something like the Phillip Hughes tragedy never happens again. Within a very short space of time helmet manufacturers were producing additions that offered some protection to the vulnerable area around the neck. Protective gear has evolved, just like the game itself, over the years. A couple of generations ago no-one wore helmets and now they are second nature, not only to batsmen but also to wicketkeepers standing up to the stumps. When you think of the batting gloves worn by the likes of Don Bradman and the ones that are used now, it is like comparing apples and oranges. And as time goes on that protection is bound to improve even further.

In May 2015 Cricket Australia announced a review into Phillip's death led by David Curtain QC, the former Chairman of the Victorian Bar Council and President of the Australian Bar Council. The idea behind it was not to apportion blame, but to find out what lessons could be learnt to ensure nothing similar happens again. And among the recommendations made when the review was published in 2016 was that all batsmen, wicketkeepers and close-in fielders in front of the wicket should wear helmets in matches and training.

The game has changed for me since November 2014 and the same is true, I think, for everyone connected with Australian cricket. I certainly look at cricket now from a different perspective, knowing it is important but also knowing, at the end of the day, it is not the be-all and end-all. It is still a wonderful sport, a sport that has given me the life I have, and I want as many people as possible to know how great it is and to have the chance to experience it for themselves, doing so in the knowledge that it is a safe sport too.

Michael Clarke was right when he said the Australian dressing room would never be the same again and my message to players now is: 'Just remember – we are not trying to cure cancer, we are just playing a game of cricket.' I want them to play, wherever possible, with a smile on their faces, because that was the way I think we all remember Phillip. There is a great photograph of him walking up the players' race in Abu Dhabi during our Test series against Pakistan that sums him up. He was not even in the side but when he looked up his first reaction was to smile. That, to me, was Phillip.

We miss his smile, but he has stayed with us through the tributes that continue to be paid to him: the applause at

4.08 pm, to match his number as an Australian Test cricketer, on the first day of the inaugural day-night Test match against New Zealand was especially poignant; the armbands with his initials that the players have retained from the Test against India in December 2014; the plaque that has been placed outside the home dressing room at the SCG, something the players see whenever they go on and off the field.

One thing that will never change is that when tragedy strikes there is nothing in the Marylebone Cricket Club coaching manual to guide you through it. As I have discovered, together with all those people touched by the deaths of David Hookes and Phillip Hughes, all you can do is cope as best you can, try to offer support to each other and then try to move forward by living your lives in the best way possible.

We knew that soon after Phillip's death we too would all have to move forward – the first Test may have been delayed, but it would have to start sometime. It did, 13 days after Phillip's life support was turned off.

What the players did over the first days of that Test match in Adelaide stand without doubt as the highlight of my coaching career.

People might think that I would nominate our 5–0 Ashes win in 2013–14 or the World Cup triumph on home soil in 2015, or beating South Africa away in 2014 and New Zealand in 2016, both of which took us back to the top of the international rankings.

But all those performances pale into insignificance when set against the way the players and staff came together to get back into action and start a Test series against India at the

Adelaide Oval on 9 December 2014, in the shadow of the death of Phillip.

Even with what I hope are years ahead of me in my coaching career, I cannot believe I will experience anything more moving and more impressive than seeing the players taking part in that Test. For them to perform so brilliantly and go on and win the match really was above and beyond my wildest dreams.

The reasons why it was so tough for everyone to get back on the horse were threefold. Firstly, there was the emotional connection we all had – and still have – with Phillip. He is cap number 408, one of us, and he always will be. Many of the players grew up either playing with or against him; he had been in the squad just a month earlier in the United Arab Emirates and was set to feature again in the first Test at The Gabba, given Michael Clarke's struggles with injury.

There was also the fact that Phillip's dreadful injury occurred while he was playing cricket. He was hit playing a shot at a ball the type of which all our batsmen had faced countless times and all our fast bowlers had delivered with equal regularity. It struck at the heart of what the players were doing. We all knew cricket was and is a dangerous sport, but the players' high levels of skill had always masked that danger; now, suddenly, that danger was thrown into the sharpest focus by an incident involving one of our own.

We were all so close to Phillip that seeing what the game had done to him and to his family gave us a feeling of hopelessness. I am sure there were some players who honestly thought: 'Is this worth it?' You could not blame them if that question crossed their minds. I thought about being hit by that Bruce Reid bouncer at the WACA, when my helmet saved me, and that time in the nets at Carlton my cheek-bone was smashed when I top-edged a pull shot into my face. I did not think so at the time, but looking back now I realise I was a very lucky man to have survived both blows.

For the players to overcome all the thoughts they had and to perform to the level they did in that Adelaide Test showed an incredible collective strength of character. It is something I will remember for the rest of my life. It really was a fitting tribute to Phillip.

And they kept it going the whole summer.

12

HIGHS AND LOWS – AND LUCK

The summer of 2014–15 asked a whole host of questions of our players and staff. They were answered emphatically and resoundingly, culminating in us holding aloft the World Cup trophy at the MCG on 29 March 2015.

It was incredible the way the players kept themselves going through the physical pain, the mental anguish and the emotional turmoil for the four months that followed Phillip's death.

The World Cup was a huge test, not least because of the history of the tournament. Yes, India had won on home soil four years earlier, but as a rule of thumb the hosts had not always done well in the game's showpiece.

It may have been down to the added pressure of playing in front of family, friends and an expectant home crowd or it may have been the added distractions that are an outcome of being at home, but before India only Sri Lanka in 1996 had been a co-host of the event and gone on to glory. And when Arjuna Ranatunga's side did that, it played its semi-final and the final away from home, in Kolkata, India and Lahore, Pakistan, respectively.

I have already referred to how we sought to get past that home-side hoodoo by tapping into the thoughts of some Australian players who took part in the failed 1992 campaign, the last time Australia and New Zealand had staged the tournament, but our preparations went well beyond that.

We also ensured the players had what we felt was the right balance between competitive action and rest during the run-up, and part of that involved Cricket Australia restoring the One-Day International tri-series, a concept that had not featured in the previous two summers. In England and India we had two competitive sides to go up against and the five matches we had – although one of them in Sydney against India was abandoned because of rain – proved just right to get ready for the main event. During the series we rotated players in and out of the squad – we used 18 in total and only six took part in all the games. That made sure they stayed fresh, and it also gave us a chance to look at our bench strength in the event of injuries during the World Cup.

Some players wanted to play every match of that tri-series and some, like Mitchell Starc, for example, revelled in doing so, getting into a great rhythm, taking 12 wickets, finding swing with the new ball and reverse swing later on in the innings, and it was form he was to replicate in the World Cup, being named player of the tournament. Others were told to rest up – Mitchell Johnson played just once – and, again, the wisdom of that move was illustrated when the trophy was lifted in Melbourne.

What happened off the field before and during the tournament was instrumental in what happened on it, as the backroom staff, and especially the medical and support team, worked to ensure the players were right to go for each match. It's worth pointing out that we actually began the tournament two players down, as James Faulkner was recovering from a side strain he picked up in Perth during the tri-series, while Michael Clarke was in the latter stages of his recovery from hamstring surgery and was available only from the second match onwards – which turned out to be a washout against Bangladesh in Brisbane.

It is true that in the early stages of the tournament we had decent breaks between each match – the seven days between our opening encounter against England in Melbourne and that Bangladesh game at The Gabba allowed us to give the players a couple of days off – but on the other side of the coin we were faced with the most punishing travel schedule of any of the teams taking part. From the time we left Melbourne after our opening-day win against England to the trip back there following our semi-final victory against India in Sydney, we clocked up almost 17,500 kilometres in travel, a mark only Afghanistan, which crossed the Tasman Sea four times and racked up almost 15,000 kilometres during the group stages, came close to equalling.

By comparison, our opponents in the final, New Zealand, did not leave home except for that match.

In one sense we were ready and willing to make those journeys – from Melbourne to Brisbane to Auckland to Perth to Sydney to Hobart to Adelaide back to Sydney and then on to Melbourne again. Being the host side, we knew that people in every capital city wanted to see us, but it was a tough ask. That meant that recovery sessions with stretching, work in the swimming pool or the sea and regular massages were very much near the top of the agenda for players during the tournament.

We were careful not to have those players attending net sessions for the sake of it, especially in the early stages of the tournament, as we had already had a lengthy domestic summer – with some of the players in action in Zimbabwe and the United Arab Emirates before that. Making sure players were having enough rest and time away from cricket grounds to freshen up was just as important as practice. Missing the odd net would not suddenly make someone a lesser player.

But when we did practise we expected the players to replicate match intensity and it was pleasing to see that they did exactly that. Steve Waugh joined us ahead of the quarter-final against Pakistan in Adelaide – and after witnessing our session told me he had never seen an Australian team training harder. Coming from a player brought up in the Bobby Simpson era, I took that as a real compliment!

The culmination of all that hard work was the success in the final, which was revenge for our narrow loss to the Black

Caps in the group stages, our only defeat of the tournament. Looking back now, that final was just about the perfect game from a coaching point of view. We found the right balance in the lead-up between preparation and rest; we had a full-strength squad to pick from, which was a pat on the back for our medical staff in getting the players to that stage of the season in one piece; in our team meeting before the match we identified what we needed to do and how we needed to do it; we picked the right XI for the conditions; the players all performed to a high level; and the captain led by example to see us home. The match may not have ended up as much of a contest for the neutral spectator, but it ticked just about every box from my perspective.

I write 'just about' in terms of that perfect game because not everything went our way. If we had won by 10 wickets or if all the batsmen who made it to the crease had passed, say, 50 perhaps we could call it perfect, but in all my years as a player and coach it is tough to think of too many occasions when we have achieved that cricketing form of nirvana. I remember watching on from the sidelines during my playing career when we beat England by 10 wickets at the SCG in 2003, bowling out Nasser Hussain's side for 117 before Matthew Hayden and Adam Gilchrist knocked off the runs in only 12.2 overs. That was just about as close as I can recall us coming to perfection against a top side, certainly in one-day cricket.

Nothing can replace the feeling of winning the World Cup as a player and to have had the chance to do that twice – and being involved in the ultimate moment on both occasions, first of all striking the winning runs at Lord's in 1999 and then taking the winning catch at The Wanderers in Johannesburg four years later – is something that will stay with me forever. They were personal highs that in my professional career I am unlikely ever to better.

Winning it as a coach was a different feeling, just as rewarding but for other reasons. Clearly there were none of the physical challenges I faced as a player because I was no longer out in the middle, but in some ways that made things harder, as I was not in control of the destiny of something I had played a major role in planning. Despite the absence of that physicality, it was actually, in many ways, far more tiring. As a player, outside of match days and practice sessions, my time was very much my own and if I wanted to rest I could; as coach, it was far different, with numerous calls on my time. There were discussions to be had with my coaching and management colleagues, selection to be discussed, emails to answer, and on match-days – especially in the knockout matches – there was the nervous energy of looking on from the sidelines hoping the players could execute their skills effectively. It all meant there was very little time to switch off. It was only after the dust had settled following the tournament that it really was possible to take in the magnitude of the achievement. That brought me a great deal of satisfaction, but comparing the successes as player and coach really is impossible – like comparing apples and bananas.

In Test cricket, the result of that 2013–14 Ashes series was just as emphatic as our World Cup final win, a 5–0 whitewash to erase the memories not only of the clash in England the previous winter but also the series loss at home against the same opponents three years earlier. The satisfaction was heightened by our use of the same 11 players throughout the series, another tribute to our medical staff, especially as one of those players was Ryan Harris who always had to battle his body in order to make it on the field.

The results in that Ashes series were perfect, certainly, but the manner in which we achieved them was not always as we would have wanted it. In every Test we were in some form of trouble in our first innings – 6-132 in Brisbane, 4-174 in Adelaide, 5-143 in Perth, all out for 204 in Melbourne and 5-97 in Sydney – but on virtually every occasion Brad Haddin dug us out of it. Our bowlers, led by Mitchell Johnson, then put England's batsmen to the sword and in our second innings we invariably rammed home that advantage. We ended up with the top six run-scorers in the series as well as four of the top five wicket-takers. With statistics like that you are always liable to come out on top more often than not.

What was most pleasing about that win was not only that it came against the old enemy, but also that it came about through us managing to keep the players focused, even after the series was won. When I played we were often guilty of taking our foot off the opponents' throats after we had wrapped up a series. 'Dead rubber syndrome' was something we were often accused of when we lost matches having secured the silverware. There was none of that in 2013–14, as the players maintained the perfect mindset, with complete confidence in their ability to always come out on the right side of the result while never straying into the realms of arrogance. The backroom staff can take some credit for that, as one of my ambitions as a coach is to ensure that every match a side of mine plays is treated with the same level of importance as every other. That starts with the preparation and goes through to the action itself. In 2013–14 we always looked to keep resetting the players' goals as the series went on, but we also made sure they never thought too far ahead. Even when the series was won in Perth it was just a case of focusing on the next match in Melbourne and then, only once victory was achieved there, did we switch our attention to Sydney.

If I had to nominate a perfect Test from a coaching perspective it would probably be the series-winning effort in Cape Town against South Africa in March 2014.

We were up against the number one side in the world in Graeme Smith's team – although we took over, albeit briefly, at the head of the ICC rankings after the success at Newlands – and came into the final match of that three-Test series off the back of a thumping loss at Port Elizabeth for the last match of a long summer following those Tests against England – plus limited-overs matches against the same opponent. All of us were dog tired.

Yet despite that we batted big, with hundreds from David Warner and Michael Clarke, secured a sizeable first-innings lead, got quick runs when it came time for us to bat again and then left ourselves enough time – just – to bowl the opposition out a second time to secure the win. Clarke's captaincy and the way he led from the front, especially with his gutsy hundred on day one despite being peppered with short-pitched bowling from Morne Morkel, was terrific to see. The beer tasted very pleasant indeed in the dressing room after the match was wrapped up.

Winning like that may seem straightforward. Let me tell you, it is anything but, and the challenge as a coach is to try to ensure that players replicate that level of performance every time. No-one has achieved it yet and all you can do is to put processes in place that allow you to try to get every last drop of potential from each player and then the rest is down to their skills, the skills of the opposition and maybe just the odd piece of good fortune along the way too.

To me, he will always be just 'Caviar', short for Black Caviar, the Australian racehorse that was retired in 2013 with a record of 25 wins from 25 starts. She was a thorough-bred, the best of the best, and the same applies to Mitchell Johnson.

Damian Mednis, the team's strength and conditioning coach, called Mitchell 'The Beast' because of his amazing strength and appetite for training, and during my time he was a fantastic leader of the fast bowlers' cartel, or FBC, the name the quicks have given to themselves as a group since the time of Glenn McGrath and Jason Gillespie.

Mitchell's success in taking 37 wickets against England in the Ashes series of 2013–14, which he followed up with another 22 in the three matches against South Africa, put him at the very pinnacle of the game and rightly earned him the award as the ICC's Cricketer of the Year.

His presence in the side – the pace and intimidation that he brought to the table – was the single biggest factor in those back-to-back series wins. Given the way he performed, it was amazing to think that during 2013 he was actually on the outer and was not selected in the squad for the five Tests against England that winter. But how much was his inclusion in 2013–14 down to luck and how much was down to planning?

I was always a fan of his because he brought those priceless assets of pace and intimidation, and as a batsman I knew how unpleasant it was to face someone who had that ability. On that basis, had I been part of the selection panel for that Test series in the United Kingdom I might well have pushed for his inclusion. But the side was already in place by the time I was installed, and although we added Steve Smith to the mix there was no room for an additional fast bowler.

That was, perhaps, a blessing in disguise in the long run for both us and Mitchell, even though we lost the series in England. It came off the back of the disappointing tour of India and the equally disappointing Champions Trophy campaign – he had featured in both – and by missing out it gave him the chance to head home, have a break with some time away from the game to work on that fitness. The fact he was able to do all those things was undoubtedly crucial in allowing him to bounce back the way he did, not only against England at the back-end of the northern summer but also during the season that followed.

I have to admit that even in my wildest dreams I did not believe he would have the impact he did, but as soon as he started to fire up in the limited-overs matches against England in September I thought we were in with a chance. He took only five wickets in four matches, but it was the way he discomforted the England top-order players that really gave me hope for the return series.

Ironically it was a match that ended up as a no-result because of rain that gave the clearest illustration of what he was capable of achieving against those players. At Birmingham he bowled just five overs, but during that time managed to dismiss Kevin Pietersen and hit Jonathan Trott in the helmet grille, making him look like a cat on a hot tin roof throughout much of his innings.

Pietersen and Trott had been two key players for England in the 3–1 series win against us in 2010–11 and the way Mitchell got them dancing around in that match at Edgbaston that lasted just 15.1 overs was almost what you might call our 'Larwood moment'. Legend has it that England devised Bodyline to counter the incredible scoring feats of Donald Bradman when fast bowler Harold Larwood upset Bradman with some short-pitched bowling during a Test at The Oval in London in 1930. And while our plan was not to replicate Bodyline, it was clear to me and to Michael Clarke and the rest of the squad that if we could keep Mitchell fit and firing for the return leg, we had a very decent chance of calling the tune.

I had no doubt in my own mind that England was a side that was on the way down, despite the fact we had lost the

Test series 3–0 in 2013. They had struggled to find a reliable opening partner for Alastair Cook following the retirement of Andrew Strauss, and with Johnson in great shape and players like Matthew Prior, Graeme Swann and Tim Bresnan all nearer the end of their careers than the beginning, there was plenty of scope for optimism.

We actually had four of the top six run-scorers in that 2013 series, along with three of the top six wicket-takers, so we knew we were not far away from them, and if we could only avoid the type of wholesale collapses we had produced at Lord's and Durham, two of the three Tests we lost, then I was confident we could succeed.

Having seen what Mitchell was capable of during the One-Day International series, we made sure we managed him effectively in the lead-up to the first Test. We took him to the limited-overs series in India that took place in October and November, but sent him home before the last match to allow him to play a Sheffield Shield game with a red ball to ensure he was in rhythm ahead of the action at The Gabba. He got 37.4 overs under his belt at the WACA against South Australia and that was all he needed to be in peak condition for that opening encounter.

The pitches in the United Kingdom for the first of the back-to-back Ashes series were absolutely dead, with little pace and bounce, and although we had no say in the way curators prepared the pitches at the Test venues in Australia, we knew they would be harder and have a bit more pace in them. Having Mitchell fit and firing with Ryan Harris at the other end was the perfect scenario. We benefited accordingly and the result was the vindication of our approach.

The stars certainly aligned for us to have a bowler of Mitchell's quality and pace available in that series and at the peak of his powers, but I am a strong believer that in many instances you make your own luck and that has been the story of much of my career, certainly when it comes to coaching.

Yes, I had the good fortune to be sounded out by Adam Gilchrist for the Deccan Chargers job, but once I had that opportunity I still had to be good enough to take advantage of it. The fact that I made a success of that position opened up other possibilities for me at Queensland, and after coaching the squad in Twenty20 cricket I got the chance to look after the state in all forms of the game in March 2011 when Trevor Barsby left the coaching role.

That was perfect for me as, like the Deccan job, it took me out of my comfort zone. The easy option for me would have been to apply for the job as South Australia's head coach when Mark Sorrell was sacked in December 2010, but I realised I needed a wider perspective than simply operating in a state where I had always lived and so I never put my name in the hat for that role. I sat tight, did the Twenty20 work with Queensland and then the chance to step up came my way. Being in the right place at the right time is one thing; taking advantage of that situation is quite another.

*

Like most coaches my record is far from flawless, and for every World Cup win or Ashes success there are series that I would be equally happy to forget. The World Twenty20 campaign in Bangladesh, the Test series against Pakistan in the United Arab Emirates in 2014, the 2015 Ashes series in the United Kingdom and the Test series in Sri Lanka in July and August 2016 are all examples of times that did not exactly go according to plan.

In Bangladesh we were not good enough. You could accuse us of not being sufficiently dynamic, but we had players there who had enough experience of Twenty20 cricket and enough experience in subcontinental conditions to have done much better than we did. It was something to use as a motivator in the future. We also played spin poorly in that tournament and one win, against the hosts, in four matches, sums up how things went for us.

That stick of being poor players against spin is one we get beaten with regularly – and after the series in Sri Lanka it was one that appeared justified – but when we lost to Pakistan in Dubai and Abu Dhabi there were other factors at play. Yes, Yasir Shah and Zulfiqar Babar bowled well and we were unlucky to lose both tosses in that series, which meant we had to bat last against those spinners, but the truth is we should have done a whole lot better in both our first innings, before the ball started turning.

In Dubai, in response to Pakistan's 454, we reached 0-133 and 3-206 – and from those positions we should not have been bowled out for 303. David Warner scored 133, but having got in he should have gone on with the job; instead, he was dismissed third ball after lunch, playing inside a delivery from Yasir, and from then on the wheels fell off. Even so, and despite the fact we lost four quick wickets on the fourth evening, we were still able to take the match deep into the final session. Then, in Abu Dhabi, we were simply batted into submission by Younus Khan and his teammates. That can happen.

The 2015 Ashes series was a let-down primarily because we entered that series as the favourite, which was probably fair enough too given the build-up we had, including a series win in the West Indies. We won two Tests there very easily, touring immediately after England, who had only managed to draw its own series in the Caribbean.

The bald statistics of my first two away Ashes series suggest we made progress, going from a 3–0 loss in 2013 to 3–2 two years later, but I have to admit both series were eerily similar in one respect: we lost the big moments. From those collapses I have already mentioned in 2013 to, in 2015, our failure to bat big in either innings in the opening Test at Cardiff, and our dramatic collapses at both Edgbaston and Trent Bridge, we failed to deal with the pressure and the conditions. That cost us dearly.

We played the moving ball poorly, there is no doubt about that, and there is no point in trying to sugarcoat that fact. The players were poor in that regard and they know they have to get better at it. But they are nothing if not hard workers and when we toured New Zealand in early 2016 the fruits of some of that hard work was clear in the way we batted.

The fact the players are such hard workers made the white-wash we suffered in Sri Lanka even more of a shock.

Once again we had no luck with the toss, and we were condemned to bat last in each of the three matches on pitches that assisted the spinners more and more as the action unfolded. There is no doubt, too, that two of the pitches, in Pallekele and Galle, were substandard surfaces. In Pallekele, if it hadn't been for rain and bad light the match would have struggled to last three days, while the pitch in Galle contributed to the action lasting just two-and-a-half days.

Poor pitches like that and taking home advantage a step too far are a bugbear of mine and they do the game no good at all, because they short-change the fans, the broadcasters who pay millions of dollars for the rights to cover the matches, and their viewers and listeners. Can you imagine what would happen if, in Australia, all the surfaces we produced were fast and bouncy and matches finished in double-quick time? Broadcasters and the public would be up in arms and rightly so, because cricket is all about a good balance between bat and ball.

Of course, having said all that, it is also true that we were substandard ourselves with the bat especially, and also that we had our opportunities in each Test in Sri Lanka and failed to take them.

In that opening encounter in Pallekele we bowled the opposition out just after lunch on day one for 117, and when you do that you should boss the game and get a far bigger first-innings lead than the 86 runs we ended up with. We batted poorly but even then we had Sri Lanka 4-86 in its second innings, and you should win from that position nine times out of ten.

Twenty-one-year-old Kusal Mendis played the innings of his life to make 176 – only one other player on either side passed 50, another illustration of how poor the surface was – but crucially we allowed the Sri Lanka tail to wag, adding 79 runs for the last four wickets, and that was to be a pattern that repeated itself in the matches that followed. In Galle, in the second Test, we had Sri Lanka 5-98 and 6-121 in its second innings, only for the home side to recover to 237. And then in Colombo, having reduced Sri Lanka to 5-26 inside the first 90 minutes of the Test, it recovered to 355. Time and again, we simply couldn't finish the job.

One bowler who was blameless in that regard was Mitchell Starc, back in Test cricket after eight months out, following the removal of floating bone in his right ankle and a stress fracture in his right foot. He took 24 wickets, including a career-best 11-94 on the most spin-friendly surface of the series in Galle, which was one of the great fast-bowling displays there can ever have been in the subcontinent. It was just a shame that no-one else could match his results.

Our spin bowling was not up to the level of Sri Lanka's and that was frustrating, given the nature of the pitches. However, it was also asking a lot for bowlers brought up in Australia to match the performances and knowledge of their rivals who had played all their cricket in those conditions and knew them like the backs of their hands.

Among the radical solutions I heard in the wake of the series loss was the idea of taking some of our promising spinners out of the state system for a season and sending them to play first-class cricket in the subcontinent. To an extent that idea has some merit. When you think that Jon Holland played just two Sheffield Shield matches in 2015–16, you could argue that he – and Australian cricket – would get much better long-term value by sending him or players like him overseas to get much more bowling than they get at home.

In a batting context going overseas certainly worked for the likes of me, Matthew Hayden and Mike Hussey as we took our games forward by playing regularly in alien conditions in England. It also meant that when we toured there with Australia we were far better equipped to cope with the moving ball.

But having said that, I wonder about the practicalities of the idea of sending young spinners to somewhere in Asia. Unlike my time in England they would need to do it during our domestic season, and that would potentially deprive the players of the chance to play in the Big Bash League which could, of course, open the door to an offer from the Indian Premier League. Whether we could persuade players to look at the long term, especially with no selection guarantee, would be open to question. And on top of that, there would need to be a willingness from one of the Asian countries to admit our players to their system, something that would be by no means a given. There are no easy solutions to the problem but the idea is just one example of the thought being given to addressing it.

As for our batting during the Sri Lanka series, apart from the hundreds by Shaun Marsh and Steve Smith in the final match at the Sinhalese Sports Club, there was precious little to write home about. It's true that the pitches were nowhere near as good as the ones I played on in 2004 – the ones in 2016 were more variable and spun more – but we had to find a way to combat conditions and we did not. What was most galling though was that we lost so many wickets to balls that did not turn. Batsmen were constantly getting beaten on their inside edges, either bowled through the gate or trapped leg before wicket. It was something everyone worked tirelessly on to combat, but once the players were out in the middle in the heat of battle and a ball turned sharply, it proved impossible, time after time, for those players to try to ignore that occasional magic delivery and instead play the line of the ball.

The loss of all three Tests meant nine successive defeats in Asia dating back to the series in India that took place immediately before my appointment in 2013, a record that we have to improve upon. In all fairness to Cricket Australia they have bent over backwards to try and help us solve the issue of playing better in the region. At the Bupa National Cricket Centre in Brisbane we now have a specially designed spin-friendly surface for the players to practise on, and sides below senior level make regular trips to the subcontinent. Several of the Test squad for the Sri Lanka tour even spent time in India before the trip, looking to acclimatise on turning pitches, we arrived well in advance of the first Test, and we drafted in Sri Lanka spin legend Muttiah Muralitharan to provide advice and guidance for the squad ahead of the series.

The 64-million-dollar question is how we can improve in Asia but, as ever, the enemy is the schedule. Trying to squeeze sufficient opportunities to play in that part of the world into an already crowded calendar is like trying to get a size ten foot into a size five shoe. And with our own pitches at home like Sydney and Adelaide no longer displaying to the same degree the characteristics that allowed players to experience playing against spin on turning pitches – something that means so-called specialist players of spin are also thin on the ground – we will need to be even more creative to solve a problem that is a blot on our record.

As a coach in such circumstances, there is no value in ranting or raving. The players are under enough pressure without the person who is meant to be their mentor tearing them off a strip too. It might make me feel better but what would it actually achieve? The bottom line is we all have to work together to produce game plans that they can enact on a consistent basis and that is something we will continue to strive to do. When the squad for the Sri Lanka series was selected I do not recall too many raised voices saying, 'Why have you picked such-and-such a player?' or 'Why haven't you selected so-and-so?' We picked the best available players for the series but those players, by and large, failed to deliver – it is as simple as that.

As a selector and head coach of the side such failure poses a big question: the next time there is a tour of the subcontinent, do you go with the same players that failed previously if they are still producing good numbers elsewhere, on the basis that having toured the region and been exposed to the conditions and the pressures they will be better equipped to deal with them next time around? Or do you decide that those players blew their chance and on that basis it's time to look at other options? Either way it is a call based more on gut feelings than anything else and one that you will either be praised to the heavens for if the decision turns out to work, or hammered if it doesn't. When you are a coach and a selector at the highest level that is what you have to be prepared for.

No matter how badly we played in the third and fourth Tests of that 2015 Ashes, there was also no getting away from the fact that the surfaces for those two matches were poor, something all too obvious by the fact both matches almost finished in two days. Both pitches were far too heavily weighted in favour of the faster bowlers, but then that appears to be the pattern around the world now, with more and more countries going over the top in preparing pitches that suit their strengths.

Home advantage is one thing but spoiling matches as contests is quite another. The simple answer is to prepare a good pitch, by which I mean something that offers a little bit of something for the quick bowlers first up, flattens out to be at its best for batting on days two and three and then starts to offer turn, with some variable bounce on days four and five. That is the ideal, but it seems as though it is being adhered to less and less these days. I will be keen to see what the ICC does if the trend continues, because while it may satisfy home fans and players in the short term, there is no way it can be good for the game.

13

HEALTH SCARE

If life was straightforward it would be boring, so I have heard it said, but I can certainly do without too many more bumps in the road of the sort I experienced on Saturday 23 January 2016 when I was diagnosed with deep vein thrombosis (DVT).

The day had begun much like any other during the summer. We were all set for the final match of our One-Day International series against India, at the SCG, with us 4–0 up in the five-game contest and looking to make it 5–0, in keeping with the philosophy I had pushed since taking over as coach. As I reminded the players after we had won game three in Melbourne the previous weekend and again following game four in Canberra, there would almost certainly be occasions in the future when we toured India that their players would be all over us like a rash, winning games with ease in their own conditions, and so when the boot was on the other foot we had to make the momentum count in our favour.

The match was part of a tough schedule at the back-end of our home summer with the five one-day games, all of them day-night, in five different cities, as we flew from Sydney, the location for the rain-ruined third and final Test against the West Indies at the beginning of January, to Perth, then back across the continent to Brisbane before moving south to Melbourne, on to Canberra and then by bus back to Sydney (stopping at the Bradman Museum at Bowral, as mentioned earlier).

The matches against India had taken place, for the most part, in very high temperatures and, with bat dominating ball in all of them, there were some tired and sore bodies on both sides as the show rolled into Sydney once more, something we recognised by giving everyone – players and support staff – a total day off on Friday, the eve of the match, realising that everyone needed a break.

Day-night matches take an especially hard toll on those involved as they rarely end before 10 pm. By the time everyone has gathered their thoughts and tried to unwind following the team debrief, it is rarely the right side of midnight. It can be difficult to switch off and sometimes sleep might not come until one or two o'clock in the morning. With travel the next day, it means the danger of injury through fatigue is an ever-present threat.

Wherever possible we try to minimise that sort of risk and, in the case of all-rounder Mitchell Marsh, who had suffered from soft tissue injuries in the past when called upon to play an intense schedule that also involved lots of flying, we opted to give him a break, so he missed the second match of the series in Brisbane. The thinking was that not only did it mean he could take one less flight – Perth to Melbourne ahead of game three rather than Perth to Brisbane and then onto Melbourne – but it also gave him a few days to do some fitness work on his own to increase his durability. Plus it meant he had two extra days at home with family and friends. That was an especially important consideration as, with Perth so distant from the rest of the country, we knew if he did not have that break, he would not get the chance to return home before the end of the tour of New Zealand the following month.

Flights, for me, had always been my own little slice of heaven. They have long been the time I could not be telephoned, could not be emailed or texted; they meant a rare chance to unwind and relax away from the hurly-burly of life in the fast lane.

Boarding a flight was actually the equivalent of flicking a switch for me as, quite often, I was asleep even before the plane's wheels had left the tarmac. In 1999, when I was part of the World Cup-winning squad in the United Kingdom, I actually slept all the way home from London to Sydney, albeit after three days of partying that followed our success. And, more recently, my sleeping was the subject of a video that went viral on the internet as Mitchell Marsh and Peter Siddle tried to 'interview' me on camera as I dozed during the trip from Brisbane to Perth after the first Test against New Zealand in November 2015. I knew I needed to get up and move around a bit, but the urge to rest took over.

Fast forward from that point to the day of the match in Sydney and I knew that something was not quite right. I had been for my usual morning exercise, a walking session on the treadmill, at the Quay West Hotel, and at the end of it my left calf felt stiff and a little tight, tighter than it should have been. At that stage, however, I just shrugged it off; I am no spring chicken anymore and aches and pains come with the territory these days, especially after two decades of playing professional sport.

In keeping with my usual routine, I was one of the first to get to the venue and that gave me the chance to have a look at the pitch, which had been under cover from late on Friday afternoon because of a torrential storm that struck the city. From there it was on to playing a part in the players' warm-ups and catching drills that precede any match, but in the back of my mind I knew something was not as it should be with my calf.

Once the action got underway, with us batting first, I settled down to watch from the seating just out the front of our dressing room, alongside the other coaches, all of us discussing how the match was unfolding. I even found the time to move inside and have a brief chat with our media manager about Channel Nine's requirements for access during the three Twenty20 Internationals that were set to follow on from the one-day series. I am fully aware of our duty to sell the game to the public and make it as attractive as possible, and having our players available to the host broad-caster, even on occasion during matches, is one way we look to do that. I believe we are more accessible than any other side in world cricket and the only one of Nine's requests I put a line through was the one to have a fixed camera in the corner of the dressing room. It has been something that has been used in the football and rugby codes, but in those games the players barely use the rooms. In cricket, by contrast, the dressing room is a location where players and coaches spend hours at a time and is their only place to have time to themselves. It is their one private area in any stadium and I wanted to keep it that way.

But all through my discussions I knew I had an issue with my calf and I knew, too, that I would have to raise it with the medical staff – our team doctor John Orchard and Alex Kountouris, Cricket Australia's Sports Science and Sports Medicine Manager, who was working with the squad as physiotherapist during the limited-overs series. You see, I recognised the symptoms.

It was back in 2007 that I had first suffered DVT, also in my left calf, following surgery on my Achilles tendon. My Achilles had been a problem for the final four years of my career and in the latter stages of my time in the Australian side I had to resort to unorthodox methods to dull the pain, even having a beer during a One-Day International against Zimbabwe in 2004 to try to take the edge off it and allow me to bowl. That beer got me through that match.

When I eventually had the surgery, the procedure was followed by my foot being immobilised in a padded support – or 'moon boot' – but I allowed myself to become inactive and a clot developed as a result. My leg started to feel hot, I went for a check-up and was rushed into hospital, where I was put on a course of blood thinners that, over the course of a couple of months, eventually cured the problem.

Alex and John, both experienced medical personnel, had their suspicions immediately – they knew I was not the sort of person to make a fuss over something trivial – and in Alex's case he also had firsthand knowledge of the condition, having suffered from DVT himself in the past. They both knew my history too and, on that basis, were not taking any chances on what might be wrong with me.

It was here that a bit of good fortune came into play. The complex around the SCG is a sport hub, with the Sydney Football Stadium adjoining it, and part of that complex includes the offices of PRP Imaging, a state-of-the-art medical facility that is set up to conduct just the sort of scans and tests that I needed, given my symptoms.

John and Alex made the call to their staff and within a matter of minutes, as the match continued, I was on my way out the back of the Members' Pavilion and up the incline that threads between the cricket nets on the left and tennis courts and a swimming pool on the right, off to have my condition assessed. I was able to walk but the tightness in my calf still remained. My leg was scanned and very quickly it became apparent that I had a clot, so there was no time to waste and I was taken by car to the Royal Prince Alfred Hospital for treatment.

Oddly enough, I actually felt relatively relaxed. I knew the seriousness of the situation, but having experienced it previously I knew it could be addressed and that it could have a positive outcome.

Treatment was administered to thin my blood as quickly as possible to lessen the threat of a major clot and I remember John telling me that he knew things were heading in the right direction when the hospital staff tried to get a needle into me only to be greeted by spurting blood that, for a short while, showed little sign of stopping. That meant that the blood-thinning regime was working and that the imminent danger to my health was slowly lessening.

It was only later that Alex told me his take on the gravity of the situation when the clot had been discovered. 'You flagging this with us when you did probably saved your life,' he said. If the clot in my calf had worked its way up to a vital organ, the chances of me surviving would have been greatly reduced. It was a sobering thought.

All the while that I was being diagnosed, whisked off to hospital and then undergoing the start of my treatment, the match had been continuing. We had reached an imposing 7-330 off the back of a brilliant hundred by David Warner and a maiden three-figure score for his country by Mitchell Marsh, but India was able to chase it down in the final over thanks to some blazing batting on another very batsman-friendly surface, aided by some sloppiness in the field from us as we dropped two crucial catches.

The fact we were in the field during the second half of the match meant that there were no players in the dressing room to notice my absence and they were only told afterwards, following the presentation ceremony, about what had happened to me.

As soon as my situation was confirmed, team manager Gavin Dovey had called Andrea to let her know what had happened, but initially he had been unable to make contact with her; all he could do was leave a message asking her to get in touch as soon as she could. Once she knew the situation, she booked a flight from Brisbane to Sydney the following day, knowing by that stage that I was out of any imminent danger.

After I was settled at the hospital, John and Alex returned to the ground, informed the players after the match, then the media. I saw no point in hiding my condition. I was not going to be on the flight the next day to Adelaide, my old home city and venue for the first of three Twenty20 Internationals, so the media would have found out anyway. I was content that as long as my family, the players and the relevant people within Cricket Australia knew, then it could be publicly announced without an issue.

The latter part of that Saturday afternoon and evening is all a bit of a blur. Once I was in bed in hospital I do recall feeling a bit ropey – not helped by the news of our defeat. But by Sunday morning, following a decent rest and helped by the medication taking effect, I started to feel much more like my old self and in late afternoon, as the squad was arriving in Adelaide, I was discharged back to the Quay West, where I was joined by Andrea. It was the start of what was, on the one hand, a very relaxing week and, on the other hand, a very frustrating one.

The relaxation came from the fact that I was off work, with instructions to take it easy. I was not allowed to fly home to Brisbane, but I did have the knowledge that after what had happened in 2007 I still had to get up and about. It meant that Andrea and I played tourists around Sydney for the week, even catching the ferry to Manly.

As for the frustration, that came from the way we performed in games one and two of the Twenty20 International series, losing in Adelaide on Australia Day and then Melbourne. I am a poor watcher at the best of times, but watching on from a different city when the team was underperforming was a new and none-too-pleasant experience. As I admitted when I spoke to the media after the squad arrived back in Sydney for the third and final match of the series, I came close to putting my foot through the television on more than one occasion.

There were plusses to my exile from the team, not just in that it allowed Andrea and I to have a very pleasant few days together but also because I was able to get on top of my correspondence. Seven days after I was diagnosed I had just two emails left in my inbox. I can receive between 50 and 100 emails per day during a home summer, and if they are not addressed promptly things can get out of control pretty quickly, so the chance to tidy them up was a relief.

By the end of the week Andrea was content that I was well on the road to recovery and she returned to Brisbane to rejoin Ethan and Amy, and when the squad did arrive back in Sydney I was a very relieved man. I had missed the involvement, especially with the side losing, and there was plenty to chat about, not least the two losses and also the hamstring injury to captain Aaron Finch that had occurred in game two in Melbourne, which placed a question mark over his involvement in the World Twenty20, set for March in India.

Officially I was still on sick leave and the side was still under the control of Michael Di Venuto, who had been handed the reins by Pat Howard in my absence, but it was a useful exercise for me to be around and observe things with a slightly detached air. I could see how people were feeling after three successive losses across two formats amid multiple changes to the line-up as we tried to discover our best combination for that World Twenty20.

I was feeling perfectly well and on the afternoon of the final Twenty20 International was able to walk without discomfort from the team hotel, located at The Rocks, not far from the Sydney Harbour Bridge, to the SCG, a stroll of 55 minutes. I also gave the team's medical staff a fright by joining in with some of the pre-match drills, including taking throws from the players with a baseball catcher's glove. The danger for me now was being struck by the ball, as the blood-thinners I was taking made me liable to bruise and bleed more easily than was the case normally, something that brought dangers of its own. I knew their concerns and I like to think I was sensible enough to stay out of harm's way.

As an aside, the issue of players and coaching staff being struck by the ball while practising had become an increasingly hot topic within Cricket Australia and among our medical team during the course of the summer. Call it workplace safety gone mad, but there was a recognition that with batsmen now stronger than ever before and with bats getting bigger all the time, the old adage of 'never turn your back in the nets' was no longer sufficient protection to people anywhere near where action was taking place.

International cricket had already seen just such an injury, when Zimbabwe seamer Keegan Meth lost his front teeth as the ball was whacked back at him in his follow-through in a match against Bangladesh. My old South Australia teammate John Davison, working with the Australia side as spin bowling consultant, decided to take his own precautions by wearing a baseball catcher's facemask when giving throw-downs to batsmen and it is something I have tried out too.

Eventually I was given the all-clear to fly home on the morning of 2 February, two days after our last-ball loss in Sydney confirmed a 3–0 Twenty20 International series defeat to India, a disappointing way to end a home summer that included the high of the first day-night Test match. I had already been ruled out of any involvement in the limited-overs series in New Zealand, but after my trip to Brisbane went off without incident I was passed fit to head to New Zealand on 6 February, arriving in Wellington to see the final stages of our victory in the second of three matches, then staying put in that city with the Test players while the One-Day International squad moved on to Auckland.

That international flight across the ditch is not a really long one, but it incorporated all the changes the medical staff wanted to see from me when flying. I made the trip wearing compression stockings to aid blood flow, ensured I stayed hydrated and regularly moved about the cabin – all common sense measures, especially for someone recovering from DVT.

The issue brought into sharp focus the need to alter my lifestyle in a number of ways, and not simply in the way I behaved on flights. A renewed desire to give up smoking was very much back to the top of my agenda. Ahead of the DVT incident I think I must have tried to quit at least half a dozen times, using all sorts of aids, including nicotine patches and gum.

Nothing worked and as I embarked on the trip to New Zealand I found myself contemplating hypnosis as an option to overcome the cravings.

The episode reflected the fact that life on the road is not always healthy. You never truly get away from your work and the absence of home-cooked food can present its own challenges. But the health scare I suffered crystallised my desire to look after myself as well as possible, not only for my own sake but also for the sake of my family.

The incident in Sydney was a wake-up call, no doubt, not only to me but also, perhaps, to other coaches around the world crisscrossing the globe. From a personal point of view I realised the key was to take onboard the lessons and so ensure it did not become something with the potential to affect my longevity in the role. I resolved to do everything I could to ensure those lessons were learnt.

14

WHERE DOES THE GAME
GO FROM HERE?

There is a good argument for saying that the modern game has never been stronger than it is right now. We have three terrific formats – Tests, One-Day Internationals and Twenty20 Internationals. How many other sports can boast that? It means cricket has something for everyone, whether it is the casual observer or the tradition-loving purist.

However, that is not to say the game is without issues and challenges and some of the main ones, at least in my opinion, lie in Twenty20 cricket.

This is not my way of biting the hand that has fed me, or at least biting the hand that started me off on the coaching road. If it was not for Twenty20 cricket and, in my case, the Indian Premier League, there is every chance I would not have had the opportunity to coach Australia, as it gave me my chance to show what I could do.

And unlike the coaching careers of people a generation older than me, my whole life within cricket after I packed up playing has taken place with Twenty20 very much a central feature of the landscape. It is not as if I was set in my ways only to suddenly have the shortest format dropped into my world with chaotic results.

For the record, I am a huge fan of Twenty20. The value it has brought to the game is evident. Just look at the number of fans who flocked through the turnstiles for the KFC Big Bash League in Australia alone in 2015–16 for the proof of that particular pudding. Also, look at the way players have developed different shots and now have a different mindset about what is possible. Chasing 12 an over? In my time that was regarded as impossible; now, especially over a short period of time, a batting side will actually fancy its chances.

Having said all that, I believe Twenty20 cricket has an identity issue, at least at international level, and that is something I would love to see addressed.

Administrators and broadcasters need to decide what it is – a bit of fun or a serious part of the sport. At the moment its identity appears to be blurred.

On the one hand broadcasters want to use it as a vehicle for trying different things, like cameras on players' helmets and umpires' hats and microphones on players during play. Players are expected to be available for interview on the sidelines during matches too. The whole air is of a bit of fun, as far as TV is concerned. At the same time, we are expected to be fully focused on the action at hand because every four years there is a World Twenty20 tournament.

My view is that you cannot have things both ways: it is either a bit of hit-and-giggle or a full-on international format, but not a bit of both. I am not saying that our players do not take the format seriously; they certainly do, as do the coaches. But the peripheral demands around the game can make it tough to be fully focused at all times. Those fun additions are all well and good at domestic level, but when players are playing for their international futures it can be a hindrance.

Also tough is a schedule that makes continuity of selection and establishing game plans for Twenty20 Internationals very difficult indeed. Take our build-up to the 2016 World Twenty20, for example. It is true we had three matches against India at home in late January and then three more in South Africa in early March, immediately prior to the tournament.

But before those games against India, we had just one match, against England in Cardiff, in the previous 14 months. What that meant was that when it came to the India matches – and with a tour of New Zealand to prepare for too – we ended up using 19 players in an attempt to look at different combinations and cover for absentees, hardly an ideal way to go about playing one of the best sides in the world in Twenty20 cricket. India, by contrast, selected the same 11 players in all three of the matches – and won the series 3–0.

I am not apportioning blame for this situation; it is the classic scheduling issue: the need to fit too many matches into too small a space, the cricketing equivalent of getting a quart into a pint pot. But faced with this situation, I think administrators can go one of three ways: retain the current status quo where Twenty20 Internationals still take place but are a bit of an afterthought; play more of the format, even though, with packed schedules, it would be to the detriment of either Tests or One-Day Internationals; or play virtually no Twenty20 Internationals at all outside of the World Twenty20.

I know administrators are reluctant to sanction more Twenty20 Internationals for fear of the effect that might have on interest in the other formats. Since Twenty20 cricket was first discussed, the fear has been that it would cannibalise Tests and One-Day Internationals.

In Australia we have five or six Tests at home each summer, most if not all of them very well supported by the public, and when you throw in a couple of One-Day International series too, there is precious little room for anything else. That explains why Twenty20 International cricket has been squeezed in the way it has.

If you gave me a choice about which direction the game should go in – despite what I said earlier about the issues created by too few Twenty20 Internationals –my decision would be for the format to be virtually phased out at international level, outside of the World Twenty20. In its place, and alongside the already existent domestic leagues around the world, I would like to see the club or franchise system strengthened still further, even perhaps along the lines of a global tour, so that it runs in parallel with international cricket, similar to what happens with the rugby union sevens series.

Players could opt to play on that circuit, but all of them would know that international cricket is where you make your reputation, and nation versus nation is still where the hearts of the vast majority of people lie. Providing the issues of pay for players in some countries can be sorted out – and I accept that is a big 'if' in some places where television rights and sponsorship are not as lucrative as they are in Australia – I do not believe it would represent a threat to Tests and One-Day International cricket.

Players would be selected for the ICC World Twenty20 on the basis of their performances for clubs and franchises, and by limiting the number of Twenty20 Internationals outside of the global event then hopefully that event would become even more prestigious than it already is.

The Twenty20 circuit could include a stop in the United States, a country that could also be targeted for hosting a World Twenty20, which would be the best way, at least in my opinion, of breaking the game there.

Cricket can undoubtedly be a success in the US thanks to the already significant supporter base that exists there among its large Asian community. And a global event has the potential to capture the attention of those not necessarily interested in the sport already.

Soccer took the World Cup to the USA in 1994 and the benefits of doing that can now be seen, two decades on, with the growth of Major League Soccer, while rugby union has also grasped the nettle by awarding its 2019 World Cup to Japan, a country it sees as its next big market. The venues for cricket's major events through to 2023 have already been confirmed, but there is no reason why a World Twenty20 cannot be considered for the USA after that time. The Caribbean Premier League has dipped its toe in the water by staging matches in Florida in 2016, so why not take things on a stage or two further than that?

I mentioned players' pay as a key issue in helping to ensure the best talent continues to play international cricket – as opposed to opting for franchise cricket instead – and I know the International Cricket Council is looking to assist in that matter through its provision of a Test match fund that can be dipped into by countries to help cover the costs of playing the longest format, something that in some countries, with scant crowds, can be a loss-maker.

At the same time, I also see the issue of pay for coaches at international level as being a critical issue. The truth of the matter seems to be that more and more coaches are opting for a life in the Twenty20 leagues instead of the more rigorous grind of international cricket. That is a worrying trend.

To an extent it is understandable: why would you opt to spend most of your year on the road when you can earn the same or, in some cases much more, from a few months looking after a franchise? National pride is one thing, but financial and family realities are quite another.

Ultimately it is the game as a whole that suffers if some of the better and brighter minds in the coaching world opt to give international cricket a miss, but with an ever-increasing number of leagues and franchises, that is an issue that will not go away.

At Manchester United, Sir Alex Ferguson insisted, albeit at the back end of his career, that he earn the same amount as his highest-paid player, Wayne Rooney. By that stage, in 2010, after more than two decades at Old Trafford, he was in a position of strength, but as he said in his book *Leading*: 'What message does it send out to the team if most of them are being paid more than their boss?'

That, of course, is soccer, which has considerably more money to throw around than some cricket boards around the world. And while that remains the case, the prospect of top coaches not working in international cricket remains a very real one.

When it comes to Test cricket I am old school and still regard it as the pinnacle of our sport. I accept Twenty20 represents a significant challenge to that – and to the health of One-Day International cricket too – but the biggest challenge to the longest format, for me at least, comes not from Twenty20 but from the surfaces on which matches are being played.

Put simply, those surfaces are either far too bland or, conversely, are far too heavily weighted in favour of the home side. In both instances that does Test cricket no good at all.

On the other hand, no-one wants to see 600 plays 500 on pitches that offer the bowlers nothing. Producing tracks like that is the surest way to kill off the format.

We are fortunate that in Australia – and in England too – people have always tended to support Test cricket, but if we keep producing flat surfaces of the sort we have seen to an increasing degree at home over the past few years even the patience and support of that loyal fan base is liable to be put in jeopardy.

I accept it is a balancing act for curators across the world. If they go too far in the other direction and produce result-orientated pitches that make batting anything from difficult to a lottery, that is no use either. If matches finish well ahead of time, broadcasters and the public miss out.

My solution to ensure the best possible pitches are produced is, at international level, to do away with the toss, with the visiting side given the option of whether they want to bat or bowl. That way the result is not decided by the toss of the coin, host boards have a greater incentive to produce decent pitches that are fair to both sides and the chances are that after five days the better side – rather than the one that has called correctly and thus been able to take advantage of favourable conditions – is the one that will come out on top. The England and Wales Cricket Board looked at a variation of this at domestic level for first-class matches in 2016, with the visiting captain being offered the option to bowl first; if he declined the toss took place as normal.

I know tradition is a big thing in cricket and the toss is certainly part of that, but I wonder whether some of the pitches we saw on our travels in 2015 and 2016 would have been quite as they were had we had the choice of batting or bowling. Thinking about those Sri Lankan pitches of 2016, would they have been as dry and shaved as they were if we had the chance to bat first, or would they have been the type of pitches we encountered on the tour of 2004 when I was a player, ones that produced good contests between bat and ball?

The pitches on which we lost the third and fourth Ashes Tests in 2015 were so heavily weighted in favour of the home side that it helped to ease my conscience about our heavy losses to some degree. Yes, we were not good enough in the key moments and we played the moving ball very poorly, but the pitches on which those matches were played could hardly be said to have produced an even contest between bat and ball.

Day-night Test cricket is a great innovation and I am all for it. Anyone who was at Adelaide Oval for the inaugural Test under lights in November 2015 will, I am sure, share my view, as it was a terrific match that went right down to the wire and, most importantly of all, saw people flock to watch it, with more than 120,000 passing through the turnstiles.

The recipe for the continuing success of the concept is twofold: a recognition that it is not something that is going to work in every country and at any time of year, and the need to get the ball right.

In Australia, I see little need to switch the Melbourne or Sydney Tests, over the Christmas and New Year periods, to day-night, because – as they are both played at a time when most people are on leave from work or school – attendances are already great. But playing in early summer, as was the case in Adelaide, was and is ideal, as it gives working people and children the chance to come and watch.

In England Test attendances have remained high for many years – in 2015, for example, more than 550,000 people watched the seven matches against New Zealand and

Australia – and you could argue that climatic conditions would work against matches under lights in that, when it is dark enough for those lights to take full effect, in early and late season of April/May and September, it is too cold to sit around for hours on end at cricket grounds. That may be so, but there is no reason why the authorities could not try playing twilight Tests starting at 12 noon or 1 pm in mid-season, taking advantage of long summer evenings with the option of lights if needed, if they felt the need to do something different should crowd numbers ever fall.

The most pressing need to make day-night Tests work is on the subcontinent, where attendances have been poor for a number of years. And somewhere like the United Arab Emirates, where Pakistan plays its home matches and where we played two Tests against it in October and November 2014, is perfect.

Our matches were played, for the most part, in front of virtually empty stadiums in Dubai and Abu Dhabi. despite the fact that there is a very large expat community in the country. There was a very straightforward reason for that: people who live in the UAE are there for work, and many of those expats work six days a week. The only times they are free to watch cricket is on a Friday, the Muslim day of rest – and we saw a terrific attendance on the Friday of the Abu Dhabi Test as Younus Khan moved towards a double-hundred against us – or after working hours.

When Australia played a limited-overs series in Abu Dhabi, Sharjah and Dubai against Pakistan in August and September 2012, the matches started at 6 pm due to the high temperatures and humidity, which meant the finish time was after 1 am. Even so, the matches were hugely successful, with big crowds at each of the venues, primarily because that was the time when those supporters could watch.

It emphasises a simple truth that sometimes we forget in our cricketing bubble: that we are there to entertain the public. Thus we should play at a time that suits the public.

As for the ball for day-night Tests, that is still a work in progress. The pink ball certainly assisted the bowlers, especially under lights, in Adelaide and a three-day Test, although compelling viewing, showed that things were tilted a little bit too far in favour of them – just for once. The balls' lasting qualities were also an issue, which was one reason why more grass than normal was left on both the playing surface and the surrounding pitches.

One comment from batsmen after that Test against New Zealand was that it was difficult to pick up the seam. On a red ball the white stitching can be seen very easily. The difficulty in seeing the light seam on a pink ball was especially important when facing slower bowlers, as it was harder to work out which way the ball was spinning as it came down the pitch.

That issue was addressed for Sheffield Shield matches in late season with a darker stitching on the seam, something that made it stand out from the pink. However, the reports I got back from those matches were that many of that batch of balls struggled to retain their hardness, which made it difficult for bowlers to extract bounce from the surface and for batsmen to time attacking strokes.

These issues are not deal-breakers and I am all for what Cricket Australia – and New Zealand Cricket – did in taking the plunge and trying something new. If we never innovated then developments like coloured clothing, day-night one-day cricket and even Twenty20 would never have become reality. And at a time when bat has been dominating ball to a great extent, it was fascinating to see a match in which, for once, the bowlers held sway. All the same, the issues raised demonstrate that work still needs to be done to get day-night Test cricket to where it should be, which is that the only difference between it and playing during the day is the colour of the ball, rather than the way the ball behaves.

Two divisions for Test cricket, and even a Test Championship, have been other ideas that have been floated to give the format additional relevance. While I am in favour of both in principle, in practice I need to be convinced that either idea would work.

International cricket is made up at the moment of a series of bilateral agreements between countries as to when, where and how often they play each other. In the case of Australia, matches against England and India are, without doubt, the most lucrative. They get the biggest crowds, they get more media coverage and they are also the most lucrative for the broadcasters that buy the rights to show them too, as they can generate the highest levels of return from advertisers, which in turn make them the most lucrative for cricket boards, as they push up the price of the broadcast rights.

In Australia's case it would be a disaster if England or India ever ended up in the other division. The only way to play them would be additional fixtures, which would lack the context of taking place within that divisional system, and also create problems by adding volume to the already hectic schedule.

It might not be all that palatable for some people to hear but the revenue generated by those three countries really does help make the cricketing world go around, at least in the current economic environment, and so the ICC team-ranking system, imperfect though it may be, is perhaps the best way to rank sides.

One option that has been suggested is that the broadcast revenue earned for all Test series is pooled. That would mean the countries that traditionally get less money from broadcasters would benefit, which would be one means to sugar the pill if they ended up playing in the second division. But whether sufficient sides would agree to that is very much open to question.

Since the rise of Twenty20, One-Day International cricket has appeared to be under threat, likely to be squeezed out. I do not see it that way. From where I stand, the format is enjoying its best health for quite some years.

Yes, I am a huge supporter of one-day cricket because I grew up playing it and with two World Cups in the locker as a player and another as a coach you could say I am more than a little biased about it.

What it offers is terrific: you get a game of cricket done and dusted in a day but which, thanks to its duration, allows for a degree of ebb and flow that Twenty20 cannot provide. And thanks to the rise of Twenty20 cricket, batsmen have realised that far more is possible than was previously considered. They are going harder for longer and 300 has become the new par score – and, in many cases, below par.

Like Test cricket, I tend to think the biggest threat to the format comes from pitches that are simply too batsmen-friendly. Take our series against India in January 2016 as an example. The games featured the most runs in history in a five-match series – 3159 – and it got to the stage where you might as well have put a bowling machine at either end of the pitch, so little help was there for the bowlers in any of the surfaces.

The feedback I heard from Channel Nine was that the high-scoring matches were very popular with viewers across the country, but I think you have to have some variety. Surfaces that offer the bowlers something – anything – have to be better than batsmen-dominated run-fests.

How you create that is another matter, of course, and, as with day-night Test cricket, I think the ball is key.

With two balls, one at either end, the most wear one ever gets is 25 overs' worth and that is not usually enough to allow the ball to scuff up sufficiently to help generate reverse swing, unless conditions are especially dry and abrasive. Under the previous regulations, where one ball was used at both ends for the first 34 overs of an innings, that gave the chance of the ball reversing. The replacement ball was old enough to reverse swing too.

I am not necessarily advocating going back to those previous regulations, but scores were certainly lower when they were in place and, in addition, the fact the ball became a little softer meant there was the possibility of spinners playing more of a role than they have done in many of the matches I have seen over the past year or so.

Perhaps the answer is a slightly bigger or more prominent seam – something I know the ICC Chief Executive Officer David Richardson flagged as a possibility in June 2015 after the organisation's annual conference – or even the use of the pink ball that moved around during that day-night Test. I would certainly be willing to experiment to see if we can get the balance between bat and ball back into One-Day Internationals. Whatever is decided has to be given time to bed in so players can get used to it before the World Cup in 2019. It will be interesting to see whether the ICC opts to remain with the status quo or looks to tweak the format again.

The other major talking point around the game and how it is played at the moment is the size of bats. Barry Richards wrote recently that the only things in common between the bats he used and modern ones were that they both had a handle and were made of willow. Some of the bats, such as David Warner's Kaboom, look more like railway sleepers than the sort I used during my career.

As long as bats get no bigger than they are at the moment, I am content. Yes, some edges of current bats can be up to 45 millimetres thick, a far cry from the 10 to 13 millimetres that was common when I started out, and there is a view that their size has helped shift the balance too far in favour of the batsmen.

It's not often appreciated that bats are actually no heavier than when I played; instead, they are prepared in a different way, with the wood having a far lower moisture content which allows for volume – if not longevity – without the extra weight.

Much more important in my opinion is that we ensure that boundary sizes are maximised, so that only a good shot clears the boundary for six. Venues where the playing area is reduced in the hope of increasing the six count are a far greater threat to that bat-ball balance than any chunk of wood wielded by a batsman.

In any case if we do restrict the size of bats, are we not railing against the march of time and technology? One thing that that visit to the Bradman Museum taught me was that bats, along with every other piece of cricket equipment, have evolved over time. Putting artificial limits on that develop-ment, such as limiting the size of bats, is not necessarily in the best interests of the game.

I wonder what other sports would think if something similar was suggested to them. How about going back to wooden tennis rackets? Or leather soccer balls? And how about a return to wooden drivers in golf? Cricket, like any sport, will always develop, and as long as that development is monitored and policed – and the Marylebone Cricket Club, in charge of the Laws of Cricket, is very diligent in that regard – then I see no problem.

I am in favour of the promotion of the leading Associate teams towards the top table of international cricket. The idea of the top second-tier side having the carrot of Test cricket if it beats the lowest-ranked Full Member in a play-off is a great innovation. That is due to happen in 2018. But the elevation of another side to Test cricket also presents problems. To start with, when would we ever play them? Our fixture list is crowded enough as it is, and it would be tough to see where we could possibly add any more matches.

Over the past few years we have done our best to play matches against the leading Associate sides, recognising that the only way they are going to develop is by playing better opposition more often. That was part of the idea behind Australia A's matches in Ireland and Scotland in 2013, as well as the senior side's One-Day International matches against Afghanistan in 2012, Scotland in 2013 and Ireland in 2015. I know one-off matches like that are far from ideal for our opponents, especially if it rains, but in the absence of anything better, given how full our schedule is, we are happy to play our part, playing Ireland again, in South Africa in September 2016.

The gulf between the Full Members and the top Associates is certainly much less than it was when I played – I played against Namibia in the 2003 World Cup when we bowled them out for 45 and the following year, at the Champions Trophy, our match against the USA was done and dusted in 31.5 overs, with Ricky Ponting saying afterwards we would have been better off having a gym session for all the value we got out of it. The gap does remain, though, as was shown during our matches in the 2015 World Cup. Non-competitive matches are often the least enjoyable to play in.

I am open to ideas that help bridge that gap, as the reality is that the game will only become stronger if more and more countries are playing it and playing it well.

15

A DREAM TEAM

It is a question I am often asked: who is the best player you have seen? And it is a tough one to answer as, over the course of almost 30 years in the game, I have come into contact with plenty of greats – Shane Warne, Muttiah Muralitharan, Sachin Tendulkar and Brian Lara, to name just four.

Choosing just one, or even a handful, is a task beyond me so, instead, I will pick a side, including a 12th man, made up of players I regard as the best from those I have had the privilege of coaching.

My criteria for selection were the ability to play across all three formats, to entertain and to change games. I only wish I could have seen this side play together!

If I had believed all I heard and read about **David Warner** before I started my job as Australia's coach, perhaps I would not have taken it in the first place. Or, if I had taken the job, and I had believed the stories, it is unlikely that David would have been part of the set-up.

Right from the get-go his talent was undeniable, as he showed on his never-to-be-forgotten international debut against South Africa in a Twenty20 International in January 2009, scoring 89 from just 43 balls, facing an attack including Dale Steyn, Makhaya Ntini and Jacques Kallis.

But in the early days, and for some time after that, his tendency to self-destruct was equally undeniable, with a misplaced word or action, something that made him, at least in the eyes of the public, hard to love. There was an overtly aggressive attitude on the field and off it too, with Twitter rows with journalists and even fellow players, as well as that infamous clash with Joe Root during the Champions Trophy in 2013.

As I said to the players when I took the Australia job, it was a clean slate for all – but from now on there were certain standards to which everyone had to adhere. After our initial conversation in which I explained what I expected of him, David has never given me a moment's trouble.

He has knuckled down and, because he opens the batting, he knows it is his role to set the tone for the way we want to play. For me, he really has become a leader, including what he does off the field.

David's initial struggles with the pressures and expectations of life as an international cricketer were a perfect illustration of the problem I identified earlier, of players coming into international cricket with all the talent but not necessarily all the experience required to make the step up.

His Test debut against New Zealand in 2011 was only his 12th match of first-class cricket. No matter how gifted you are, it will take something remarkable for you to have developed the necessary match awareness and maturity in so few matches.

In time, of course, he has done exactly that and a Test average in excess of 50 after 50 Test matches is a testament to how good a player he is. Those are the sorts of numbers I could only dream of when I played.

David is the first player I can think of who has made the leap from the shortest form of the game to the longest and done so with barely a blip. He has shown that the journey is possible, but I am not sure we will see too many more making that leap, at least with his level of success, in the near future.

Yes, playing Twenty20 cricket in tournaments like the IPL or the KFC Big Bash League means you are given the chance to test yourself against some of the best players, and it also means you are exposed to coping with the demands of performing in front of big crowds in pressure situations. But the fundamental requirement to make that transition is a sound technique. That is something David possesses, and something he demonstrated as early as his second Test match, when he carried his bat for an unbeaten 123, almost taking his side to victory against New Zealand in a bowler-dominated Test in Hobart. It can get lost in all the chatter about his ability to destroy an attack, but the truth is there are very few chinks in his batting armour.

I am a steadfast fan of his for a whole host of reasons, but let's stick with two that stick out. He plays the game in exactly the way I want, taking on the opposition, putting them under pressure from ball one and seeking to dictate the course of the match. Also, he has not always conformed – and in this respect I see some of myself in him, although I did not have his exceptional talent.

There are numerous examples of him dominating a match from the start, but the ones I remember most are two innings he played in Perth, both in 2015. The first was his innings of 178 from only 133 balls against Afghanistan in our World Cup pool match. Why should an innings against a team playing in its first World Cup stand out? Well, what mattered to me was the way he went about his business. He was ruthless in the way he punished every error in line or length but he also continued to drive on, dismissed in only the 38th over when a different, more self-centred, approach could have seen him cruise to 250 or even more.

That is what I am constantly asking my players to do, to challenge themselves, which John Buchanan liked to do as coach when I was a player. If we have wickets in the shed going into the closing stages of a one-day innings then I would much rather see us bowled out trying to score 350 in an attempt to put the game beyond the opposition than have us finish up at 3-300. I want us to explore what is possible, what is achievable, and David's approach is a manifestation of that.

The other innings of his that stands out for me during our time together is his 253 against New Zealand in the second Test of the Trans-Tasman series. It was remarkable for the fact that 244 of those runs came on day one, including 115 in the final session. That illustrated both his mental strength and his fitness, as well as an increase in that game-awareness I mentioned earlier. New Zealand's bowlers were flagging after tea and David went for their throats with brutal effect.

The incredible thing is that he could just as easily have been a right-hander, which is exactly what he was for a year as a junior. He still plays golf that way today. It is another illustration of what an exceptionally gifted sportsman and a wonderful talent he is.

My opening partner for David came down to a choice between two players, both of them wicketkeepers – **Adam Gilchrist** and Brad Haddin.

Both are players I would have in my side every day of the week, not only for their abilities on either side of the stumps, but also because they are great team men who galvanise dressing rooms through words and actions. In the end I went for Gilly. Although 'Hads' was absolutely pivotal to both the Ashes series win in 2013–14 and the World Cup success of 2015, Adam is someone who, quite simply, changed the game of cricket.

When he came into the Australia Test side, the expectation was that wicketkeepers averaged 25 with the bat; if they averaged 30 they were exceptional. Gilly actually averaged a touch over 47, which is top notch for a specialist batsman. Add to that the facts he got those runs incredibly quickly – his strike-rate was 81 per hundred balls – and that he accumulated more than 900 dismissals in the three forms of the game for his country, and you have an unbelievable, once-in-a-lifetime cricketer.

Of course, my criteria for selecting players in this dream side of mine is the impression they have made on me from a coaching standpoint and Adam was a wonderful person to work alongside at the Deccan Chargers and Kings XI Punjab in the IPL. When we won the IPL with Deccan in 2009 he was a very hands-on captain, in the sense that he set the standards in training and led by example. That made my job as coach so much easier.

When the key moments presented themselves he was also the one who invariably stood up and was counted. In the semi-final of that IPL season in South Africa we faced Delhi Daredevils, and after Ryan Harris had dismissed both their openers, Gautam Gambhir and David Warner, for ducks in the first over, their remaining batsmen got away from us to reach 8-153.

It looked a challenging target until Gilly walked to the crease. Within one over any tension we had felt within our dressing room had evaporated completely. In that over, bowled by Dirk Nannes, Gilly smashed five consecutive fours and when you threw in a wide to the total as well, we were suddenly 0-21 and on our way.

He went on to score 85 from just 35 balls and, amazingly, we actually reached our target with 14 balls in hand, as his approach removed all the pressure from his partners at the other end. All they had to do was give him the strike and he did the rest!

Gilly's record as a player – and three-time World Cup winner – meant that when he spoke others listened, and I am sure if you speak to any of the young Indian players in our dressing room in that tournament they will tell you how inspirational he was. But he was also someone who liked a laugh, a joke and was more of a night owl than perhaps people realise. He had the ability to bring a side together, but was meticulous in his preparation and expected the same of everyone else.

I remember one of the juniors in our squad in that IPL season asking me, with concern on his face, what was wrong with the captain when he saw Gilly sitting in the dressing room, his knees wrapped in ice packs after a training session. There was actually no issue; that was just Gilly, doing what he had done throughout his career, ensuring his joints got all the love and attention they needed after all the bending and squatting he did.

It was another tough call to settle upon the captain of my fantasy side as I have selected a team of leaders, but in the end I went for **Steve Smith**.

'Smudge' is a player who has improved more than any other I have ever worked with. He is one of *the* best players in the game today, alongside the likes of AB de Villiers, Joe Root and Virat Kohli.

I first spotted him when I was coaching Queensland and he was playing for NSW. I knew he had talent, that was clear to see, but he was unorthodox and that can lead to people putting question marks against a player.

Right from the outset, however, that unorthodoxy has actually been one of his great strengths, as he has the unerring ability to get the ball to places where the fielding captain and bowler are not expecting. Steve is a terrific manipulator of the field, in that he will work a ball into a gap, force a captain to plug that gap and then he will exploit the place where the fielder has been taken from. It drives the opposition mad.

I can relate to Smudge as I was never the prettiest of players, but my attitude has always been that runs on the board are always far more important than technical excellence. Yes, you need a sound basis on which to build your run-scoring, but technique is nothing without an end product.

I first worked with him on the A tour of the United Kingdom in 2013, before I was handed the chance to take over the senior side. Straight away I was struck by his work ethic, which was incredible. If ever practice was optional, he was one person you could be guaranteed would attend. He saw that A tour not as the second-place ticket in the lottery – it is hard to believe now that he was actually left out of the original squad for that summer's Ashes series, although you could argue he had still to do more to justify his spot – but as the chance to impress and push his case for further honours. He did exactly that from day one.

By the back-end of what was a relatively short trip I made it quite clear I liked what I saw and that I felt he should be drafted into the senior side immediately. He was, although it took until the end of that 2013 series for him to make the breakthrough with his maiden hundred at The Oval. Even then, it still took him another year to become a regular in all three formats. Now it is hard to imagine any Australian side without him.

The work he has done during my time as coach falls into three categories – physical, technical and mental. The physical side of things can be seen by the way he has changed his body shape. I heard as an aside on that 2013 A tour that my predecessor Mickey Arthur had told him he needed to shape up and get his skin folds down, a message he took to heart. He became one of the most diligent trainers in the squad and has developed an impressive upper body that has helped him add power to his batting.

The technical work he has done has been alongside former Australia batting coach Michael Di Venuto. If I had a dollar for every ball that 'Diva' has thrown to Smudge over the past two years I could comfortably retire and never work again. Theirs has been a great partnership, only ending when Diva took up the role of Surrey's head coach in England in the winter of 2016. Diva knew Steve's game inside-out and knew what worked for him, while Steve trusted Diva's views implicitly. It was the perfect player-coach relationship. I remember ahead of a match in the tri-series against India and England in early 2015 when Steve spoke to Michael about the fact he was not getting the runs he felt he should be, and he asked whether Diva thought he was out of form. 'No, you're hitting the ball as well as you ever have and the runs will come, believe me,' was the coach's reply and, sure enough, Smith's response was a hundred as captain in his next innings to win us the match against England in Hobart. Sometimes a coach's job is simply to offer reassurance rather than try to come up with some mysterious solution to a problem that is not really there.

Steve's play against spin is an example to all of us that you do not have to get too funky in order to succeed. He drives slow bowlers to distraction with an utterly simple method: if the ball is short then he gets right back and if it is flighted or full then he gets right forward, trying wherever possible to get down the pitch to put the bowler off – just like Barry Richards advocated to me at South Australia all those years ago. Allied to that game plan is his ability to read length very quickly, a combination that will test the abilities of any spinner who operates against him.

The mental side of Steve's development as a player has been twofold: his ability to absorb pressure and the way he has learnt from how players such as Ricky Ponting and Michael Clarke went about their business. His calmness out in the middle comes from a complete confidence in his ability and the knowledge that you cannot make runs in the pavilion. He has a full range of shots at his disposal so is willing, if necessary when bowlers get it right, to allow the run rate to climb, confident that he has the game to get back on track later in the innings. And, as a disciple of Ponting and Clarke, he watched closely how they prepared for games and also took on board what they looked to achieve as captains, with the fields they set and the plans they wanted the bowlers to stick to.

The first question you should always ask as a captain is 'What does the opposition least want me to do?' And whatever the answer is, go ahead and do it. It sounds simple, but sometimes it can get lost in the midst of those opposition players playing well or even because of pre-existing plans you may already have, plans that might not always work out as you wish.

Steve's instinct is to attack and he will always err on that side, just like Clarke and Ponting, realising the best way to stop the opposition is to get them out. He is my type of captain and he will not back down, even if what he does may make him unpopular. The prime example of that was Ben Stokes' dismissal for handling the ball in the One-Day International at Lord's in September 2015. The popular thing to have done would have been to withdraw the appeal; Steve's instinct was that the handling of the ball was deliberate and he pressed on – quite rightly in my opinion – with the appeal, which was upheld. We love to be liked, but international cricket is not a popularity contest and Steve showed he was prepared to take the hard decisions.

I saw another example of his mental toughness – and he needed it after the Stokes incident as he was booed by the English crowds for the rest of that tour – in his innings of 100 against a rampant South Africa attack at Centurion in February 2014. Batting at number six he came in with the score at 4-98 and, alongside Shaun Marsh, coped with an exceptionally tough situation as though he was playing a weekend Grade match. Conditions were difficult – the pitch offered variable bounce and there was sideways movement too – but he adapted to the situation brilliantly. And if there is one word you will hear from Steve's mouth more than any other, especially in team talks, it is that one: adapt. He wants players to become better in different conditions, as he knows that is the only way for Australia to get to the top again and stay there. He is the perfect player to learn from.

Although he is not the captain of my dream team, I like to think I have a strong bond with **Michael Clarke**, born of some pivotal factors. He was Australia's captain when I took over as coach and he proved himself to be an exceptional leader of men in the aftermath of the death of Phillip Hughes.

It is true that we did not see eye to eye at the start of the summer of 2014–15, as we had different views of how he should go about proving his fitness following injury, but all that was forgotten as he played a central role in rallying us together in the wake of tragedy, despite his own grief.

When I began as coach I knew that Michael had been close to Mickey Arthur and so that had the potential to make things awkward between us, but it was never an issue. He was as fed up as I was of losing to England and all he wanted was to win – plain and simple.

The latter part of his career, with injuries, poor form and being worn down by an Ashes series loss in 2015 obscures both his abilities as a tactician and his skill as a batsman. I was part of the side on his Test debut against India in Bangalore in 2004 when he scored 151 and, at his best, there have been few better players of spin for Australia in the past 20 years. He was so light on his feet, getting down the pitch at the drop of a hat, that he was a nightmare to come up against if you were a slow bowler.

His stand-out innings for me as coach was the unbeaten 161 he made in Cape Town in the series decider against South Africa in March 2014, a match that saw us go back to the top of the ICC rankings, albeit for a relatively short time. We had lost the previous match at Port Elizabeth and Morne Morkel gave him a fearful working over from round the wicket – even, it turned out later, fracturing his shoulder in the process – but he never backed down, helped us get a substantial score on the board, which was the foundation for our win. It was the perfect illustration of leading from the front.

As a player I found him to be as tough as teak – he had to be to defy the pain of a longstanding back complaint – and if you set him a task, no matter how difficult it was, he would invariably come up with the goods. As selectors, we had some critics in the World Cup summer of 2014–15, not least our mutual mate Shane Warne, when we imposed a timetable on Michael to either prove his fitness for the tournament or pull out, but like all great players he took that as a challenge and responded accordingly. He was up before sunrise for weeks on end working on strengthening his suspect hamstring, knowing that we could not and would not allow any passengers in the squad. He proved his fitness and then led the side to success, a fitting finale to a terrific One-Day International career, which actually began when he replaced me in the starting line-up in Adelaide back in January 2003.

When Michael announced he wanted to test the water about a comeback in January 2016 I was surprised but, at the same time, pleased. I know from experience how difficult it is to let go of something you love – my forced retirement as a player from South Australia is testament to that – and even if a return to action does not work out, I hope it means a return to the game in some form. The experience Michael has accumulated over so many years can only benefit Australian cricket.

My choice of **Glenn Maxwell** in this fantasy line-up might surprise a few people because there may be a perception that I am his harshest critic.

It is true that I do ride him hard at times, but that is only because, having worked so closely with him, I have seen firsthand what he is capable of and I want him to fulfil his potential.

The choice for me in this fantasy side lay between 'Maxi' and another wonderful talent, Andrew Symonds. In the end I went for Glenn and relegated 'Roy' to 12th man, on the basis that as this team is all about my impressions of and experience with players from my coaching standpoint, I only got to work with Andrew at the back end of his career when his best days were just about behind him. For Glenn, those golden days are still very much in the future.

There are actually plenty of similarities between the duo, both of them incredibly gifted, breathtaking and brutal with the bat, handy with the ball and stunning in the field. My job as a coach is to find the happy medium with Glenn. On the one hand I want him to play with the type of freedom that can drive attacks to distraction while, on the other hand, I want him to discover that extra degree of consistency that can turn him from a good player into a very good, or even great player. It is a fine balance.

As I wrote earlier, I am fine with Glenn adopting an aggressive, attacking mindset as long as he has a clear plan of how he intends to do it. As long as he has that he will never get any stick from me. He has all the shots in his locker and it is just a case of realising when to use them.

He was one of our stand-out players in the World Cup. To score 324 runs in that tournament with a strike-rate in excess of 182 really was exceptional. He has some of the best wrists I have seen, which let him manipulate the ball into different areas of the ground, something that makes him extremely difficult to set a field to. His innings against Sri Lanka of 102 from just 53 balls was as destructive an effort as I have ever seen from an Australia batsman. One of my stand-out memories of all the matches we played in that World Cup campaign was his partnership with Shane Watson in that encounter in Sydney. The pair added 160 in 14 overs and it really was like one long highlights reel.

To an extent Glenn has been a victim of his own success, another player who has risen through the ranks quickly without a vast amount of first-class cricket behind him. His ability and form of the sort he showed in that World Cup has demanded his inclusion in the limited-overs line-ups but that, in turn, has counted against his ability to push his case for selection in the Test arena, because it means he simply does not get the chance to play as much red-ball cricket as either he or, ideally, we selectors would like him to.

What has impressed me about Glenn is that he is not prepared to settle for simply being known as a white-ball specialist, even though that approach would make him an extremely wealthy man; his desire to wear the baggy green again, following three caps in India and the United Arab Emirates in 2013 and 2014, was shown by the way he went to England in the winter of 2015, even turning out for Yorkshire's second XI, in an attempt to get more exposure to the red ball in alien conditions. That is the type of hunger and self-motivation I want from my players.

Think of Glenn and invariably you will think of that term that is bandied around in cricket circles these days when people talk about a player capable of something special – the X-factor. I know that is a label Glenn hates and is desperate to get rid of; he wants to be known as an outstanding, but also consistent, cricketer. It is my job to help him fulfil that aim.

India's **Rohit Sharma**, who I worked with at the Deccan Chargers, has as much natural talent as any player I have coached.

He was player of the One-Day International series for India against Australia in January 2016, even though his team lost the series 4–1. Admittedly the pitches were loaded in favour of the batsmen, but we still never really looked like finding a weakness.

He made 171 not out, 124, 6, 41 and 99 – 441 runs at a strike-rate of 110 opening the innings – and by the end of that series and the Twenty20 Internationals that followed (he made 31, 60 and 52 in those matches), our bowlers were left just shrugging their shoulders about how best to approach bowling at him.

One of the first impressions he made on me at Deccan was the time he had to play his shots. When you watch really good players it is as if they are operating in slow motion as, no matter how fast the bowler up against them is, they always seem to be able to get into position and ease the ball away without looking rushed. Rohit has that ability and I recall him taking four fours off Dale Steyn's bowling, one of them a pull shot and the others through the covers, and thinking to myself: 'This guy can really play.'

In the early days with Deccan he gave the impression of being a little laid-back and I know he had enjoyed a fair amount of success at age-group level, playing with the India under-19s in the 2006 junior World Cup, the same tournament that featured David Warner. Don't be mistaken: he was utterly dedicated and eager to learn as much as he could.

For a young Indian player to enjoy the success he did in the season we won the IPL in 2009, playing in utterly foreign conditions – he was the tenth highest run-scorer with 362 runs, despite celebrating only his 22nd birthday during the tournament – spoke volumes for his ability. My only surprise, having seen him in the formative years of his career, is that he has not kicked on and enjoyed a stellar Test career to go with his limited-overs exploits.

But right from the first time I saw him I felt he had something special about him, and that feeling still persists almost a decade after that first sighting.

Shane Watson is a much-maligned figure in Australian cricket, but he is someone I place in the top bracket among modern players.

Just like Mitchell Johnson, he has the ability to change a game completely, especially in the shorter forms of the game, and he has always been one of the first names I put down on any team sheet.

As I said earlier, I allowed myself to be seduced by his talent to the extent that I probably should have pushed for us to look beyond him at Test level sooner than we did.

But given his skill set, why would I not have been seduced? After all, in an era where all-rounders could hardly be said to grow on trees, he did offer himself up as a terrific all-round cricketer: as a batsman he could slot in anywhere in the top order, although his preference was always to open, and with the ball he was genuinely quick when he first burst on to the scene. Then, as injuries took their toll, he throttled back and became a really clever operator, with nagging accuracy combined with clever and subtle changes of pace. When you add in the fact that he was one of the best slip fielders I saw, with hands like buckets, he was an irresistible package when fit.

Those last two words are the key to Shane, as he endured more injuries than any player I can think of in the modern era. I am not sure how I would have coped with so much time away from the game, but he kept bouncing back. Whenever he did his ability made it impossible for the selectors to overlook him.

Those comebacks speak of a player with tremendous strength of character – how many times was he knocked down only to bounce back up again? And allied to that strength I always found him a great asset in the dressing room. He was a good thinker on the game, invariably cut to the heart of the matter in any team meeting and in my experience was happy to put the team ahead of himself, as shown by the way he took on the captaincy when Aaron Finch was injured during the Twenty20 International series against India in January 2016. The fact he then responded with an unbeaten 124 from just 71 balls was all the proof you need about his ability.

I first worked alongside Shane on the 2002 tour of South Africa when he was given the chance as something of a project player. Australia was on the lookout for an all-rounder and he fitted the bill. He had already shown his ambition by heading to Tasmania in search of first-class cricket, leaving his native Queensland when he found his way barred, and that single-mindedness has always been one of his hallmarks.

Part of me wonders how good he could have become if he had just focused on his batting, but it was the fact he was always such a terrific talent with bat and ball that made him the real deal in my eyes. I did feel there were times when he had the tendency to be too critical of himself and despite his significant imposing physical presence I found him to be someone who, one-to-one, sometimes needed to be reminded just how good he really was.

His quality shone through in his 176 against England at The Oval in the final Test of my first series as coach of the national side. Over the 10 Tests of the home-and-away Ashes series in 2013 and 2014 he scored 763 runs, impressive figures at a time when our top order generally struggled.

I thank my lucky stars that my first home summer as Australia coach coincided with the absolute peak of **Mitchell Johnson** – and I am also grateful that I never had to face him at his peak.

The prospect of being 22 yards away from him when he had the ball in his hands was enough to turn plenty of England and South Africa players weak at the knees in 2013–14. No wonder, given he was propelling it at speeds around 150 kilometres per hour.

I cannot imagine there has been a better spell of sustained fast bowling in the past generation than Mitch's 5-16 in five post-lunch overs at the Adelaide Oval in the second Test of the series against Alastair Cook's side.

It is true that some spells in the series that followed, in South Africa, ran it mighty close, including his opening bursts in both innings of the decisive Cape Town Test, but Adelaide stands out as a wonderful memory, for me and I am sure a large number of other people who were privileged to witness it. Even Jeff Crowe, the match referee for that Ashes series, recently nominated it as a highlight of his officiating career.

What Mitch had at his best – and I was fortunate to see plenty of that best as coach – was the ability to scare batsmen. It was something that had gone out of fashion in international cricket since the halcyon days of the West Indies and, to an extent, the prime of the Pakistan duo of

Wasim Akram and Waqar Younis but Mitch brought it back in thrilling fashion and the world game was the richer for it.

If you wanted my model of the perfect cricketer, I think Mitch would be pretty close to it, and not just for his ability with the ball but also because of his very underrated batting ability. During my time around the Australia squad, both as a player and a coach, there have been few cleaner strikers of a ball.

Why did it take him so long to fulfil his incredible potential? Partly, I think, it was because he may have suffered from the weight of expectation generated by the terrific raps he received from the get-go from the likes of his great mentor Dennis Lillee and also from the fact that he was the next cab off the rank after the retirement of the great Glenn McGrath. Those boots were pretty big ones to fill.

He needed to be comfortable with his own body too, and physical maturity allowed him to find that comfort, as did personal happiness with wife Jessica and daughter Rubika. That allowed him to relax and just release the handbrake.

Also, I think, he really was a thoroughbred – and thoroughbreds need to be looked after. He was never going to be a bowler who you could simply wind up at the start of a season with the instruction to keep going; in horse-racing terms he was someone who needed to be raced lightly, handled with care and unleashed at the right time. That was something that Michael Clarke and I both came to appreciate in the lead-up to the 2013–14 Ashes series and it was an approach that bore delicious fruit that summer.

The cliché of a fast bowler is of a mean, ruthless enforcer but, although he slotted into that role, Mitch was as far from that stereotype – and as free from ego – as can be. He was content to slip down the pecking order as player of the tournament Mitchell Starc cranked up the speed gun with the new ball during the World Cup, and his retirement from international cricket was as low-key as could be, given we were saying farewell to a bowler with almost 600 wickets in all three forms of the game.

We lingered long into the night in the dressing room in Perth at the end of his final match, as every player and member of the support staff relished a last chance to be alongside the great fast bowler in Test match mode. Mitch brought so much quality and ability to the Australian dressing room during my time as coach. He tested the waters as a commentator on ABC Radio during our One-Day International against India in Perth, and I am sure he will bring those same traits to a career in the media if that is the path he decides to go down.

I have seen plenty of players go through the pain barrier but the lengths to which **Ryan Harris** went to make it on to the field for Australia take the biscuit.

During our series in South Africa in early 2014 he was on high-strength painkillers and having his knee drained of fluid seemingly nonstop, but once he left the dressing room he put all that to one side in a single-minded pursuit of wickets.

He was the straight man to Mitchell Johnson's Joker in our series wins against England and South Africa that summer, pounding away on an immaculate line and length and hitting the bat hard. That was one of his traits – he bowled the archetypal 'heavy' ball. If runs had been easy to come by at the other end from Mitch's pyrotechnics, we might not have enjoyed as successful a run as we did in those eight Tests, but 'Rhino' gave nothing away and tightened the noose before 'Johnno' released the lever to the trap door.

I captained Rhino on his first-class debut, for South Australia against Tasmania in November 2001, and he broke down with a damaged pectoral muscle after bowling beautifully with the new ball. It was to be the start of a career that was hampered by injury. If he had remained fit for long spells there is no doubt in my mind he would be regarded as one of the greats, and his figures show that very clearly. When he retired, no Australian bowler who played more than 20 Tests had a better strike-rate than Rhino, who, on average, took a wicket every 51 balls.

When he finally had to concede defeat to injury, at the start of the Ashes tour of 2015, I moved quickly to ensure we kept him inside the tent. He stayed on and worked alongside Craig McDermott and then, at the back end of our home summer, when Craig headed to New Zealand for the start of that tour, he came back in again to work with the bowlers during the Twenty20 International series against India. He has always had an easy way about him, relates well to other players and has the potential to be a terrific coach. He was always one of the first names on any captain's team sheet and he remained that way for me as a coach.

When selecting a spinner for my line-up, it came down to a choice between two: Nathan Lyon and **Daniel Vettori**, and in the end I went for Vettori, who I worked with during my time in Queensland, simply because of his extra experience in all formats.

'Gazza' Lyon has been great to work with and has been a go-to man for his captains at Test level during my time as coach, after seeing off an early challenge from Ashton Agar on that 2013 Ashes tour. You could also argue that the fact he spins the ball more sharply than Dan did in the latter stages of his career should give him a leg-up at my selection table. But Dan eventually won the day because, when we worked together, he proved himself to be a great operator in 50-over and Twenty20 cricket.

By the time we met up his Test days were all but behind him, and as a result of various back injuries – which may have scuppered the careers of less determined players – he certainly got less action on the ball than at his very best.

But what he lacked in revs he more than made up for in subtlety, using the crease and changes of pace and length to great effect. Like all top-class left-armers he had a great, curving arm ball, and he had the ability to always keep the batsman guessing, a great asset to have.

His other advantage, something that was not always visible to those watching on television, was his great height. From 1.91 metres he was able to generate disconcerting bounce and, again, in the absence of sharp spin that was something he exploited to the full.

On top of that, he also had his batting as an additional, resounding string to his bow. He was an unorthodox but highly effective player capable of batting anywhere in the order – I remember he opened the innings against us in the 2003 World Cup in Port Elizabeth – and a Test batting average of 30 with six hundreds marks him out as a genuine all-rounder.

By the time we worked together he had both a very clear idea of what he needed to do to perform and also an obvious desire to move into coaching. He took over from Stuart Law at the Brisbane Heat in 2015–16 and although the side did not pull up any trees in his first season, I still expect him to go on and have an excellent career behind the clipboard.

Why? Because he knows the game inside out, having played at international level for two decades but, more importantly – and this is something I keep coming back to – he has the right temperament to be a leader in the dressing room. He is undemonstrative and calm and that, allied to his experience and the fact his record commands respect, means he is exactly the type of person that players will naturally gravitate towards and follow.

I worked with **Dale Steyn** for two years at the Deccan Chargers and he was a player who made an immediate and positive impact on me.

He was a big-name player with a massive reputation who joined us from Royal Challengers Bangalore and what I liked about him was that as soon as he arrived he sought to set the standard for others, and in particular our young players, to follow.

If he were asked to do something at training, for example some fitness work, he would do it – and then do some more. He did that extra because (a) he knew he could, (b) he clearly loved to push himself and (c) he wanted to set an example. That is exactly what you want from a senior player.

Deccan underperformed in the two seasons that we worked together, but you could never attach any blame for that at Dale's door. In 2011 he took 14 wickets with an economy rate of 6.57 and the following year he managed 18 wickets and an economy rate of 6.10. More often than not sides opted to survive against him and look to exploit our weaker links at the other end.

I will always hold up Dale as what I regard as the perfect example of how a fast bowler develops: invariably they explode onto the scene, full of fire and brimstone, and then as age catches up with them they add guile to the mix.

Anyone who saw Dale's dismissal of England captain Michael Vaughan, my old Yorkshire teammate, on his Test debut in Port Elizabeth in late 2004 would have sensed, even then, that they were seeing the start of something special and so it proved.

The delivery, bowled at high speed, seemed to be angling in at Michael's pads and he opened up his body to clip it through wide mid-on, only to find the ball swinging away late and plucking his off stump out of the ground.

Even nearer the end of his career than the beginning, Dale has shown himself capable of slipping himself and a spell he bowled to Chris Gayle for Deccan against the Royal

Challengers Bangalore still sticks in my mind. Gayle is one who is not backwards in coming forwards, but Dale well and truly showed him who was boss on that particular occasion, making the big man hop and jump about.

Allied to his insatiable desire to train and lead by example, I also found Dale to be great at knowing when to relax and help put other players at ease. If he was Australian you would mark him down as a terrific country boy and I found he was not afraid to tell a joke against himself and had a nice dry sense of humour.

One story he told me was about his start in first-class cricket. He was batting against fellow fast bowler Andre Nel, and Andre was never short of a word or two to opposing batsmen.

With a name like Steyn, a not uncommon name among the Afrikaner community, Nel started sledging the newcomer in that language. Dale failed to react to any of the abuse and Nel walked away thinking he was up against a very cool young customer. However, Steyn told me later that English was the only language he spoke and he did not understand a word Nel was saying.

Andrew Symonds slots in as 12th man both for his prodigious talent and the fact that if any player – aside from the wicketkeeper – was injured I know he could slot in and do a very fine job in their place. And I reckon he would be great at mixing the drinks for the other players too!

A brutal hitter, a handy medium-pacer and a capable off-spinner, he was also one of the most agile fielders I ever saw, especially given his imposing frame.

He played eight matches for the Deccan Chargers in our IPL title-winning season of 2009 in South Africa, linking up with us after Australia's limited-overs series against Pakistan in the United Arab Emirates, and made a massive contribution to the success, scoring 249 runs with a strike-rate of 150, and also finished as our fourth-highest wicket-taker with seven victims despite playing only half the matches.

He was not enjoying international cricket at the time – the tournament came just before he was sent home from the World Twenty20 in the United Kingdom in 2009 for breaking a drinking ban, his last involvement with the national side – and I think the chance to perform away from the spotlight of Australian cricket, and in a country where he had enjoyed such tremendous success during the World Cup of 2003, was just what he needed.

I needed no convincing about his ability, having sat on the sidelines watching his maiden One-Day International hundred against Pakistan in the opening match of that World Cup. With me suspended, Michael Bevan recovering from a hamstring injury and Shane Warne on his way home after failing a drugs test, we were selecting from just 12 that day and up against the side that we beat in the final at Lord's four years earlier.

At 4-86 and then 5-146 we were really under the pump but 'Roy's response was to play the innings of his life, 143 not out from only 125 balls against an attack including Wasim and Waqar. It was an effort that not only helped define the team's tournament, but also set him on the path to four years of excellence at international level.

'Symo' took his time to find his feet for Australia and it is easy to forget now that he was a controversial pick for that tournament, selected on a hunch rather than having solid numbers behind him, thanks to support from Ponting and coach Buchanan, who had worked with him at Queensland.

My role as coach when he came to Deccan was to make him feel valued and also give him downtime when we were not training or playing, and he responded by being an absolutely terrific team man.

He was someone who played it hard on the field and he lived for his friends in the dressing room, but he was not someone who relished the limelight and the 'Monkeygate' controversy, at least in my opinion, took a lot out of him and sapped his desire to keep performing at international level.

You could argue that his was a talent unfulfilled, but a couple of World Cup medals, from 2003 and 2007, plus numerous other honours, is still a pretty good haul in anyone's language.

16

THE FUTURE

As a coach, I may be many things – mentor, friend, teacher, taskmaster – but one thing I am not is a clairvoyant. Even so, I am certain the role of the coach in the future will continue to evolve, just like the game itself.

Coaches will continue to look for the so-called one per-centers in our preparations, things that we believe can help tip the scales in favour of our side in a crucial moment. We will come up with those ideas either by having revelations of our own during practice sessions or by picking up things from other coaches. I would be lying if I said we did not always keep a lookout at what opposing teams did in practice and warm-ups, and I am sure they are doing just the same. It is almost a case of a cricket coaching arms race.

Even in the past few years I have seen a whole host of innovations brought in by players and coaches to enhance their ability to train better and smarter. To start with, I can think of the ball-thrower pioneered by former England batting coach Graham Gooch – originally a device to hurl balls for dogs to fetch and now used by coaches across the world to give throw-downs to players – and there are plenty more besides that.

There was also a cut-down bat I saw Graeme Hick use in the late 1990s when he played for England. The sides of the bat either side of the splice were removed so that it was just one long narrow strip of wood, the idea being that because the bat only had a middle it encouraged the player to watch the ball more closely, given he no longer had any margin for error afforded by a wider blade. 'Hicky' used the bat when he first went into the nets to help him focus on the ball and would then switch to a normal bat once he felt he was middling it regularly.

While I was playing for Australia Adam Gilchrist used to practise his wicketkeeping with a 'nicking bat' that he had specially made. It had a normal handle and a flexible plastic blade. The batsman would play a shot and even if he hit the ball, the fact that the blade was soft plastic meant the ball would still go through to 'Gilly', standing up to the stumps, albeit with a slight deviation. Like Hicky's bat with no edges, it was something that encouraged Gilly to watch the ball more closely.

On top of all these things are more recent innovations, such as the small plastic ramp that is a modern version of an old-fashioned catching cradle, with the coach kneeling down in front of it, throwing balls into the ramp for the fielder to catch. That fielder would usually be wearing thin leather fingerless gloves with padding in the palms to take those catches, something intended to allow him to practise catching for long periods without the risk of damaging the hands.

More recently, on our tour of New Zealand in early 2016, we experimented with the prototype of a device to help bowlers monitor whether or not they were keeping their front foot behind the line during practice sessions, a sort of cricketing version of tennis's electronic eye. You could argue that one of the coaching staff should go and umpire to save the need for something like that but, when you have 14 or 15 players in the squad, sparing a staff member to do that rather than actually watching a bowler's action, for example, might not be the best use of that coach's time.

Australia was one of the first teams to look beyond cricket when John Buchanan brought in baseball coach Mike Young to work on the side's fielding, but even before that I remember former England fitness coach Dean Riddle, who also worked with the Yorkshire squad when I started there, telling me how he left a tour of the Caribbean for a few days in 1998 to travel to Florida and watch baseball spring training, again to see whether there was anything he could learn from the way the players in that sport went about their business.

Video analysis has developed a lot too. Our video analyst emails video clips to players of their own performances or those of an opponent and they can download and watch them on their mobile phones and portable devices whenever they want, rather than having to watch in a team meeting. Technology is developing in leaps and bounds and cricket coaching is feeling the benefit of that advancement.

The next stage of my personal development as a coach is to dip into what other sports are doing and to see what scope there is to improve our preparations, something Cricket Australia is very supportive of. The only problem with that idea is the relentless treadmill that is the international cricket circuit these days. Just about the only period in the schedule when Australia is likely to be out of action is the time when the Indian Premier League takes place, but that is the best time for me to plan for the next series and also recharge my batteries and spend time with family and friends, something that is absolutely vital given the amount of time the side spends on the road, not only overseas but also domestically.

That has been the main difference for me between coaching domestically and coaching internationally. When I worked with Queensland I had the whole of the winter to plan for the next season and also to work with the players, often on a one-to-one basis. The opportunity for that downtime, to focus on the challenges to come and also to freshen up, is much more restricted on the international circuit and it is one reason why a coach of a national side needs a much larger support network around him.

Whatever the future holds, I am under no illusions. The life of an international coach is a finite one, and not just because of the toll the role takes on family life due to the high volume of travel. I know that as more and more money comes into the game, expectations rise and the demand for results increases. Whether we like it or not, cricket is going down the road of many other sports where, in the absence of success, the coach is the most likely person to get the sack.

What I can say with absolute certainty is that international cricket will never see the equivalent of a Kevin Sheedy or a Dick Reynolds, who both spent more than 20 years at AFL club Essendon or even, looking further afield, an Arsene Wenger or a Sir Alex Ferguson, in charge of Arsenal and Manchester United respectively for well over two decades. In teams where the action is confined to a domestic season with a break to follow you can have those lengthy periods with one person in charge, but in international cricket, with tours taking place in off-seasons, it is simply not possible. Indeed, nowadays even the tenures of John Buchanan and Duncan Fletcher, in charge of Australia and England for eight years apiece, look unlikely to be beaten.

I have gone on record as saying that the end of the winter of 2019 looks like a decent jumping-off point for me – and in August 2016, I signed a contract extension up to that point – as that year will include the next World Cup, when we will defend our title in the United Kingdom, as well as an Ashes series straight afterwards. We have not won a series against England away from home since 2001. The chance to finally put that record straight after two failed attempts on my part as coach will certainly be a strong motivator.

On top of that, by then, I would have been in the role for six years and I think every coach in every role has a shelf life. I read in the autobiography of Leigh Matthews, the hugely successful AFL player and coach who led both Collingwood and Brisbane to championship flags, that he thought the optimum length of time for a coach in that sport was between five and seven years. After that there was a danger that the coach's messages would start to sound stale and that players might need a fresh voice and fresh ideas to continue to spur them on. Specialist coaches coming and going within the set-up may remove an element of that, as they can bring with them their own enthusiasm to refresh a group, but Matthews' underlying message is probably not far off the mark, even in cricket.

Of course, all that assumes that our results continue to be decent – and the Test series loss in Sri Lanka in July and August of 2016 and the questions that followed was a reminder that you are only as good as your latest results – my own appetite for the role remains intact and Cricket Australia's board have not got sick of me. They are all factors that are impossible to predict. I may even find that by the time 2019 rolls around I have a second wind, and if family life permits and results are still positive then I may wish to continue. But whatever happens, the positive sign from Australian cricket's perspective is that the powers-that-be are already thinking in terms of a succession plan.

The idea of Western Australia head coach Justin Langer taking over the reins for the limited-overs tour of the Caribbean in the middle of 2016 was twofold: to give me a break and allow me to plan for the tours and series following that tri-series against the West Indies and South Africa and also to give him the chance to dip his toe in the water at the next level. Already hugely successful as a coach in the west and a former batting coach with the national side, the tour gave 'JL' – and Cricket Australia – the chance to see if he could be the right man when my role next becomes available.

The talent pool of Australian coaches working at a high level is impressive and not just limited to our domestic game with its six first-class states. My old Australia and South Australia teammate Jason Gillespie has had considerable success in charge of Yorkshire in the English county set-up and also came home to work with the Adelaide Strikers in 2015–16, while Michael Di Venuto's move to Surrey deprived us of an outstanding batting coach but gave him the opportunity to take a step up the ladder by running a side, something that will provide him with invaluable experience and an even more attractive curriculum vitae.

The role of Australia's coach is an attractive one from the outside, with the chance to shape the direction of the national side working alongside the country's best players. But with the almost constant travelling, it has the potential to lose its appeal very quickly. You certainly need an understanding and supportive family behind you, and I have been lucky enough to have that. The alternative attractions of roles in some of the many lucrative Twenty20 leagues around the world, bringing as they do significant rewards for far less time away from home, represent a threat to the flow of talent behind me, but I know that is something Cricket

Australia is acutely aware of and it has worked to make the role as attractive as possible. That threat is not limited to just Australian cricket either, as England discovered when it recruited Trevor Bayliss to take over from Peter Moores in 2015. England travel around just as much as us and the prospect of doing that has the potential to be off-putting to even the most enthusiastic candidate.

One option to keep coaches fresh and enthusiastic and extend their longevity is to split the role and, for example, have one person looking after the limited-overs squads and another in charge of the Test team. It has happened with the captaincy of many international teams so, the argument goes, why not do the same thing with the coaches?

We have done that with members of the staff in the past but as head coach, the person in charge, I am not keen on the idea of handing over control. I have always wanted to remain on deck overseeing the operation and I think that is very important.

It might sound like I am making a rod for my own back and I may sound like a control freak, but hopefully this book has shown that I regard delegation as a key part of the role of head coach and I trust my staff to get on with their own roles without me breathing down their necks. At the same time, however, there are plenty of players who play all the formats and looking after all of those formats as coach provides a source of continuity. Splitting the role opens up the potential for conflict and confusion, which was high-lighted to me by the then England head coach Andy Flower, the ex-Zimbabwe batsman and a former teammate of mine at South Australia, following the Ashes series of 2013–14.

The England and Wales Cricket Board was keen to retain Andy as, under his direction, the side had gone from also-rans to the top side in the Test arena and had also landed its first global trophy by winning the World Twenty20 in the West Indies in 2010, but everyone recognised the nonstop demands of the role were an issue.

The solution was that Andy agreed to split his role, remaining in charge of the Test side while Ashley Giles, the former England spin bowler, took over as coach of the limited-overs side.

But while that looked good on paper, Andy told me it created problems in terms of who was actually in charge of the overall running of the England team on a day-to-day basis, and the issue of whether or not Kevin Pietersen was persisted with became an open sore. The split role was dispensed with following the World Twenty20 in 2014.

From my perspective, having one person take the overall responsibility for the direction of the side is the best set-up, even if that comes with the downside of potentially reducing the length of time it is possible for a person to do the job.

The number of players we lost either to retirement or long-term injuries in the period after our success at the Cricket World Cup in 2015 was a problem and did present a number of challenges, but the upside was that it brought about the need to introduce lots of fresh faces to the set-up. Those players brought with them a high level of enthusiasm and also challenged me as a coach to ensure they were brought up to speed on the demands of international cricket as quickly as possible.

In the 16 months before the 2015 World Cup just two players made their One-Day International debuts – Sean Abbott and Gurinder Sandhu, neither of whom featured in our squad for the tournament – whereas in the year that followed that success we had six players receive their first caps in the format. Despite the team's relative inexperience, we were still able to win both in England and against India in 2015–16, and in doing so retain a comfortable lead at the head of the ICC rankings.

By the time we get to 2019 we should have a group of players who are experienced enough to give it a red hot go in seeking to win the World Cup again. It will be hard, but challenges are there to be undertaken. I believe that the pathway to our elite side is a good one and that the future remains bright for Australian cricket.

INDEX